INSIDE THE
GREEN LOBBY

For Jackie —
Hope you enjoy
the book. Of
get up to the Ark
Park!
— Brennan

INSIDE THE GREEN LOBBY

THE FIGHT TO SAVE THE ADIRONDACK PARK

BERNARD C. MELEWSKI

excelsior editions

AN IMPRINT OF STATE UNIVERSITY OF NEW YORK PRESS

Published by State University of New York Press, Albany

For information, contact State University of New York Press, Albany, NY
www.sunypress.edu

Library of Congress Cataloging-in-Publication Data

Name: Melewski, Bernard C., author.
Title: Inside the green lobby : the fight to save the Adirondack Park / Bernard C. Melewski.
Description: Albany, NY : State University of New York Press, [2021] | Series: Excelsior editions | Includes index.
Identifiers: LCCN 2021012590 | ISBN 9781438486697 (hardcover : alk. paper) | ISBN 9781438486680 (pbk. : alk. paper) | ISBN 9781438486703 (ebook)
Subjects: LCSH: Environmentalism—New York (State)—Adirondack Park. | Adirondack Park Agency (N.Y.)—History. | Green movement—New York (State)—Adirondack Park. | Environmental policy—New York (State)—Adirondack Park. | Land use—New York (State)—Adirondack Park.
Classification: LCC GE198.A2 M45 2021 | DDC 320.5809747—dc23
LC record available at https://lccn.loc.gov/2021012590

This book is dedicated to Mollie, our sons Matt and Dan,
and to their children and their children's children.
May they all enjoy the wild places that
have been preserved for them.

Figure D.1. Ansa at dusk on Lake Mohegan *Source*: Matthew Melewski.

CONTENTS

List of Illustrations   ix

Acknowledgments   xiii

Introduction   1

Chapter 1   The Land Campaign   7

Chapter 2   The Bowler Boys   97

Chapter 3   New York's Big Secret   103

Chapter 4   The Canal Canary Sings   107

Chapter 5   The Prison in the Park   113

Chapter 6   Mary-Arthur and Me   121

Chapter 7   Well, I'll Be Damned   125

Chapter 8   Timber Rustlers   131

Chapter 9   The New Chairman   137

Chapter 10   Year of the Moose   141

Chapter 11   The Air Campaign   147

Chapter 12   The Art of Lobbying   237

Notes   253

Index   255

ILLUSTRATIONS

Figure D.1   Ansa at dusk on Mohegan Lake.   v

Figure I.1   A locator map of Adirondack Park.   1

Figure I.2   A map of land ownership in the park.   3

Figure 1.1   Cover of the *Commission Report*.   8

Figure 1.2   A property rights letter.   17

Figure 1.3   George Davis at a hearing.   22

Figure 1.4   Mario Cuomo, Maurice Hinchey.   36

Figure 1.5   Cover of the governor's proposals.   38

Figure 1.6   Topridge boathouse.   53

Figure 1.7   Ceremony for a bill signing, Environmental
              Protection Fund.   56

Figure 1.8   Clarence Petty, Gary Randorf, Greenleaf Chase.   63

Figure 1.9   The summit of Whiteface Mountain.   66

Figure 1.10   Sign-in sheet for the governor's meeting.   69

Figure 1.11   *New York Times* ad, Adirondack Park up for grabs.   72

Figure 1.12   Whitney Park cartoon.   77

Figure 1.13   Paddlers on Grasse River.   82

Figure 1.14   Brian Houseal, George H. Cannon, and the author.   89

Figure 1.15   Follensby Pond.   91

Figure 1.16   Preston Ponds and Duck Hole.   91

Figure 1.17   OK Slip Falls.   93

Figure 1.18   Boreas Ponds.   94

Figure 1.19   The Whitney estate.   94

Figure 2.1   Lewis Lehrman's letter to the governor.   101

Figure 4.1   Canal lands cartoon.   110

Figure 5.1   Wild Center in Tupper Lake.   119

Figure 8.1   Timber theft bill signing.   136

Figure 10.1   Indian Lake Moose Festival.   145

Figure 11.1   The mechanics of acid rain.   149

Figure 11.2   Mike Finnegan's note to the author.   155

Figure 11.3   Senator Alfonse D'Amato with the author.   163

Figure 11.4   Senator Joseph Bruno with a certificate.   166

Figure 11.5   Cover of an acid rain brochure.   169

Figure 11.6   New York attorney general Dennis Vacco with
               the author.   171

Figure 11.7   *National Acid Precipitation Assessment Program
               Report* cover.   173

Figure 11.8   An invitation to testify.   174

Figure 11.9   *New York Times* acid rain ad.   176

Figure 11.10   Congressman Sherwood Boehlert with ad.   177

Figure 11.11   Cover of the Department of the Interior book.   178

Figure 11.12   Hillary Clinton thank you letter.   182

Figure 11.13   Cover of Government Accountability Office report.   185

Figure 11.14   George Pataki bill signing.   186

Figure 11.15   A hotel note.   197

Figure 11.16   President Bush on Earth Day.   216

Figure 11.17   Toy loon.   223

Figure 12.1   Black Fly Tour sign.   244

Figure 12.2   Great Camp Sagamore.   245

Figure 12.3   Elk Lake.   247

ACKNOWLEDGMENTS

I want to thank my fellow staff members at the Albany office of the Adirondack Council: David Greenwood, Scott Lorey, Lisa Genier, Radmila Miletich, and John Sheehan. They were all very willing to recount with me the adventures we had together. In particular, Lisa gave generously of her time to help identify people, places, and events. Tyler Frakes of the Council provided key research assistance. The recollections of William "Wild Bill" Cooke were also appreciated.

Dr. Michael Wilson encouraged me years ago to write this book. Despite this, I still consider him a friend. Early on, I received thoughtful advice from Carol Melewski, a dedicated librarian and her husband, my favorite brother, Peter.

My primary editor, Arthur Dalglish of Boulder, Colorado, a retired copy editor for the *Washington Post*, took my drafts and shaped them up significantly. I deeply appreciate his professional assistance.

Finally, I am grateful to have worked for fifteen years with all the staff, interns, members of the board of directors and supporters of the Adirondack Council, whose dedication to the protection and enhancement of New York's largest park is beyond commendable. I also wish to acknowledge the staff of many other environmental organizations, large and small, with whom I have had the pleasure of working on many issues over many years. Their contributions to the protection of our natural resources have been invaluable to the people of the State of New York.

All photographs, unless otherwise identified, are by Nancie Battaglia, an extraordinary photographer working in the Adirondacks. Special thanks to Carl Heilman II, who contributed one of his outstanding Adirondack photos.

INTRODUCTION

December was a time of transition for the professional staff in the State Assembly and Senate. The members of both houses were up for election every two years. In law, that meant that every two years a "new" legislative body took their seats. The reality was somewhat different. The vast majority of members of both houses were reelected time after time. They held the benefits of incumbency—ready access to their constituents, free mailing privileges, and staff members who not only solved small problems for folks

Figure I.1. A locator map of Adirondack Park. *Source*: Adirondack Council.

1

in their district but often worked as campaign staff at election time. Senior staff in both houses would joke with each other that they did not work for the Democrats or Republicans, but for the "incumbent party."

This working fiction of a "new" legislative body every two years produced some interesting twists. Under the legislature's ethics rules at the time, staff members were prohibited from lobbying on issues they had handled while in the legislature, until the next legislative session convened. But if you left on December 31, the day before the next legislative session convened, you could begin working as a lobbyist immediately—on the same issues you had been assigned and with the same staff and members you had been working with, perhaps for decades.

It had been five years since I had taken my environmental advocacy and lobbying skills from the private sector to the state, becoming counsel for the New York Legislative Commission on Solid Waste Management.

I enjoyed my job and my status as a senior staffer in the State Assembly. But it was apparent to me that the Solid Waste Commission had completed its primary task—to close leaking landfills and to set the state in a new direction of reuse and recycling. The task going forward was to find the money to carry out the new state policies. I was not the only one who felt that way, and several of my colleagues had already left for greener pastures.

Despite my feelings that it was time for a career change, I decided to stay with the commission into the New Year. Two months into that next legislative session, our executive director, Richard D. Morse, called me into his office and told me that an environmental group in the Adirondacks wanted to establish a lobbying presence in Albany and had approached him about the job. He asked me, as a friend, for advice. I urged him to get an opinion from the Assembly's Committee on Ethics and Guidance before making a decision.

I thought that he might have problems because he also worked as a senior staffer advising the Assembly speaker on any number of environmental issues, including the Adirondacks.

Sure enough, Rick confirmed that the ethics committee had issued an opinion that he should avoid working for two years on exactly the issues for which the environmental group wanted a lobbyist. It was disappointing, Rick said, but the group was moving on in its search.

"Do you know anybody I could suggest to them?" he asked.

"What about me?" I replied, to my own surprise.

I had no ethical conflict under the rules. My work had been all garbage, all the time.

The group looking for help turned out to be the Adirondack Council. The Council was created with one overriding mission: "To ensure the ecological integrity and wild character of the Adirondack Park."[1]

The park, created by the Legislature in 1892 to protect timber and water resources, is the largest protected area in the lower forty-eight states. Bigger than Yellowstone, Everglades, Glacier and Grand Canyon National Parks combined, its six million acres covers almost 20 percent of New York state. Almost one-half of the land in the Park is publicly owned "forever wild" forest preserve.[2]

Almost an additional 775,000 acres of private land are subject to publicly held conservation easements.[3] (See figure I.2.)

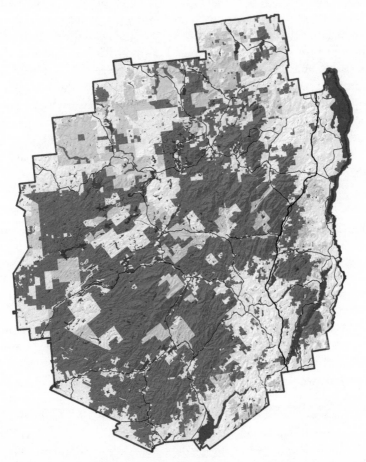

Figure I.2. Land ownership in the Park. State lands shaded dark, easements in gray, private lands in white. *Source*: Adirondack Council.

While the High Peaks region with forty-six tall peaks is most widely known, the Park includes the headwaters of five major drainage basins: Lake Champlain and the Hudson, Black, Saint Lawrence, and Mohawk Rivers. There are thousands of miles of rivers, brooks, and streams and approximately 2,800 lakes and ponds.[4] Conservationists nationwide revere the park, one reason that the Council's members come from all fifty states.

For much of its history, one of the strongest environmental laws in the world, the "forever wild" clause of New York's Constitution, adopted in 1894, has protected the public lands in the park. It reads: "The lands of the state, now owned or hereafter acquired, constituting the forest preserve as now fixed by law, shall be forever kept as wild forest lands."[5]

Over the decades, this ideal had come under pressure in the sprawling, complex Adirondack Park. Inside the Blue Line, as the park boundary is known, lies a six-million-acre patchwork of public and private land, in roughly equal parts. More than a hundred town or village boards control the private lands, and the public lands are managed by several state agencies.[6]

In 1970, an alarming report highlighted the dangers of this arrangement. Most private land in the park was not subject to land-use regulation, and a Temporary Study Commission on the Future of the Adirondacks, appointed by Governor Nelson A. Rockefeller, warned that there was an imminent danger of large-scale, uncontrolled residential development. It found that most town and village governments lacked the land-use and zoning laws to control development within their borders, not to mention the resources to enforce such rules, even if they were in place.[7] This situation would soon change, and change drastically. The very next year, the legislature approved Governor Rockefeller's proposal to create an Adirondack Park Agency to oversee the planning and management of both state and private land in the Park. In effect, the state took the unprecedented step of establishing a parkwide planning and zoning board to regulate development in the towns inside the Blue Line.

The environmental community soon responded in kind. The Adirondack Council was created as a privately funded organization in 1975 to monitor the work of the Adirondack Park Agency (APA). The nonprofit, nonpartisan council would be a "green voice" as regulations for lands within the park were drawn up, adopted, and implemented. The Council was, at its inception, an organization of both individual and organizational members. Many of its board members represented national and regional environmental organizations with an interest in the future of the Adirondack Park. These predecessor organizations had already done outstanding work, especially the venerable Association for the Protection of the Adirondacks.

Over the following years, the Adirondack Council expanded its agenda beyond the APA to all matters involving the private and public lands in the park. By 1990, it had an annual budget of over a million dollars and staffers working not just at its Elizabethtown, New York, headquarters but also in the state and US capitals. It had become widely recognized as the "watchdog of the Adirondacks."

It was at this point that I entered the scene as a job candidate.

I had met Gary Randorf, the council's executive director, years before when we joined forces to lobby the legislature to expand the state's Wild, Scenic and Recreational Rivers program. Gary was a short, nimble, and fit fellow with a huge beard, an easy laugh, and a twinkle in his eye. (Later he shaved the beard, saying that too many people told him it made him look like an elf.)

Gary's accomplishments included paddling all waterways in the wild rivers program, along with the legendary woodsman Clarence Petty.

Gary led the fight to stop acid rain in the Adirondacks for years, and was successful in ending the aerial spraying of pesticides to kill black flies inside the Park. He was also a celebrated photographer of the natural beauty of the Adirondacks, whose prints were highly prized gifts to patrons of the Adirondack Council.

Gary explained that the council's board of directors had recently decided it needed a full-time lobbyist. The impetus was an impending report like the one produced under Rockefeller in 1970. It was coming from a new panel, appointed by Governor Mario M. Cuomo, called the Commission on the Adirondacks in the Twenty-First Century.

The Adirondack Council thought that this report, like the original one, would set off a drive for new policies toward the park. He wanted his board of directors to be positioned to influence the results in the legislature.

Gary set up a meeting for me with the chairwoman, Barbara L. Glaser. Barbara was and remains a major force for conservation in the Adirondack Park, and in her hometown of Saratoga Springs. She would become a good friend.

I got the job. Having gone through the revolving door at the Capitol from not-for-profit lobbyist to legislative staffer, I now exited the way I came in. Back to the environmental community. I could not have been more thrilled at the prospect. Growing up only minutes south of the park boundary, I had spent many days hiking, paddling, fishing, camping, and hunting in the Park. Until now, most of my professional work on environmental issues had been focused elsewhere.

Just as I joined the Adirondack Council, the Park's natural resources were facing two great threats to their survival: environmental damage from acid rain and a potential sell-off of huge tracts of privately held timberlands.

Acid rain, laden with sulfur and nitrogen oxides, was killing trees in the Park; many lakes and streams had become acidic and could no longer support native fish, and the health of not just wildlife but also the Park's human residents was being endangered by mercury and lead. The main source of these pollutants was coal-fueled power plants and factories, most of which were located out-of-state, hundreds of miles away and out of the reach of New York's legal authority.

The push to obtain large tracts of private land for development inside the Park was a fairly new phenomenon. For more than 100 years, the owners of timber companies and large family estates took their responsibility to preserve and protect the hundreds of thousands of acres of forest, rivers, wetlands, and meadows they owned quite seriously. Few people realized that when they climbed to some high vista and looked across the vast forests and lakes below, they were likely looking at private land.

Now, market forces were rapidly changing the timber industry and the older generation of landowners was dying off. Large holdings were being sold off and subdivided at a rapidly increasing pace, with the development now focused on new vacation homes. The sheer scale of the turnover represented a potential catastrophe for the Adirondack Park. The legislative compromises that had been struck to create the Park Agency's regulatory authority, particularly the weak rules on waterfront development and protection of the backcountry, were now exposed. It was hoped that the new Governor's Commission would issue recommendations to address these new land use challenges in the Park.

The Adirondack Council and other environmental organizations would meet these two great threats to the future of the natural resources of the park by staging unprecedented lobbying campaigns at the state and federal level. In addition to this challenging work, the Council, in its self-declared role as the Park's "watchdog," faced other new issues large and small.

We would tackle them all: the reintroduction of moose; the construction of a prison in the park; a proposal to dump chemicals into the "Queen of American Lakes"; the fate of the Park's major river corridors; even the need to corral timber rustlers. All these events occurred in my tenure as legal counsel and legislative director of the Adirondack Council from the year 1990 to 2005.

I helped lead those campaigns. These are my stories.

CHAPTER 1

THE LAND CAMPAIGN

It was early 1990, and Dan Plumley and I had just settled into our seats. The train was gathering speed when Dan leaned down and pulled something out of his well-tooled cowboy boot.

"What 'ya got there?" I asked.

"The report from the Commission on the Adirondack Park in the Twenty-first Century."

"How did you get that?"

"I pried open a box with my penknife and hid one in my boot," he nonchalantly replied.

"Holy shit!" I said. My mind flashed back to Dan asking the way to the men's room and then going off alone, past the high stack of boxed reports.

Dan and I were headed to New York City for my first meeting with the Board of Directors of my new employer, the Adirondack Council. Dan had previously been the sole government liaison for the Council. I was the new guy, taking charge of lobbying at the state Capitol. Dan would now focus on the review of development projects pending before the Adirondack Park Agency.

On the way to the Albany train station, Dan had suggested we stop by the offices of the Commission on the Adirondack Park. Governor Mario M. Cuomo had created it the previous year because, he said, large land sales in the Adirondack Park threatened to bring on "an era of unbridled land speculation and unwarranted development." The Commission's work had been completed with the printing of its report *The Adirondack Park in the Twenty-first Century*.[1]

Dan introduced me to several Commission staffers who were cleaning out their desks before returning to their other lives. In a corner, stacked four-high, were cardboard boxes full of the completed but not yet distributed report containing the panel's recommendations. Cuomo had asked Commission Chairman Peter A. A. Berle to delay its public release. That delay had extended to several weeks, and now the lease on the rented Commission offices was about to expire.

The report was obviously going to be a topic of conversation at our board meeting, and our visit to the Commission was aimed at finding something new to tell the directors. We enjoyed a nice chat with the remaining staffers. They said they would love to tell us what was in their report, but could not. They hoped for a public unveiling in the next few business days.

Now, thanks to Dan, I held a copy in my hand. "You ought to read this before we get in," he said. (See figure 1.1.)

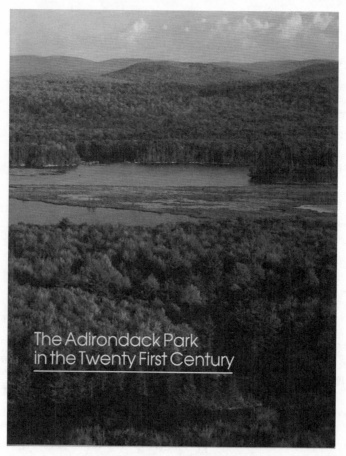

Figure 1.1. Cover of the *Commission Report*. *Source*: author, public domain.

Rumors had been swirling ahead of the report's release, particularly in the Adirondack Park's hamlets and small communities, about who was really in charge of the Commission's work. Chief among the theories was that control of the Commission lay in the hands of the environmental community, particularly the Adirondack Council. This conclusion followed from the common belief that rich people from New York City—"flatlanders," as the locals called them—dominated the Council, leading the Council to care only about maintaining a wilderness playground, not working in the interests of local residents. Fueling these suspicions were the undeniable links between the Council and the Commission. George D. Davis, executive director of the Commission had just completed the research necessary for the Adirondack Council's multivolume 2020 Vision document. In it, the Council had proposed that the state acquire hundreds of thousands of acres of privately held land in the Park "to secure and complete the Adirondack Wilderness System."

The Commission's chairman, Peter Berle, also brought strong environmental credentials. At the time of his appointment, he was president of the National Audubon Society. He was also a former Commissioner of the State Department of Environmental Conservation (DEC). As a member of the New York State Assembly, in 1973 he had led a successful effort to pass comprehensive legislation regulating development in the Adirondacks that had been proposed by the Temporary Study Commission on the Future of the Adirondacks.

And finally, Commission member, Harold A. Jerry Jr., then a member of the State Public Service Commission, had also served been as executive director of that first Commission, established by Governor Nelson Rockefeller. His reputation for strongly held environmental beliefs could be seen in the earlier Commission's conclusions, including the antidevelopment recommendations that Peter Berle had later shepherded into law. Jerry, who owned land inside the Park near the village of Speculator, was also a member of the Adirondack Council's board and an unabashed advocate of protecting both private and public lands in the Park.

Over the next two hours aboard the train, I ignored the lovely views of the Hudson River as I pored over the Commission's still-secret recommendations on the future of the Park.

I found political land mines throughout the document.

"You know, they are going to piss off a lot of people with this," I told Dan. "They have two hundred and forty-five recommendations in the ninety-six-page report and no priorities. The proposals touch almost everyone that lives, works, or visits the Park, and not necessarily in a good way."

The recommendations ranged from sweeping all of the state agencies operating inside the Park into one consolidated Adirondack Park Administration to a plan for removing abandoned cars from the roadsides.

Most notably of concern, the Commission called for the following:

- An immediate moratorium on any new development in the Park,

- Increasing state control over the use of private lands,

- Expanding the Park into adjacent private lands, and

- Imposing new fees and taxes.

As the train rattled on, I made a list of all the people who might hate the recommendations. It was impressively long: developers; motel owners; people with shoreline lots; and people who owned boats, snowmobiles, all-terrain vehicles, jet skis, or recreational vehicles, not to mention local government officials, large landowners and the forest products industry. You might even add the governor of New York to the list. Cuomo was preparing to run for a third term in 1990, and annoying large numbers of people was probably not in his campaign plan.

The report urged that all the Commission's recommendations be considered as a package and not individually, because "pulling a single thread could unravel the whole sweater."

If that was the case, this thing was going nowhere. I had seen lots of legislation fail in Albany not because the main thrust of the bill was a bad idea, but because the bill collected so many opponents, each with their own minor problem. At the Capitol we called it the Lilliputian effect after the tiny characters who tied down the "giant" in the Jonathan Swift novel *Gulliver's Travels*.

MINORITY REPORT

Our directors were shocked to discover that I could report exactly what the Commission was about to recommend. (I didn't tell them how I knew.) No one was more surprised than Harold Jerry, who confirmed my summary in general terms.

It wasn't clear if Jerry was more upset with the governor, who was being blamed in the media for delaying the release of the troublesome report, or me, for telling the board that I thought it was going to be a public relations disaster.

I didn't know it that day, but Jerry was aware of another looming problem. He knew what Bob Flacke was about to do.

Robert F. Flacke was another member of the Commission. He owned a resort on Lake George inside the Adirondack Park and had enjoyed a successful career in politics and government. He had risen from a local elected office to be the appointed chairman of the Adirondack Park Agency, which oversaw development inside the Park, and then Commissioner of the Department of Environmental Conservation succeeding Peter Berle. Flacke had returned to the private sector to run his lakeside hotel before his appointment to Cuomo's commission.

Flacke was a burly former football player who I knew from many meetings during his tenure at the DEC.

The consensus among environmentalists who dealt with Flacke in that job was that he "just didn't get it." He seemed to like talking to me, however, often commenting that "You don't bullshit me." Apparently, I was also one of the few environmental lobbyists who didn't yell at him.

One time, he invited me into his office for a "man-to-man" session prior to a larger meeting with the environmental community.

"You think I don't know what you guys are really after—but I do!" he said.

Years of experience had taught me to respond in deadpan fashion.

"How so?" I replied.

"I've been reading this, and it is very clear to me now."

He waved a book at me. After a pass or two past my face, I saw the title: *What Environmentalists Want*.

Unable to muster a better reply, I just said, "You got me now, Bob."

He seemed satisfied with that response.

Flacke (nobody in the environmental community called him by his first name) was also famous for his temper. His nickname was "Thermometer Bob," because you could watch the red color rising on his neck as he got more and more upset in most meetings I was in with him. I always expected him to suffer a stroke right before my eyes.

To his credit, Flacke held himself in check and was civil to all, even though his neck sometimes gave away his true feelings. There was one memorable exception. He was a guest at an Environmental Planning Lobby reception, when he got into a heated argument with a citizen advocate from Syracuse. Partygoers claimed a physical altercation had ensued and Bob had lifted the other fellow off the ground—by his neck. All I saw was a commotion. Later, I defended Flacke to my colleagues—I had always found the other guy to be a pain in the ass. No one disagreed with me on that point.

Now Flacke was on the Governor's commission, and our paths were crossing again.

Whether by coincidence or design, Flacke took advantage of the delay in the release of the commission majority's findings to issue his own "minority report." The "Flacke Report," as it came to be known, undermined most of the recommendations supported by the majority.

Flack wrote, "The Commission bases its conclusions and recommendations largely on a premise that a development crisis exists in the Adirondack Park, when it does not." He contended that the supposed development crisis "is mostly the creation of an unfortunately effective, massive campaign by the Commission's main support group, the Adirondack Council."

He said the law governing the Adirondack Park Agency was "still one of the most stringent in the nation." He argued that improvements could easily be made within the existing administrative network, and that "there is absolutely no need for a one-year moratorium on land use and development in the Park." Flacke offered forty-four recommendations of his own, including new legislative commissions, studies and agency audits intended to challenge the assumptions in the commission's report.[2]

Bob would later predict that economic opportunities for residents of the communities in the Park would be crippled if the recommendations of the commission were adopted, leaving them only the prospect of "selling trinkets to tourists by the roadside."

Many people are surprised to learn that there are more than 100 towns, villages, and hamlets with more than 130,000 residents inside the Park. This is because of its huge size and unique makeup. Within its six million acres, more than one-fifth of the state's total footprint, lies a checkerboard of public and private lands in roughly equal proportions.[3] Despite proposals over its 100-year history to redefine the Park's boundaries to exclude human settlements, it has remained a sprawling political and biological experiment in compatibility between humans and the wild.

This coexistence has always created tensions between conservation and development. After proposals for extensive residential development were announced and his brother Laurance continued to press the governor and others to create a national park in the region, Governor Rockefeller named the first blue-ribbon commission on the Park's future in 1968. The Commission's report, released in 1970, led Rockefeller to ask the legislature to impose new controls on land use and development in the Park, and within a few months the sweeping measure was enacted. It created a new entity, the Adirondack Park Agency, and gave it the authority to impose new controls over the use and development of most of the public and private land in the park. The APA's powers superseded the zoning authority that had been held, though seldom exercised, by the local governments.

Adirondack residents resented the new agency deeply. Most of them lived in communities with no zoning or land-use controls, and seemingly overnight they found themselves subject to oversight by a state authority that they perceived had the power to decide whether someone could subdivide his or her own property or build a boathouse next to the lake.

Feeling powerless in the face of what they saw as an overbearing intrusion into their lives by "flatlanders," residents put up fierce resistance. They dumped manure at the APA's door and emptied their guns at state vehicles. An arson attempt against the agency's headquarters was famously thwarted by a staff member, a former football player, who made a saving tackle in the agency's darkened hallway.

Most Adirondackers would learn to tolerate the APA over the next twenty years, but they never grew to like it. Their resentment floated just below the surface like a mine in a harbor, capable of exploding if something hit it hard enough. And Flacke's minority report hit it hard.

Despite the dreams of Chairman Berle and others, history would not repeat itself. The 1990 legislative session ended without any action on the Berle Commission's report.

A BUCKET OF SNAKES

Fifty years ago, one of the biggest driving forces for the first commission on the future of the Adirondacks was a proposal by a few developers for massive housing developments. Environmentalists were convinced their construction would create a precedent that would eventually change the character of the Adirondack Park and compromise the biological integrity of the publicly held wild lands. The commission proposed new land-use controls that would at least require sound planning in the development of new subdivisions.

Twenty years later, another burst of new development, this time of second homes and vacation homes, led to Governor Cuomo's creation of a second commission. The land-use controls that were adopted in the 1970s by the new Adirondack Park Agency, which were considered far-reaching and progressive at the time, were now deemed ineffective in keeping development away from the "back country," the most sensitive lands in the Park.

Simultaneously, an enormous shift in land ownership was beginning inside the Park. Private family holdings, some larger than 10,000 acres, were beginning to break up as the owners grew elderly. Their children and grandchildren had priorities other than maintaining the grand estates and paying taxes on them.

Similarly, new pressures were affecting one of the Adirondacks' core industries. While government and tourism now employed most Adirondackers, vast tracts of private land were under active timber harvesting and management. Changes in demand and competition had shifted the market to benefit foreign producers. Many people were certain that the extensive commercial holdings of northern timberlands would soon be sold off to housing developers. Indeed, in 1988, the timber company Diamond International sold over 900,000 acres in the Park to Lassiter Properties Inc., a developer. Despite the State's keen interest in protecting much of Diamond International's property, its cumbersome and lengthy acquisition procedures led the timber company to sell to another willing bidder. In a blistering editorial in the *New York Times*, John Oakes took Governor Mario Cuomo to task for his administration's failure to buy and thus protect lands of such ecological significance.[4] Under pressure from environmental groups, a few years later Cuomo would pay a premium to buy conservation easements from Lassiter on some of the same lands.[5]

"Death by a thousand cuts" was how Robert C. Glennon, executive director and counsel at the Adirondack Park Agency, described the slicing of large unbroken tracts into smaller "ranchettes" to meet the increasing demand for vacation homes. As for the timber firms whose business model was clear-cutting, green groups called the practice "cut and run."

Green groups across New York began to realize they had common concerns. Environmentalists in the Hudson Valley were also seeing large estates and private lands changing hands rapidly. On Long Island, a land and farm preservation movement was gathering momentum.

Unfortunately, the state had exhausted its funds for land acquisition, and local governments did not have the resources to compete with private developers. The consensus among environmental groups was that a new bond issue with an emphasis on land acquisition was needed. At the same time that Governor Cuomo's commission was completing its work, green groups around the state were successfully lobbying both the governor and their legislators to put a two billion dollar borrowing package before the voters in November.

In anticipation of new public funds from the proposed Twenty-First Century Environmental Quality Bond Act, then DEC commissioner Tom Jorling initiated contacts with a number of owners of land in which the state might have an interest. Some of the most scenic and environmentally sensitive tracts were in the Adirondack Park.

In 1990, the state had sought to acquire a parcel on Pine Lake in the Adirondacks from a landowner who was losing his patience. The environmental department's policies and practices caused it to move with tortoise-like efficiency, and it was outmaneuvered and eventually outbid for the parcel by a Syracuse-area dentist, Vincent J. Vaccaro.

Jorling had a quick and lively temper, as I can attest, having been dressed down by him more than once. So I believed it when I heard that he blew his top over "that dentist," Vaccaro. Jorling soon declared to me, among others, that his department would start eminent domain proceedings, if necessary, to wrest the parcel away from Vaccaro. That proved to be a critical error in judgment.

Eminent domain, in which the state condemns property and pays the owner "fair value" in return, is widely used for all kinds of infrastructure projects from roads to power lines. In this case, commissioner had the legal authority to protect a parcel of "special use and value to the People of the State." But the use of eminent domain to condemn the Vaccaro property was unusual; to my knowledge it had been used only once before to protect a state historic site.

"That dentist" would prove to be a formidable opponent, traveling across the state and appearing on radio and television to portray himself as the victim of an abuse of power by the state of New York. Vaccaro also sued Jorling, but the courts eventually upheld the state's right to exercise eminent domain.

These simultaneous events—the Commission's report, Flacke's minority report and the Vaccaro public relations disaster—soon became something larger than the sum of their parts, stoking anger that focused on the new bond act.

Large landowners joined with the still-fuming Adirondack property rights advocates to weave an implausible but oddly compelling narrative that got wide media coverage. The bond act, as the conspiracy theory went, would finance a huge land grab in the Adirondacks, and private landowners who resisted would see the state take their land by eminent domain.

I went to see Bob Flacke in Lake George before the November 1990 vote on the bond act referendum. His minority report had set the stage for the conspiracy theorists to portray a plot by the rich flatlanders at the Adirondack Council. He had also helped organize an opposition group, wryly named the Blue Line Council to mimic our organization's name, composed of banks, large landowners, and timber and business interests. It was well funded and had hired its own public relations firm.

Reporters had asked Flacke to comment on whether the state would use money from the bond act to exercise eminent domain in the Adirondacks and "herd the people into the hamlets." Declining to dispel the false fear-mongering, his response added fuel to the fire by implying that it was unlikely, but that he could not rule it out. Flacke's views carried weight among Adirondackers, because as a member of the Commission, "he ought to know."

In my visit, I called him on it. I was growing very concerned at the rising anger at public meetings in the Park and the potential for vandalism and violence. I told him that I thought it was irresponsible for someone of his stature to scare people for a strategic advantage. He knew better, I said. I asked him to clarify his remarks publicly and do what he could to help calm people down.

It was a short meeting.

Flacke said, "I was surprised that you took that job. How can you work for those people?" He meant my board of directors at the Adirondack Council. He muttered that he soon would be heading to Florida until the spring and was done making public statements.

Then he thanked me for coming.

Things got worse for the bond act. A lawsuit was filed alleging that taxpayer funds had been illegally used to produce millions of promotional pamphlets (not educational materials) in support of the act and sent to voters. A court agreed and ordered state agencies to halt distribution of the pamphlets.

By Election Day, the bond act was enveloped in a cloud of public ignorance, confusion, and concern. Environmental groups mounted a desperate media campaign to save it, but even a large supportive turnout in New York City was not enough. Voters rejected the 21st Century Environmental Quality Bond Act by a margin of 51 percent to 49 percent.

I later received a personal note from Carol LaGrasse, the founder and president of the Property Rights Foundation of America. It read in part, "You and yours have no future." (See figure 1.2.)

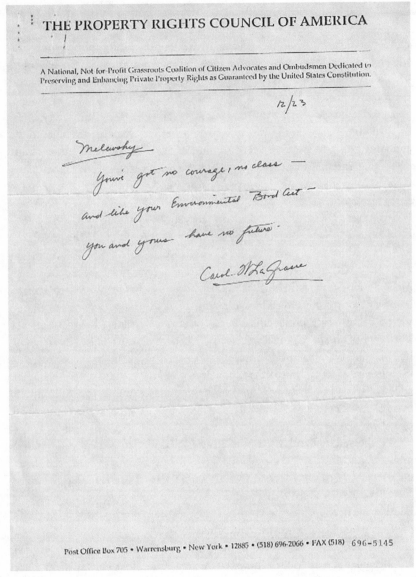

Figure 1.2. Letter to author from Property Rights Council of America. *Source*: author's own material.

As my friend and Council executive director Gary Randorf was fond of saying, "What a bucket of snakes."

UNDER SIEGE

It did not take long for the release of the Commission report to tear the Adirondack Park community apart, including the Adirondack Council itself.

Gary Randorf told me that old friends in the Park had stopped talking to him and that he had barely avoided a fistfight in a bar. Other staffers who resided in the Park reported similar hostility in the community.

Internally, the staff was split over whether the Council should be endorsing the Commission report enthusiastically or should be more cautious. That internal dispute surfaced at a board meeting in New York City, where to our surprise, the whole staff was asked to step outside except for Gary, our executive director.

"What's going on?" I asked my colleagues in the hallway. They told me they had heard there might be an effort to oust Gary for his failure to publicly endorse and promote the Commission report.

They said one of our directors, Harold Jerry, who had been a Commission member, was behind the effort. Supposedly, he wanted to replace Gary with our communications director, Dick Beamish, whom Jerry considered a hard-core preservationist and a stronger leader. In my relatively short time with the Council in Albany, I had rarely met Dick. In fact, our first meeting was very unusual.

Just after I had joined the Council in 1990, I ran into an old acquaintance in a Capitol hallway who said he would see me at the Adirondack Council news conference later that day. The press event was certainly news to me!

I showed up and there was Beamish, alone, introducing our latest publication. Afterward I introduced myself, but Dick was understandably eager to talk with reporters and we had only a brief exchange of greetings.

I was embarrassed that I had not known about the news conference or the new publication. I decided to call our executive director at the Council's main office in Elizabethtown, New York.

Gary Randorf knew about the publication, but he had not known that Beamish was holding a news conference until that day. In fact, Gary had not seen the finished product.

I mentioned to Dick later that it would be good for me, as the Council's lobbyist, to know about events being planned in Albany. He acknowledged that it would have been better if I had known, but added that he couldn't see how that would have changed anything. I made a mental note to find a way to improve the coordination between the new legislative effort I was heading and our outreach to the media.

In what could only be called a fortuitous coincidence of timing, Gary learned that he had finally found a publisher for his book about the Adirondacks. He had previously mentioned to me that he would be stepping back from the Council's leadership if this happened. Now, in the midst of the Council's internal disagreements over the Commission report, Gary and the board agreed that he would step down as executive director and serve the Council part time as senior adviser and staff photographer.

But because of the growing factionalism within the Council, the board decided to avoid choosing a new leader and asked me to step in as acting executive director (ED). My virtue, apparently, was that I was a new guy untainted by internal politics. I was assured that the search for a new ED would take no more than three months.

In my new role, I began splitting my time between Albany and the Council's headquarters two hours north in Elizabethtown. Every week, I found the staff there more divided and dispirited. One staffer came in every morning, closed his door, and never reopened it till he left for the day.

I asked our Chairman to have a member of our Board of Directors visit Elizabethtown to meet with the staff and buck them up. Instead, a board member arrived with a message of tough love. He told the staff that continued carping would not be tolerated. Although I was only the acting ED, I had the full backing of the board, he said, and anyone who did not like it could leave.

By the end of the year, Dick Beamish had left the Council, as had our development director.

As if internal strife were not enough, outsiders continued to make verbal threats to Council staffers and physical assaults on our offices. Staffers would arrive to find tacks in the parking lot, or a pile of manure at the front door. In an incident that took place after a new ED had taken the helm and I had returned to lobbying in Albany, the front of our rented building in Elizabethtown was spray-painted bright blue. We asked for and received police protection, and we put up a surveillance camera outside the front door.

The staff was rattled. People were afraid to come to work and in a hurry to leave.

The worst was when a young staff member, Eric Siy, had to defend his pregnant wife and Elizabethtown home from an angry group of residents that appeared at his door. They demanded that he leave town. They lacked only pitchforks and torches. His neighbor, a deputy sheriff, had saved the day by breaking up the mob.

The Council decided to expand its rented office space in Albany and relocate Eric and his understandably rattled wife to Albany. I had named Eric the acting communications director when Beamish resigned, but I thought he had more potential as a lobbyist. Eric stayed with our legislative office only a short while, however, leaving in the middle of the legislative session to join Beamish in establishing a rival group called the Adirondack Campaign. The new group worked with the National Audubon Society under Peter Berle, who had rejoined Audubon after his work leading Cuomo's Adirondack Commission.

Gary Randorf not only secured a book contract, he also found a new lady friend. I stayed in his usually empty farmhouse in Wadhams when I was working at the Elizabethtown headquarters that winter. At first, given the vandalism at the office, I worried about having the house burned down around me. But finally, it was the cluster flies that got to me.

I had never heard of cluster flies, and Gary had said nothing about them. The first night in his farmhouse, I put a lamp on so I could read through the box of mail that I had brought from the office. Large black flies suddenly appeared on the ceiling. They started to swarm above me, and then started dropping dead on top of me. *Boink! Boink!* I barely got any sleep that night. Gary later instructed me to first turn on a light at the far end of the room before climbing into bed to read. (It was always too cold to read anywhere else.) The flies rushed to "cluster" above this light and I was free to read with only the occasional *boink* on the head.

Things were equally annoying on the policy front. The Cuomo commission's executive director, George Davis; its chairman, Peter Berle; and member Harold Jerry, our director, had apparently convinced themselves that, just as in 1973, their report would lead to swift legislative action. The governor would introduce a bill based on the Commission's findings and the bill would become law within months.

But things were much different in 1973. Back then, Republicans controlled both houses of the New York legislature. The governor, Nelson Rockefeller, could impose his will on the state Senate when he needed to. And it was more likely than not that the Assembly would follow suit. Rockefeller's commission members had unanimously agreed on all its recommendations, with no minority report. And there were few fax machines or other devices to help organize opponents and spread their arguments to the media.

In 1990, by contrast, groups opposed to the commission's recommendations immediately sprang up in the Adirondacks. Besides the Blue Line Council that Bob Flacke had helped organize to ensure that timber interests and large landowners had a seat at the negotiating table, the Adirondack Solidarity Alliance became a prominent player. Calvin Carr, a relatively unknown activist who popularized the notion among his fellow Adirondackers that the state was trying to "herd us into hamlets," led it. The Alliance was committed to defending "true Adirondackers" from the "flatlanders," who wanted to tell them what to do with their land and lives. Several more grassroots opposition groups sprang up as well.

Flacke's minority report spurred much of the early opposition. He released it months before the Commission's report itself appeared, meaning that the only information available on the Commission's recommendations focused on how damaging they would be to those who made the Adirondacks their home. Meanwhile, the delay in releasing the Commission report led to rampant rumors that it did not even have the support of the governor. Key Commission staffers unwittingly nourished that notion by explaining to the press, off the record, that the reason for the report's delayed release was that the governor was holding it back.

Months after the release of the Flacke report, the Commission's report finally appeared. George Davis and his staff conducted public information hearings on its findings in communities within the Park. The hearings drew larger and larger crowds and became more and more contentious, to the point where it was deemed necessary to have a police presence at the events. (See figure 1.3.)

Demonstrations and vandalism at the Council's office in Elizabethtown continued for nearly two more years, but those weren't the only statements made by angry locals. Major highway signs welcoming the public to the Adirondack Park were destroyed. A barn belonging to Anne LaBastille, an environmentalist and author who served on the Adirondack Park Agency, was burned to the ground. And there were two incidents of violence directed directly against persons.

The first occurred after the state DEC trucked in large stones to barricade a road in the Pharaoh Lake Wilderness, blocking motor vehicles' access to the popular Crane Pond. The department was blocking vehicle access to comply

Figure 1.3. Commission Executive Director George Davis at a hearing. *Source*: Nancie Battaglia.

with the State law that forbade vehicles in wilderness areas, but local residents, who had been using the road for years, were furious. Some, allegedly led by a transplanted Long Islander named Donald H. Gerdts, hauled away the stones blocking the road in the dead of night. Fearing violence, the department did not intervene when vehicles starting using the road again.

But wilderness advocates were not so inhibited. A few months later, members of the Earth First! advocacy group camped in the middle of the illegally reopened Crane Pond roadway. That led to a confrontation with residents in which Maynard Baker, supervisor of the town of Warrensburg, knocked down one of the Earth First! advocates with a sucker punch to the chin. A news crew from the CBS-affiliated TV station in Burlington, Vermont, was on hand, and the knockdown appeared in a segment on the property rights movement aired by the network's magazine show, *60 Minutes*. No charges were ever filed.

Sucker punching again was the theme some months later. The State Assembly was poised late in the 1992 session to approve legislation containing most of the Commission's proposals. About 200 Adirondack residents came to Albany to protest. They drove slowly down Interstate 87, occupying several lanes in a kind of rolling blockade, which they correctly calculated would tie up traffic and bring media attention to their cause. To add to the spectacle, the protesting motorcade included a trailer hauling the very stones that had blocked access to Crane Pond. The defiant display of the "Stones of Shame," stolen from state property, would appear on local television stations across New York that night.

From the Council's Albany office, we monitored the developments and then joined hundreds of other gawkers to hear the fiery speeches as the protesters rallied on the Capitol steps. State Senator Ron Stafford, who represented much of the region, had just reintroduced a bill to abolish the Adirondack Park Agency, and many protesters carried placards reading, We support AdiRONdacks STAFFORD. Everyone, including us, wanted to hear what Stafford would say to his gathered constituents.

John Sheehan, our communications director, wandered into the crowd to speak to reporters. He came back red in the face and looking a little worse for wear.

"What happened to you?" I asked.

"I have to go to the Capitol police station," he said. "Cal Carr sucker punched me."

John explained that when he arrived at the front of the gathering, Calvin Carr of the Adirondack Solidarity Alliance had recognized him. Carr threw a drink in John's face and then punched him.

Now, John is a big guy. He was a lineman on his high school football team. John put Carr into a headlock and pounded his ear with his fist until bystanders separated them.

Carr got the worst of it. Blood seeped from his ear. The Capitol police investigated, but no charges were filed.

The altercation left no lasting damage, but it was a turning point in the saga of the Adirondack Commission.

An hour after the fight, I got a call from one of Senator Ron Stafford's aides asking me to visit immediately. When I arrived, I was ushered into the senator's office for a private meeting.

"I heard there was a fight at the rally," he told me. "Did you know about it?"

"Yes, sir. John Sheehan was walking by and Cal Carr threw a drink in his face and then sucker punched him."

"Is he okay?"

"Yes, sir. Frankly, I think Cal got the worst of it."

Stafford, not really addressing me, shook his head slowly and said, "This has gone on too long. That's the end of it."

Then he looked up and said, "Thanks for coming in."

From that moment on, Stafford made himself unavailable to the Adirondack Solidarity Alliance and to many of the other groups who had come to rally in his support. The groups quickly took notice, and the harshness of their rhetoric fell off sharply. The exception was Don Gerdts, the instigator of the Crane Pond raid and the self-declared leader of the "Adirondack Rebellion." Gerdts had his own style and a much better sense of the media than most people. Reporters loved to quote his pithy, colorful comments.

But Gerdts had a darker side. If he disliked something you or your organization did or said, he would write you a short note and fax it to your office from a store. These "Gerdts Grams," as we called them, usually contained a vague threat such as "I hope I see you in a dark alley someday." Collector's items.

GIVE US A SIGN

Large signs along the major highways welcomed visitors to the Adirondack Park. Defacing or destroying those signs became a popular way to protest the recommendations of the Governor's Commission. One of the largest signs was at the southern boundary of the Park along Interstate 87 near Lake George. Someone had taken a chainsaw to its wooden supports.

The sign had been down for many months and no effort seemed to be under way to replace it. The Adirondack Council occasionally asked the regional office of the DEC about plans for its replacement, but after several inquiries, we were told that there were no immediate plans to replace the sign because "they will just knock it down again."

That made no sense to us. Vandalism is an irritating fact of life, but the rest of us carry on. We paint over graffiti. We put cemetery monuments back on their pedestals. We buy another pumpkin. And we press the authorities to catch the little bastards that were responsible.

So we redirected our efforts to the DEC's main office in Albany. The staff got back to us in a day or two. The sign was scheduled to be replaced, they said, and soon.

But weeks went by and still there was no sign welcoming visitors at the busiest entrance into the Park. We asked again, and this time, we got a strange reply.

A replacement sign had been created, we were told, but the department did not have the wooden supports to which the sign would be affixed. They were waiting for the state Department of Transportation to give them two wooden poles.

Now, it was not unusual for reporters trolling for a story to call John Sheehan, our communications director, to see if anything interesting was happening. Fred LeBrun, a local columnist for the Albany Times Union newspaper, happened to call John that week. John had no news of particular importance to pass along, but in the course of chatting he did tell Fred about our efforts to restore the sign and the reason the bureaucrats had given for the delay.

The tale caught Fred's fancy. In the next Sunday edition of the Times Union, he lampooned the state department of environmental conservation for its inability to find two sticks in a six-million-acre state forest.

The next day at the office, we were all chortling at Fred's clever column. Later that morning, the phone rang and John picked it up. At that time our Albany office was a small room in the back of a law firm on loan to us while we searched for a permanent location. There was just enough room for three desks—one each for John, Eric Siy, and me and we could easily hear one side of each other's phone conversations. But this time I could hear the caller as well. He was shouting at John, who held the phone several inches from his ear.

After a few minutes, John said, "I will put you on hold for a second, and put him on." Then he turned to me.

"Who the hell is that?" I asked.

"It's Tom Jorling," he said. "He wants his goat back."

I took the call. LeBrun's column had indeed gotten the environmental commissioner's goat. He had plenty of abuse left after finishing with John, and he gave it to me with both barrels.

According to Jorling, the Council had nothing better to do but to harass him. Apparently, I did not appreciate that the continuing sign issue was distracting his department from more important tasks in protecting our environment. Among my personal faults was my lack of ability to distinguish the important from the mundane, which also demonstrated how naive I was. Everyone knew that all our organization wanted was to have our name in the paper so that we could raise more money.

I made the mistake of correcting him. "Commissioner, the story did not even mention the Adirondack Council."

That was a bad idea. Now I was "playing games" with him.

Jorling found a third barrel, which he proceeded to unload on me as well. Then he hung up.

The commissioner had claimed during his rant that LeBrun had identified the Council as his source. LeBrun later told us that he too had taken a call from the enraged commissioner in which Jorling had threatened to cut off his access to the department if he did not reveal his source. LeBrun did not say if he gave up his source, which would be considered an ethical breach by most reporters. But because it would not take a detective to deduce that we were the only people making inquiries about the sign, we were likely behind the column. So we gave LeBrun the benefit of the doubt and thought none the less of him.

The new sign went up that week. It had steel posts. Thanks, Fred.

MEL MILLER LOVES ME

The unexpected defeat of the bond act in 1990 devastated those environmental groups seeking funds from New York state for land acquisition inside the Park. No other source of money appeared on the horizon.

The bond act defeat was a political disaster as much as a financial one. Land protection groups had assured both the governor and the legislature that the voters would endorse their approval of a statewide referendum on the bond act. We had put all our proverbial eggs into that one basket, and now they lay broken on the ground. It took a long time for the groups to shake off the defeat and decide what to do next.

A key moment arrived while many of us were attending a meeting that winter at Camp Eagle Nest on Blue Mountain Lake, now the Blue Mountain Center. There, the Nature Conservancy revealed, for the first time the status of its negotiations with landowners throughout the Park. They had identified thousands of acres of timberlands and privately held estates whose owners were looking to sell.

Our biggest fear was that land speculators would jump in and complicate the situation. In prior years, opportunistic companies had done just that, acquiring prime properties in a manner that left much forestland divided up in a way that threatened their sustainability. The prospect of new speculators or residential developers was alarming. The fact that the land-use regulations proposed by the governor's commission were facing relentless attacks only deepened the anxiety.

One valuable idea emerged from the Blue Mountain Center meeting: a list of the top ten properties we all agreed needed to be protected. That then raised the question of whether we should make that list public. Releasing a top-ten list could drive up the price if the state did try to acquire the parcels. Our relationship with the landowners would also suffer if they resented seeing their properties on the list.

The groups decided that the risk was worth taking. We needed to remind state legislators of how many "Jewels of the Adirondacks" could be lost if nothing was done to either purchase these properties outright or otherwise rein in the speculators. The Association for the Protection of the Adirondacks printed a flyer with photos of the properties, which we distributed to state legislators, potential donors and the media. The Adirondack Council published the list as a special edition of our newsletter.

In the state legislature, the flyer barely moved the needle. Lawmakers who had been on the fence about buying more land hopped off—to the wrong side. Most saw the failure of the bond act as the voters' rejection of the very idea of more land acquisition. And since it was the environmental community that had pushed them and the governor into proposing the bond act, the environmental community was the focus of their anger.

Our meetings as the next legislative session began were peppered with dismissive remarks from members and staff: "The voters have spoken," or "The public doesn't care," or "I guess you didn't get the message."

The Adirondack coalition's "Jewels of the Adirondacks" flyer, its best effort to blow on the fading embers of public land purchases, had seemingly failed. The prospects for land acquisition seemed as good as dead.

Personally, I was at a loss. I had just left a secure, influential, well-paying job in the state Assembly on the assumption that the bond act would pass. I had envisioned spending the next several years going from one ribbon-cutting ceremony to the next as spectacular new tracts of land were opened to the public for the first time in generations.

Instead, I had to look at the glum faces of the Adirondack Council's directors. They asked the question to which I had no clear answer: What happened?

The drive to put the bond act before the voters had been led by the Democratic majority in the Assembly who, in turn, were led by Speaker Melvin H. Miller. Miller was a lot of things, but an environmentalist was not one of them.

Even though many of the speaker's top staffers had spoken up for the bond act, they felt betrayed by the vote and feared for the potential damage such a political loss would do to their careers. They blamed the environmental community for what they perceived as our incompetence at "bringing home the bacon."

Even before the bond act debacle, my own relations with Speaker Miller were not as good as some had assumed, given that I had worked in the Assembly as counsel to the Legislative Commission on Solid Waste Management for five years prior to joining the Adirondack Council in 1990. In that role, I had worked well with Miller's senior staff, although we had occasionally clashed over policy matters. I had particularly rubbed the Speaker the wrong way by refusing to support legislation that a friend of his from outside the legislature was pushing. The senior staff met with me twice in an effort to convince me that I should change my position. The third time we met, I was reminded pointedly that staff members served at the pleasure of the speaker. Message received but unheeded.

My boss, Assemblyman Maurice Hinchey, backed me up. That probably saved my job, but in the end we were both rolled and the bill passed over my now silent objection.

In the early months of the 1991 legislative session, green lobbyists dutifully arranged meetings with key legislators and staff in order to promote a revised agenda as the new legislative session began. The green groups arrived at their appointments only to be stood up, screamed at, or insulted. A dark humor spread among them as they joked about "going in for another beating." And then they pretty much gave up all hope for their land-use agenda that year.

There was one notable exception, David Gibson at the Association for the Protection of the Adirondacks. That group, founded in 1901, consisted of the original advocates for protecting the Park. I was inspired by Gibson's conviction that if we just presented the facts we would prevail in the end. Plus, having worked both inside and outside the power structure, I knew that the worst situations often created the best opportunities. Nobody sees you coming.

I saw a new opportunity when Speaker Miller shuffled his staff and put a newcomer to the legislature in charge of environmental policy. Alyse Gray was a smart lawyer and, as far as I could recall, the first person of color to be in charge of environmental issues at the Assembly.

Alyse knew little about the Adirondacks, but was open to new information and wanted to understand the issues. I saw her as a new conduit for my message. I could get directly to the speaker through her without having to run the gauntlet of longtime staffers tending their fresh wounds and holding old grudges.

When the time was right, I pitched her. Mel Miller is a blank slate on environmental issues, I said. That's not his fault; it just wasn't his area of expertise. The previous Assembly speaker, Stanley Fink, and the current chairman of the environmental committee, Maurice Hinchey, had simply dominated the field for years.

"But Mel is the speaker, and he can lead," I said. He certainly could. While Mel or the previous Assembly speakers would consult and confer with their majority members on important issues, the Democrats dominated the Assembly chamber and the speaker ruled the roost.

I said there were a lot of reasons for the failure of the bond act, but the public's lack of interest in saving priceless Adirondack parcels was not one of them. I showed her a poll commissioned by the Nature Conservancy just before the November vote that demonstrated public support for the state's purchase of key parcels in the Park. (Thank goodness, Alyse did not ask me why that support did not translate into easy passage of the bond act.)

"Mel Miller can make his mark in Adirondack and New York history," I continued. I told Alyse that the speaker had a golden opportunity to personally save some or all of the ten "Adirondack jewels" that we had promoted in our flyer. Miller should put money into the budget to save the parcels that were placed most at risk of sale to developers by the failure of the bond act, I said.

The need for action was urgent, I reminded her. The timber giant Diamond International Corporation had divested itself of all of its lands in the Adirondacks just a year or two earlier, which had forced Governor Cuomo to scramble to find the funds to protect key tracts. And just a month ago the Heurich estate, the largest undeveloped tract of privately owned shoreline on Lake Champlain, had been advertised for sale following the collapse of the bond act.

Miller should focus on three to five parcels with a price tag of "only five million dollars—tops," I said. And now was the perfect time to do it! Next year would be the centennial year of the Adirondack Park, and there could be no better way to celebrate its creation. If Miller put money in the budget this year, the land purchases would take place during the centennial and the speaker would be on hand to accept his well-deserved applause at the ribbon cuttings.

The Adirondack Council, I promised, would dub Miller a "champion of the Adirondacks." We would deliver the support of the other Adirondack groups and many more organizations statewide for the "Speaker of the Assembly Mel Miller Adirondack Park Centennial Initiative." We would also deliver to the speaker the editorial support of the *New York Times*, I blithely assured her.

To my pleasant surprise, Alyse reacted like a co-conspirator. We met again to refine the pitch, and Alyse said she would raise it at dinner with the speaker that very week. Miller was known for sweeping into Albany restaurants with his staff entourage. The boisterous crowd would occupy a large table, supposedly to conduct Assembly business after office hours.

Alyse called the very next morning and invited me to her office. I was quite excited when I arrived and was ushered into her office immediately. She greeted me warmly, closed the door and sat down.

She said that Miller had asked that she personally deliver his response to my funding suggestion. "I am to deliver the message exactly as he asked," she said.

"Let's see, hmm." She thought for a second and then said, "Oh, yes."

"Mel said," and then she shouted, "FUUUCKK YOOOUUU!"

The office door quickly swung open and Alyse's secretary, with a look of concern, asked if everything was all right. Alyse waved her off.

I sat stunned for a moment. Then I remembered that I never had liked Mel Miller and could not see why anyone else did.

"Well, that message is precise and quite clear," I replied. "Thanks for asking him."

Then I left.

For good reason, I never mentioned this episode to my boss or to my colleagues. Plan B would not come to me for some time.

THE LOST YEAR

Following the bungled release of the new Commission report, the defeat of the bond act at the polls, and my failed outreach to Speaker Miller kept most of 1991 a dead zone for Adirondack policy-making.

But to his credit, Governor Cuomo started laying the groundwork for a comprehensive bill that would shape the future of the Adirondack Park. The governor traveled that fall to meet with the Adirondack North Country Association and announce that he intended to work with local leaders and other stakeholders to forge consensus legislation on the Adirondacks in the 1992 legislative session. He instructed his staff to sit down with moderate town supervisors, large landowners, and representatives of the environmental community. The recommendations in the Commission report would be the jumping-off point for these discussions in the form of a "study bill."

The administration's main representatives in the talks were Frank Murray, the governor's longtime deputy secretary for energy and the environment, and Murray's new assistant secretary Joe Martens.

Joe had worked at the Assembly Ways and Means Committee and the Adirondack Park Agency before Cuomo asked him to join his staff. Joe knew a lot about the Park and environmental policy, and it did not hurt that he also had a nice jump shot. He was immediately drafted to play on the governor's basketball team in Cuomo's weekly games at the New York State Police Academy.

Frank and Joe met frequently with various interests in the Park, including Bob Flacke's Blue Line Council; local officials at the Adirondack Planning Commission, an arm of the Inter-county Legislative Committee of the Adirondacks, and environmental groups including the Adirondack Council. For the most part, they excluded grassroots groups in the Park that were openly hostile to the governor and the Commission report. The chosen groups met separately with officials in the governor's office, and at times with each other, often at remote locations away from the Capitol. Frank used the meetings as an opportunity to find out what was important to the various stakeholders and to bounce ideas off them.

The Blue Line Council and the Adirondack Council were invited to submit ideas for legislation. Both went further and drafted complete bills that were delivered to the governor's office.

Bob Glennon, who had worked with Joe Martens as both executive director and counsel at the Adirondack Park Agency, was brought into the inner circle to sort through the various ideas and draft a legislative proposal for the governor to submit in 1992.

In many ways, Glennon was the last person you would to ask to forge a compromise on the future of the Adirondack Park. For one thing, his sympathies were squarely with the Commission report. It was widely believed that he had been the author of the draft legislation that was poised to turn the Commission's recommendations into law.

Glennon also had a difficult relationship with the Adirondack Park Agency even as he was serving it as executive director. He felt that APA members were too concerned with being liked by Park residents, and thus were reluctant to use their powers to restrain or control development to protect natural resources.

Glennon believed that the regulatory scheme that the APA oversaw would allow a significant build-out of new homes in the Park over time, which he often publicly described as the Park "dying by a thousand cuts."

He also was not shy about telling others that he saw one aspect of the original Adirondack Park Agency Act as a complete failure. The act creating the agency had adopted a carrot-and-stick approach to regulating development. First, it had taken the power to regulate most land use other than in hamlet areas away from local towns that did not already have zoning in place and given it to the APA. It was a new layer of regulation. But towns could regain the power if they adopted local zoning laws that were at least as protective of natural resources as the new state law. There were more than 100 localities with land inside the Park's boundaries, but only a handful had chosen the carrot and moved to adopt modern zoning. That left the state agency in charge of regulating much of the Park—everything from a homeowner's boathouse to a developer's dream of fifty summer homes around a lake. And the legislature consistently gave the APA inadequate staffing to do its job.

Local residents blamed the APA for being an intrusive regulator even as they turned a blind eye to the failure of their own local governments to step up and take responsibility and control. Glennon feared that under pressure from the residents, the state would capitulate in any new compromise and restore local land-use control without adequate protections for the Park's resources.

Other flaws in the Act were apparent both to developers and environmentalists. In a political compromise to win its approval, the act allowed much more construction near waterways than was ecologically sound. A new boom in second-home development was squeezing through that loophole, threatening not only to divide the backcountry into mini-estates but also to mar the scenic beauty of shorelines and pollute lakes and streams.

Despite these head winds, Glennon was a damned good lawyer who knew the Park like the back of his hand. The governor's office needed his expertise to draft the new compromise bill.

Eventually, the draft came out of Frank Murray's office and was distributed, to my knowledge, to only two groups for private comments: the Blue Line Council and the Adirondack Council.

The next time I saw Murray, he was apoplectic. He was on the phone when I walked into his office, and as soon as he hung up, he turned to me and exclaimed, "Fucking Glennon!"

It was highly unusual for Frank to swear in front of me. I soon learned that he had just heard from the attorneys representing the Blue Line Council, and they were not happy. I got the impression that Glennon had buried some of his own ideas in the draft bill and Frank had not been aware of them. Now he was embarrassed.

"If it's any solace, we liked the draft," I offered.

Without a word, Frank waved me up from my chair and out of his office.

That may not have been Glennon's only stealth attempt to shape the bill. As the governor's negotiations on a grand Adirondack deal continued, environmental groups began receiving anonymous letters and faxes from the "Black Loon." This mysterious figure was very well informed. The messages were a mix of advice, information, and warnings about what might happen. As far as I know, no one tried to learn the Black Loon's identity. When I asked my colleagues, they all said they assumed it was Bob Glennon.

To their credit, the governor's team persevered. They made the most progress with the Adirondack Planning Commission, led by the Richard Purdue, supervisor of the town of Indian Lake. The Adirondack Council participated in joint sessions with Purdue's group and the governor's staff, and tangible gains were made on several fronts. Purdue would be rewarded for his efforts with denunciations from some local officials and shunning from others, all of whom seemed afraid to say yes to anything.

Rumors began swirling that a deal on the Adirondacks was possible during the 1992 legislative session. Inside the Park, the newspapers and local government officials were on edge. It was in this atmosphere that I had a weird encounter with state Senator Ron Stafford. Not my first, mind you, but one of the most memorable.

Stafford was careful to cultivate different images for himself in his home district and at the Capitol among his fellow legislators. At the Capitol, he was a dealmaker, a veteran legislator who knew how to exercise power and when to compromise. But in his sprawling Adirondack district, Stafford was known as the orphan boy, adopted and raised in the shadow of the state maximum-security prison in Dannemora, who became a successful lawyer and a powerful state senator. He was a "good ol' boy giving 'em what fer down there in Albany." As he accumulated seniority, the senator also accumulated, and distributed, pork-barrel funding for his constituents—two thousand dollars here for new fire equipment, one thousand dollars there for a senior center, and so forth. For that, too, he was beloved.

On the speaking circuit in his district, Stafford railed against big government (although government was a major employer there), New York City residents (whose taxes largely paid for his pork-barrel projects), and especially environmentalists from Downstate "trying to tell everybody in the Adirondacks what to do with their own damn property."

The senator's longevity in office helped him build a broad support network. In effect, Stafford's district had become a political organism.

When he needed to show the voters were behind him, the word would go out from his office via a telephone tree to his supporters. Then his district would come alive! Local governments would approve a hail of resolutions endorsing his position on virtually any topic. Commentary in the local newspapers' opinion pages and letters to the editor would adopt the same point of view. The writers usually praised Stafford for defending his people from some threat, real or imagined. Whether the issue involved property rights, the state budget, or the broader concerns of rural Upstate communities, the senator could always argue that he was responding to the will of the people of his district. He made sure of it.

Most local government officials in the Park would have been surprised to learn that at least some of us tree huggers were regular visitors to Stafford's office. The senator usually knew exactly when to expect a visit from a delegation of these local officials at the Capitol. But on one particular day, a delegation arrived several hours early.

On that day, I happened to be in the Senator Stafford's private office meeting with the senator and his senior aide, Peter G. Repas. A secretary suddenly pulled Peter out of the office, and he returned to report that the large delegation had arrived very early for their appointment. Peter made a point of telling Stafford that the visitors were filling all the chairs in the reception area and in the conference room.

There were two doors to the senator's private office. One opened onto the reception area and the other to the conference room. I was slow to appreciate the problem this posed, but Stafford immediately rose to the occasion.

He said to me, "I have some visitors waiting outside that I must meet with now. Can we finish this later?"

"Sure, Senator," I answered. "I'll follow up with Peter."

Then he puzzled me by saying, while shooting a look at Peter, "Now, don't pay attention to what I'm going to say. My staff does it all the time."

I was going to ask him what he meant, but before I could, Stafford got up quickly from behind his desk and strode to the door to the reception area. He pushed it open sharply and stood in the doorway, pointing outward.

He turned to me and said firmly and loudly, "Get out!"

Rattled by the sudden change in the senator's demeanor, I froze in confusion on his deep red leather couch.

"Excuse me, Senator?" I asked.

Projecting his voice into the adjacent room, he said in an even louder voice, "You heard me, get out!"

Startled, I started to move, but the slippery leather was hindering me from rising from the deep recesses of the low couch.

As I struggled, Stafford declared, "Don't bother coming back!" Turning to his aide, he barked, "Peter, show him out!"

Peter gestured for me to get up and follow him. I struggled to my feet and passed through the doorway, where the senator now stood acknowledging his new guests.

As I followed Peter through the reception area, I felt the eyes of every local official trained on me. We exited into the hallway, and I was still confused about what was happening.

Peter walked me some distance down the hall without speaking and then, with a quick look back, turned to me and said, "Sorry about that. We would have taken you out through the conference room, but that was full of local government folks too."

"So he threw me out of the office in front of them?" I asked.

"Yeah, well, like I said, we couldn't get you out any other way. I gotta go."

As I watched Peter walk briskly back down the hall and into the office, I could only shake my head. I had been thrown out of offices before, but not as an act of theater.

Most of the 1992 legislative session turned out to be nothing but sound and fury.

Pete Grannis, who had succeeded Peter Berle in his Manhattan Assembly district, was likewise an ardent environmentalist. He had introduced a bill essentially implementing the Commission's recommendations to the letter.

Maurice Hinchey, chairman of the Committee on Environmental Conservation, introduced his own bill in the Assembly. It differed from Grannis's in some respects, but likewise proposed consolidating state agencies in the Park into a single Adirondack Park Service and adding new protections for the backcountry.

There was no Adirondack bill in the governor's name, because Cuomo's staff continued to struggle with satisfying competing interests. But the new speaker of the Assembly, Saul Weprin from Queens, took up the issue. By the close of the legislative session in June, the Assembly had overwhelmingly approved a bill cosponsored by Weprin, Hinchey, and Grannis.

A few weeks earlier, Governor Cuomo had traveled to the Blue Mountain Lake Museum to attend a celebration of the centennial of the creation of the Adirondack Park. He spoke about his commitment to protect the natural resources of the Park and to pass new legislation.

He also came bearing a gift—the announcement that an eighteen-mile stretch of Hudson River shoreline owned by the Niagara Mohawk Power Corporation would become part of the forest preserve. (See figure 1.4.)

I remember his speech mostly for one of his adlibs. That day, the winds were calm and the notorious seasonal arrival of biting black flies was in full swing. Clouds of flies hung over the heads of the crowd, and many of us were slapping at them when they landed. I was close enough to the governor to see his face and that he was not being spared. But he stood there stoically.

Figure 1.4. Maurice Hinchey with Mario Cuomo at Blue Mountain Lake Museum. *Source*: Nancie Battaglia.

When another speaker apologized to the governor for the biting flies, Cuomo quipped that in his experience, dealing with state legislators in Albany every day was much worse than dealing with the black flies at the museum.

Meanwhile, Stafford was having none of the bill passed by the Assembly. He reintroduced in the Senate the familiar parade of doomed-to-fail anti-Park measures that he sponsored every two years as he sought reelection, including a bill to abolish the Adirondack Park Agency.

Negotiations between the two houses went nowhere. It was now two years since Cuomo's commission had put forward a comprehensive set of proposals to protect and expand the Adirondack Park, and all attempts to turn them into law remained dead in the water.

Or so we thought. The legislation was dead, but only Rasputin dead. It would prove as hard to kill as the Russian monk.

THE DEAL

The governor had finally released his proposals for the Adirondacks in October 1991. (See figure 1.5.)

The Adirondack Council knew that the governor was willing to make a deal. The Assembly was willing to compromise as well, but Stafford appeared to be simply turning his back on an Assembly-engineered bill even though it could include millions of dollars in new programs and benefits for his district.

Stafford had to reconsider, we reasoned. You don't say no to that twice. We just needed to give it one more try.

We also knew that there were too many cooks in the kitchen. Our observation was that local government officials could agree to deals, but they couldn't hold the line for more than a week without being pushed off by intense pressure from worried constituents and antigovernment activists.

The environmental community, still debating the merits of various commission recommendations, was having a hard time finding consensus itself. Hell, we even had a group of former Council colleagues, led by Dick Beamish and Eric Siy, break away to form a parallel advocacy campaign.

Amid this cacophony of opinions, we started ramping up another effort. Not publicly. Not in a coalition, but in the time-honored way of smoke-filled back rooms.

Well into the 1992 legislative session, the governor's officials reached out to Senator Stafford and asked what he wanted in exchange for new

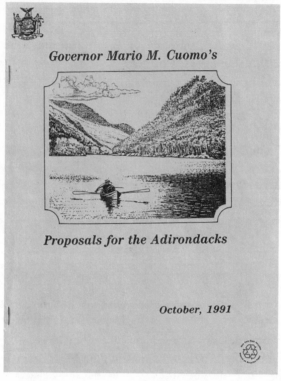

Figure 1.5. Cover of the governor's proposals. *Source*: author, public domain.

controls on waterfront development and new protections for the Adirondacks backcountry. The governor was also dangling a new economic development plan for the communities in the Park.

Shortly after that overture, I was called into the governor's office.

"Stafford isn't serious," said Frank Murray, the governor's deputy secretary for the environment, as he handed me a list. "This is what we got from his office."

It was a long list. It requested money, lots of it, for new water and sewer projects, new medical facilities and plenty more.

"I am sure that it just a starting point for negotiations," I said.

"They said they want everything on the list!" Frank said, "There is no way we can do all these things and they know it. They are not serious."

I hustled over to Stafford's office, where Peter Repas and another aide, Tom Grant, met with me.

"The governor's office just told me that you have a list of demands to do an Adirondack bill," I told them.

"We do," said Repas, handing me the same list.

"They told me that you also said that you had to have everything on the list in order to do any Adirondack bill," I said.

Repas and Grant looked at each other.

"Absolutely!" said Repas, as he tried to suppress a smile. Grant also tried, but did a poor job.

I didn't try to hide my grin. "I understand," I said. "Nice list."

Negotiations quietly proceeded in earnest as the legislative session wound down. All the state's environmental lobbyists were spending their days moving back and forth between the governor's office, the Senate and Assembly chambers, and members' offices. After all, we had another big fish to fry. We were pushing the legislature to approve a statewide fund dedicated to environmental protection, although that effort would not bear fruit until the following year.

I split my time between acting as head cheerleader, exhorting the governor's office and the senator's aides to keep talking about an Adirondack bill, and trying to be a confidential courier of information between them.

The problem was that it became increasingly difficult to hide my secret role from my fellow lobbyists. I didn't enjoy being evasive, which was necessary when the other lobbyists met with Stafford's staff and then, under the guise of reporting what they had been told—which was not much—tried to get me to confirm it.

Then it got worse. I was simply being followed. If I went to Stafford's office, ten minutes later a contingent of environmentalists would show up. Everywhere I went in the Capitol, the bloodhounds were on my trail.

Eventually, my need to move about secretly as a courier became crucial. The talks had produced a serious draft bill that would implement many aspects of the Commission report in exchange for a large number of the items on Stafford's list. The Assembly leadership had already passed an Adirondacks bill, but the leaders had essentially given the governor's office its proxy if a deal could be made with Stafford.

Tim Burke, our executive director, offered to come to Albany. As a former member of the Vermont legislature, Tim was curious to observe the end of the legislative session in New York. But more importantly, he suggested he would act as a decoy.

We asked some of our Albany staff members and interns to accompany Tim so that he would have an entourage. The other environmental lobbyists had never seen Tim in Albany except for news conferences or big ceremonial events, so they assumed, correctly, that something big was up. Tim even told them as much. He just didn't say that he was not working on it.

Our plan worked. Tim and I, as well as all the other lobbyists, tended to hang out in the Senate's lobby, which had comfortable seats and air-conditioning. When I needed to slip away for one of my secret missions, Tim and his entourage would take off for another destination. The lobbyists from the other environmental groups would tail him, and I would head off for the real work.

Eventually, the behind-the-scenes talks bore fruit. One afternoon, rumors started to filter out in the hallways of the Capitol that there was a tentative agreement between Stafford and Cuomo. Allies from other groups rushed over to Tim and me to confirm it. But having promised both sides to keep everything confidential, we acted like it was news to us.

Only an hour or two later I got a phone call from Tom Grant, Stafford's aide.

"The bill is dead," he told me.

"What happened?" I asked.

"Harold Jerry called the senator and asked him not to do it. As a friend."

I expressed my disbelief. Harold Jerry was an Adirondack Council director, and the protections for the Park in the tentative agreement were very important to us.

Tom asked me to meet him on the staircase below Stafford's office. When I got there, he handed me a copy of a phone message Jerry had left for Stafford earlier that day. It essentially begged the senator not to agree to the bill and cited their long-standing friendship.

"The senator saw the message and called Harold and told him that he would not do the bill," Tom said.

"I am in shock," I told Tom.

"So are we," he said.

When he heard the story, Tim Burke was as furious as I was.

Only the night before, Tim and I had signaled our support to the governor's office and Stafford's. Both sides, leery of criticism, had asked the Council to give its pledge of support before they would commit.

The deal provided substantial new resource protections for waterfronts and the backcountry. The key concession for Senator Stafford was that the Adirondack Park Agency would no longer be an independent state agency. Instead, like the Lake George Commission charged with protecting the water quality of the "Queen of American Lakes," the APA would technically be an arm of the DEC. Our collective judgment was that such a change merely represented form over substance, since the regulatory powers of the Agency would be unchanged, but the realignment would provide the necessary political image of a win for the senator.

The shit hit the fan at our board meeting in Elizabethtown that July, after the legislature had adjourned. In a closed session, Harold reportedly confessed to the board. He told his fellow directors he believed the proposed deal was a bad one and we were better off with the status quo. He also acknowledged that he had an obligation to either follow the organization's consensus on policy, or leave. So he resigned from the board.

For years, people would ask me why Jerry had left. We felt we could not really explain. In a private meeting some months later, Senator Stafford confirmed both the details of Jerry's call to him that day and that he had made the reluctant decision to kill the deal for his friend.

Stafford then looked up at me and asked, "Why did you throw Harold off the board?"

Thoroughly puzzled, I replied, "He resigned, Senator."

"Oh," is all Stafford said. We never discussed it again.

NO SUIT

We would make one more attempt the following year to win passage of legislation on the Adirondack Park. Much less comprehensive than the Stafford-Cuomo deal that collapsed at the last minute, the new bill focused narrowly on a topic that all interest groups seemed to agree on—better protections for water quality.

This initiative came not from the governor's office, but from the Assembly.

Working with the new chairman of the Committee on Environmental Conservation, Westchester County Assemblyman Richard Brodsky, the Council crafted a bill that was good for the environment and good for the communities that depended on clean water sources. Even Bob Flacke's minority report on the Cuomo commission's recommendations had supported more protection for water quality.

Brodsky believed, and I agreed, that a new approach aimed solely at water quality had the best prospect of gaining consensus across the Park. As a first step, Brodsky asked me to get the various environmental groups on the same page.

My former colleagues Dick Beamish and Eric Siy were still operating their own Adirondack Campaign. The heart of their legislative proposal was the original Commission report. Assemblyman Pete Grannis, a close ally of Audubon President Peter Berle, had reintroduced his bill implementing the commission report.

I invited all the lobbyists for Adirondack environmental advocacy groups to a meeting. Eric Siy responded that the Adirondack Campaign would attend, but that Harold Jerry wanted to host the meeting at his office at the Public Service Commission (PSC).

My fellow lobbyists still were not aware that Jerry had single-handedly scuttled last year's deal on the Adirondacks. He was still greatly admired in the Adirondack environmental community for his commitment to the protection of the Park. I certainly had not planned to invite Jerry, given our recent history, but it made sense to me that Siy and company would not sign on to the new bill without his blessing. If they did sign on, then Grannis would likely support the Brodsky initiative as well. I owed it to Chairman Brodsky to try.

Before the group assembled at the PSC, I had also sent a draft of the bill, at Jerry's request, to Bob Glennon at the Adirondack Park Agency. I was not at all concerned about his reaction, because I thought he would agree with most of its contents.

At the meeting, Jerry said that Glennon would not be attending, but was to momentarily fax his comments on the draft. Soon, Jerry's secretary came in and said that she had received the fax. He told her to make copies for everyone.

She hesitated, and with caution in her voice, replied, "Are you sure? I should copy the cover letter, too?"

"Yes, everything!" Jerry said, somewhat annoyed with the question.

Unbeknownst to Jerry, his secretary was the mother of one of the young basketball players I coached in our community. She knew me well and had been to my home several times.

When she returned with copies, I suddenly understood the reason for her hesitation. Each copy was topped with a cover letter that read in bold letters, "THIS LOOKS PRETTY GOOD, BUT I DON'T TRUST MELEWSKI."

Harold looked up and said with aplomb, "Well, I guess we can move onto the second page."

Most of the groups agreed to endorse the bill, except for Siy's. The Adirondack Campaign was committed to promoting the more sweeping

Grannis bill. Ordinarily, having another group say that your legislation is not tough enough can make you appear moderate and reasonable. But I had a bad feeling that their intent was not to improve our chances, but to hurt them.

Chairman Brodsky scheduled a large news conference to announce the bill in the speaker's conference room off the Assembly chamber in the Capitol.

When the Assembly is in session, security guards are posted at each of the conference room's two doors. On the day of the news conference, their job was to make sure no one entered without either an invitation or press credentials.

One of my colleagues had informed me that Eric Siy planned to crash the news conference and criticize the bill as inadequate. I had no desire to see a headline the next day reading something like "Green Groups Split on Future of Adirondacks." We owed Brodsky better coverage than that. Besides, the entire environmental lobby understood that if we made our disagreements public, legislators had a ready-made excuse for avoiding action. They could say they were ready to save the planet, but the "enviros" just could not agree on what to do.

I spotted Eric in the hallway in the Capitol and noticed that he was dressed in a short-sleeved sport shirt, slacks, and sandals. All the rest of us were in suits, which was also Eric's normal attire. I couldn't figure out if his informal dress that day was an attempt to stand out, an expression of disdain for the event, or just a rationale reaction to the weather being really hot.

The Assembly's sergeant at arms had asked the environmental lobbyists to gather at the conference room's door, and I was tasked with clearing their admission with security. As far as I could tell the whole group was there, and we filed in.

"Is there anyone else?" the guard asked me.

"I don't think so," I said. "But if I missed someone, they would be wearing a suit."

I walked in. I saw that Assemblyman Grannis was observing the news conference, which had nearly ended when a Capitol page came into the room with a message for him. The note was from Eric Siy. The security guards had refused to let him enter. By the time that Grannis came back with Eric in tow, the news conference was over.

I overheard Grannis grumble to a colleague, "They wouldn't let Eric in because he wasn't wearing a suit. Can you believe that?"

Brodsky's water-quality legislation passed the Assembly easily, but got no traction in the Senate. Senator Stafford had reintroduced all of his bills that were hostile to the Park and the Adirondack Park Agency. Some things never change.

Given Stafford's intractable opposition, the Council decided that any new attempt to enact a comprehensive Adirondacks bill would be pointless. We decided on a new strategy of breaking the Commission's recommendations into separate initiatives. Over the next several years, many of the Commission's recommendations were implemented through regulations, narrowly drafted legislation, budget provisions or other action by state agencies or the governor's office. The law creating the Adirondack Park Agency, however, which was enacted by the state legislature in 1971, would, save for one minor amendment, remain untouched for fifty years.

YOU CAN'T MAKE THIS UP

Having very little to do in the fall of 1992, I was reading a summary of the November election results in my office. I came across a surprising one. The Republican majority leader in the New York State Senate, Ralph J. Marino, had survived an unusually close race against a seemingly weak opponent. He had run against a Democrat who was an ardent environmentalist and who had attacked Marino throughout the campaign for his failure to do anything on environmental issues—and in particular, his failure to support the establishment of a statewide environmental fund.

Curious, I studied newspaper articles about the race. There was broad speculation that Marino's opponent would challenge him again, this time with strong financial backing. Some editorials and analysis pieces stated flatly that Marino should be concerned. They said the senator's poor environmental record improved the odds for his opponent, who had bona fide green credentials.

Was there an opportunity here?

Marino had several influential staff members surrounding him. His aide, Angelo J. Mangia, was chief counsel to the Senate majority and had enormous clout in the chamber. Leonard M. Cutler, a part-time adviser to the majority conference on policy issues, was my former mentor, handball opponent, and professor of political science at Siena College.

Len had introduced me as a college student in the 1970s to the more mundane but necessary elements of any political campaign. One autumn, I worked on a telephone bank. Claiming to represent a fictional polling company, we called people who had voted in the previous election and asked them for whom they would vote if the election were held today. We were careful to hide the fact that we were interested in only one upcoming election in one state Senate district. I also distributed campaign literature. One night I even prowled the streets of Albany in a sound truck, chanting slogans at unsuspecting and startled pedestrians. I am not sure that my work that night helped our candidate's campaign, but he did win.

More significantly, Cutler landed me an internship with the state Senate and several years later got me my first job there. Both positions taught me valuable political and personal lessons. I will always be grateful to Len.

The state Senate internship gave me the chance to observe the legislature in action, attend receptions thrown by lobbyists, and generally get a feel for the place and how it worked. One thing I observed helped me make the decision to enroll in law school the next year.

I noticed that however quickly bills progressed through the state Senate, they all seemed to bunch up at the Rules Committee, the final step before reaching the floor for a vote. Late in the session, people I had never seen would arrive and the legislative process came to a halt. After a few days, a torrent of bills suddenly began hitting the Senate floor to be approved. I quickly learned that the newcomers were lawyers called session counsels who seemed to have great control over legislation. They could veto deals already made and create new deals out of thin air. The power they wielded impressed me.

Now, following the 1992 elections, I was calling on Len again in hopes of gaining access to someone in the inner circle of Senate Majority Leader Ralph Marino. Len was out, but I left a teasing message stating, "You will be happy that you returned my call." When he got back to me later that day, I offered no further details but said I had a proposition to present to Angelo Mangia, the majority chief counsel. My proposition, I declared, would be politically attractive and extremely valuable to Senator Marino. My problem, I explained to Len, was that I had no relationship with Angelo and he had refused every request from me for an appointment or even to return my calls.

Len was uncomfortable about my vague request, but I kept after him, repeatedly assuring him that it would be stunning news and Angelo would be happy that he had met with me. And, I emphasized, it had to be an in-person meeting. After weeks of nagging, Len agreed to set up the meeting. He told me that "it had better be good" or it would be the last meeting I would ever have with Angelo.

The Senate majority counsel usually had a line stretching from his office into the hallway, so I was prepared to get a five-minute courtesy meeting at best. Len warned me of that possibility as he and I—wearing my best lawyer uniform of blue suit, white shirt, and red tie—waited in the exterior office. But Angelo treated me warmly and was generous with his time. He discussed his own environmental interests and his background in environmental law, citing several cases from his private practice in which he played a material role. Fortunately, I had heard about those cases and could comment in a knowledgeable and complimentary way.

We were both familiar with a the passage of a recent law that had authorized the construction of a landfill on Long Island whose sole purpose was to receive ash from new waste-to-energy garbage incinerators. The new law was challenged by a group of Long Island residents all the way to the highest court in New York, the Court of Appeals, and the law was upheld. I informed Angelo that, in fact, I had drafted the legislation while working for the Assembly and I had the bill-signing pen certificate on my office wall. He seemed suitably impressed.

Then it was time to get to the point. I noted that Marino's election in November had been closer than expected. It was likely that the same candidate would be running against him again. And I expected that having run a good race, the candidate would receive considerable financial backing from environmentalists and the Democrats. Mangia and Len both nodded in agreement.

I also said that his opponent had a point. While Marino had played a role in the passage of environmental legislation in the past—and I was careful to identify those bills—he did not have a strong environmental record over all, and green groups would be sure to emphasize that in the next campaign.

I hadn't expected to get this far in my pitch, but Mangia sat quietly listening. So I soldiered on, and went well beyond their expectations for the meeting. I said that I could deliver, with Senator Marino's help, a significant piece of environmental legislation for which Marino would get the credit as the originator and sponsor. If his Republican majority would pass it first, the bill would also win approval of the Democratic-led Assembly and the Democratic governor would sign it into law. Eyebrows went up at that news.

I pulled out the "Jewels of the Adirondacks" flyer that listed the top-ten sites targeted by environmental groups for acquisition by the state. I finished my pitch by telling them that if they could secure funding to acquire these properties, I would ensure that the environmental community recognized Marino as the person who "saved the Adirondacks."

After all that, Mangia was noncommittal. I left somewhat discouraged.

But I had no sooner gotten back to my office than I got a call from Len. He said I had made a difficult proposition. He then said it was an interesting proposition. And then he said that Angelo had liked the idea. I would hear back from them.

Apparently, I had interpreted the political situation on Long Island correctly. I had read the mood of the Marino camp correctly. Now it was all about the price tag for the properties.

After a while, Len asked me how much money we were talking about. I gave him the information, never revealing that my source was the Nature Conservancy. They said it was too much. We haggled, debated, negotiated, and ended up with a list of five properties.

I was told that the Senate majority would support new funding in the budget for those five properties, but passing it would not be an easy task. They raised that fact that nearly all of the Adirondack Park was in the district of Senator Ron Stafford, and that his district had voted overwhelmingly against the 1990 bond act. The implication was obvious. For the funding to pass, Senate leader Marino would have to roll Stafford, a powerful member of his own majority conference.

As usual, budget negotiations between the two parties dragged on well past the April 1 target date. Early in the month, I took the marble-wrapped underground walkway between the legislative office building and the Capitol building as I headed for a meeting. At the Capitol end, I rode up the escalator, and as I neared the top I saw Senator Stafford walking by on the main floor. He looked down at me. I smiled. He seemed to slow down and linger.

"Hi, Senator," I greeted him.

He looked at me. "You are with Harold's group, right?"

This was a frustrating act that Stafford put on frequently. Stafford seemed to take a strange joy in pretending that he did not know who I was or for whom I worked. "Harold's group" is what he always called the Adirondack Council. It was like, Harold Jerry was still a member of our board and Stafford was very familiar with his "cred" as an ardent environmentalist. Less well known was that Jerry and Stafford were good buddies, longtime buddies. Although the two men's philosophies about managing the Adirondack Park could not have been more different, they both loved the Park. Arguing about the Park was one of the ways they enjoyed each other's company.

I played along with Stafford. "Yes, Senator, I'm with the Adirondack Council, as you know."

I want to say he wheeled toward me, but it wasn't that fast. Stafford sort of turned and leaned into me. He said, almost in a stage whisper, "I know what you are doing."

"Excuse me?" I asked.

"I know what you're doing, and you're not going to get away with it." This statement was accompanied by a classic Ron Stafford move. When making a point, he would shape his hand like a gun and then jab it slightly toward you, making it appear that he was getting several shots off. It was equally interesting and disturbing.

I blinked and my jaw dropped. I thought to myself, what is he talking about? Then I realized he meant the Marino proposal.

"It's not going to happen," Stafford told me. "I understand why you're doing it, but it's not going to happen."

Then he walked away. That was the only discussion on the topic that I had with the senator that year.

Only a week or two later, I got a call from Len Cutler.

He said, "You might want to take a look at the budget the Senate just passed." Then he hung up. At that time, the common practice was for each house to approve its own budget, and negotiations would be held to reconcile the two with the governor's proposals before the final product was signed into law.

I rushed to get a copy of the Senate budget. There it was: Three Adirondack properties were listed—by name, which was unusual!—along with more than one million dollars allocated for their purchase by the State of New York.

Then I did something that I had not planned. I asked for another meeting with Len and Mangia, who assumed I was coming in to thank them. But when I arrived, I told them that I would still hold up my end of the agreement, but the deal was for five properties, not three.

The air went out of the room.

"Do you know how hard this is?" Len said.

I replied, "It is no harder politically to do five than three, and that was the deal."

Actually, I did know how hard it was. The *New York Times* had run a story on the Heurich estate going up for auction in the Adirondacks and the need for a permanent environmental fund to purchase such properties. Senator Stafford had told the newspaper that he was absolutely opposed to the state acquiring more land in the Adirondack Park.

Len Cutler called me back the next day, asking, "How do we know that you'll keep your end of the deal?"

"I gave my word," I said.

"We need more," he replied.

"Let me think about it," I told him. "I'll get back to you tomorrow."

I hung up feeling challenged but excited. "Fish on!" I shouted to myself from my desk. Our intern came running into my office at the commotion.

The next day, I called Len back. I said I would provide a signed, undated letter on Adirondack Council letterhead giving Marino credit for having conceived, sponsored, promoted, and won passage of the state funding to save these five priceless Adirondack jewels. The letter would say that all New Yorkers, who as taxpayers and residents are the owners of the Adirondack Park, should be grateful to the senator.

I delivered the letter later that day. I had no authorization to do so.

I had an interesting agreement with our executive director. Tim Burke was a former Vermont legislator and conservation commissioner. He loved the intrigue of the legislative process and had agreed to a devil's bargain. He would give me great latitude and tacit support for whatever legal activity I thought would advance our cause in Albany. But if things went south and it became politically necessary to maintain plausible deniability, we both understood that Tim and the organization could extricate themselves from the situation by saying, "Yeah, we fired that guy."

With my letter in hand, Marino added the other two properties to the Senate bill. It passed, even though Stafford made a passionate plea for its defeat during debate on the floor. I couldn't resist going to the gallery of the Senate chamber to listen to it.

Now it was time for me to live up to my end of the deal. In the Assembly, I made it clear to the Democratic majority that the Senate would "do the lift." In other words, the funds for the Adirondack land program would come from the Senate share of the "pork barrel"—money allocated each year for pet projects requested by legislators on both sides of the aisle. The Assembly staff confirmed with Marino's aides that the Senate would indeed do the lift, and the Assembly chamber's leadership in turn agreed to support the funding.

This left the governor no option, I figured. He had to sign off.

I was wrong.

As the legislative session neared its close, staff members at the Senate Finance Committee told me they were meeting later in the day with the governor's staff to complete the budget deal. The leaders of both parties had told their troops to wrap up negotiations on all fronts in anticipation of final action on all bills and adjournment.

Lisa Genier, my colleague and legislative assistant, and I were in a Capitol hallway as the Senate staffers walked to the meeting. They gave us a "thumbs up." It happened that we were in the same location later as the staffers returned to their offices. They looked at us, shook their heads and gestured to indicate that something had gone badly wrong.

It was after hours by this time, and the secretaries that usually controlled access to the offices of the governor's deputy secretary for energy and the environment were gone. I marched in thru the open door.

I found Joe Martens, who had become deputy secretary, chatting with environmental Commissioner Tom Jorling and his deputy, Langdon Marsh, and other staffers.

I said, "The Senate staff just told me you turned down the deal for the Adirondack parcels."

Everyone in the room hung their heads. They said nothing.

I shouted, "I can't fucking believe you did this!" and stomped out of the room. I must have looked like a madman talking to myself as I went back down the hallway. Lisa would later say that she had never seen me so angry.

I was sure it was the governor's call to walk away. His people, I saw, were clearly embarrassed to be part of the decision. They all knew that the parcels truly were the jewels of the Adirondacks.

I worried for a while that Marino would use my letter in his campaign anyway and my job would go down the drain along with the deal. But in the end, Marino's green opponent chose not to run again and the letter was not needed.

Lisa and I thought we should do something to thank Len and Angelo for sticking their necks out for us. In the fall, we invited them for a tour and an overnight stay at a historic Adirondack Great Camp, but they took a rain check.

The 1993 legislative session took a weird turn from there. The Assembly had already approved a bill to seize unclaimed deposits on bottles and cans from the state's returnable container law for an environmental fund. We worked hard on that effort, but it was blocked for the second straight year in the Senate by the soda and beer industries.

I remember watching the US Open tennis tournament on television the previous summer. During the men's singles final, there was a close-up of the spectator box immediately behind the baseline. There they were, the major Albany lobbyists for the beer and soda industries. And who was with them in those premium seats? It was Senate Majority Leader Marino and his entourage. I knew at that moment that the idea of using container deposits for an environmental fund was dead.

The fact that the Senate budget in 1993 contained money for the "Jewels of the Adirondacks" did produce an unexpected and spectacular result. Downstate groups who had been seeking to protect unique parcels of land in the Hudson Valley and on Long Island had been told repeatedly by their own state senators that because of the failure of the bond act, new money for land acquisition was not politically possible. The money for the Adirondack Jewels infuriated and energized them.

The Downstate groups launched a dynamic campaign to create a dedicated fund for land acquisition, pressuring the Senate and the Assembly with equal vigor. This time, the green lobby did not urge a specific source of funding. Just make it happen, lawmakers! The Adirondack Council was happy to join that coalition, as were other groups such as the Nature Conservancy and groups in the western part of New York.

As seemed to be always the case with environmental bills, the battle went down to the wire as the legislature wound up the 1993 session. The effort by a now united environmental community faced more obstacles along the way.

The first was an effort by some Downstate Republicans to defer any action, claiming that including any funding for land acquisition in the Adirondack Park would raise the ire of Senator Stafford, who now chaired the powerful Finance Committee. Stafford would kill the entire bill if Adirondack lands were not excluded, they said.

At least one environmental advocate took the bait. Klara Sauer of the group Scenic Hudson tried to get the other Downstate groups to agree to exclude the Park. With the help of Neil Woodworth of the Adirondack Mountain Club and staffers at the Nature Conservancy, we were able to persuade all the groups to keep the coalition together.

Then Governor Cuomo weighed in.

Cuomo invited me to come see him. Well, nine others and me.

The pressure by the coalition on Downstate senators had worked. Senator Marino and the Senate Republican majority had just announced that they were in favor of creating of an environmental fund. We had considerable support in the Democratic-led Assembly, but Cuomo was curiously silent on the matter. So our coalition increased its lobbying of the governor's office and was able to get an audience with him.

The day of the meeting, we entered a conference room on the second floor of the Capitol and waited around the table. The environmental lobbyists from the Adirondacks, Hudson Valley and Long Island included several lawyers, myself among them, wearing their best "go to court" blue suits.

Cuomo entered and wasted no time. He sat down without the customary handshakes around the room and immediately observed, "Lots of blue suits in here. That's a surprise."

Then he spoke in general terms about how the Adirondacks and the Hudson Valley were beautiful natural resources that all New Yorkers treasured, and how he would like to do more—but the state just did not have the money.

He recalled that the state's dire financial situation in 1985 had led him to sell Camp Topridge to a private buyer, which he now described as "my biggest regret." Camp Topridge north of Saranac Lake was one of the largest and most luxurious of the Adirondack Great Camps, bought in 1920 by the Post family of cereal fame and extensively renovated. I had the opportunity to visit it twice before I joined the Council to attend state conferences. Among the more than fifty magnificent log structures was a massive main lodge, most of whose furniture was covered in skins of exotic animals and whose floors were strewn with bearskin rugs. I recall having a wonderful time swimming in the lake and playing tennis on the courts. At one conference in the 1970s, Peter Berle, who had left the State Assembly to become environmental commissioner, arrived late but in style by helicopter. And the next morning, he challenged one of his staff attorneys, Langdon Marsh (who some years later would be appointed commissioner by Governor Mario Cuomo in 1994) to swim across the lake and back as I stood nearby admiring the view. I checked back on their progress just in time to see them emerge from the water. Berle looked none worse for the wear. Lang, not so much. (See figure 1.6.)

Heiress Marjorie Merriweather Post had bequeathed the camp to the state, but it was undoubtedly expensive to maintain, so Cuomo had chosen to sell it. The buyer was a Polish-American entrepreneur named Roger Jakubowski, who called himself the Hot Dog King of Atlantic City. Camp Topridge was just one of many sites that Jakubowski had rapidly gobbled up in the Adirondacks, stoking concern among local residents. He once told *Adirondack Life* magazine, "I should own the entire Adirondack Park, that's what I think." Now the Hot Dog King was looking to move on.

I spoke up. "Did you know that Topridge is back on the market, Governor?"

"Yes. And I am not buying it back," Cuomo said in a matter-of-fact manner.

That brief exchange altered the entire course of the meeting. Earlier in the day, the environmental advocates had agreed who would speak and in

Figure 1.6. Topridge boathouse. *Source*: Nancie Battaglia.

what order, so we would stay on message and not be repetitive as we made our case to the governor. But Neil Woodworth apparently saw my quip to the governor not as chit-chat, but as an abrogation of the agreement setting the order of speakers, which had Neil and me speaking last.

Neil jumped in and proceeded to pitch the governor on the merits of establishing a dedicated fund for environmental projects, with a focus on acquiring land in the Adirondacks. Neil was smart and had such a high energy level that he had acquired the nickname "the Energizer Bunny," from his colleagues. And as a former defense attorney, he loved to talk. But as he finished his Adirondacks-centric spiel to Cuomo, the Hudson Valley contingent was staring a hole in his back, steaming as he went off message.

The agreed-on order of speakers was restored, and we soldiered on. Cuomo listened intently, showing considerable patience for awhile, but eventually exhibiting signs of boredom. I was the last to speak and tried to get my points out quickly.

The big guy asked if we had finished, and then launched into a lecture. It was a classic Mario Cuomo performance, in which he asked himself questions and then answered them. We were mere onlookers as he carried on. At the end, he thought it best to give us some advice.

Senate Majority Leader Marino "doesn't care about the Adirondacks or the Hudson Valley," Cuomo said. "He doesn't care about the environment. He is not serious about an environmental fund. He is just using you."

"How is he using us, Governor?" interjected Neil.

Cuomo couldn't say. He apparently thought we would take his word for it or that it was obvious. It was an odd and uncomfortable moment.

The governor tried again. "Tell Marino that you are not going to support his fund," he urged. It was now apparent to me and others, that Cuomo was the one who wanted to use us.

A woman from the Sierra Club spoke up. "We don't work for you, Governor."

And with that remark, the meeting was over. A staff member jumped up and thanked us for coming, and Cuomo left without further word.

I had never seen the state's green groups more united than at that moment. Only a few days before, the groups from the Hudson Valley and the Adirondacks and Long Island were bickering over who deserved the most money from the environmental fund, and even whether the Adirondacks should be cut out entirely.

Now those differences would be laid aside. Ignore the governor, we agreed. We all had been pounding the hallways of the Capitol for weeks and had a pretty good sense that we were close to getting the votes we needed. We all felt that we could get the fund passed without Cuomo, that we didn't care where the money came from, and that we could bicker over who gets the loot next year after the fund is up and running.

Our renewed resolve carried the day. In the very last hours of the legislative session, both houses approved an Environmental Protection Fund to provide annual funding for projects statewide. The dedicated money would come primarily from real estate transfer fees. Senator Stafford lost again. His colleagues in the Senate majority conference dropped his demand that only two Adirondack parcels could ever be funded. Instead, a compromise provision gave local governments limited authority to veto any future state land acquisition in their towns.

Local government officials were often publicly heard complaining that public land acquisition meant a loss of tax revenue in their towns. Actually, unlike most areas of the state outside the Blue Line, the State of New York pays property taxes in full on forest preserve lands inside the Adirondack Park.

Because a large state land acquisition inside the Adirondack Park usually meant a considerable increase in a local community's property tax revenue, the green groups felt that local vetoes would be unlikely and that they could live with the compromise.

Sometime later, a gathering of the environmental lobbyists was discussing the fight for the Environmental Protection Fund. Someone said that he still did not understand why the Senate had proposed to fund five Adirondack land purchases in their one-house budget proposal. Did anyone have any idea?

I said, "Sure, I know," and I told the group the whole story.

The group was silent for a while, and then Neil Woodworth said, "That's a great story, Bernard, but no offense, I can't believe it is true."

Another colleague said, "I do."

"Why?" said Neil.

"Because you can't make this stuff up."

We all laughed.

In the fall of 1994, Lisa Genier and I decided we should renew our offer for Len Cutler and Angelo Mangia to visit the Adirondacks, and this time they accepted. They had plans to attend an annual conference held by the Business Council of New York State at Lake George, where Senate Majority Leader Marino was to speak. Afterward, they would drive west one and one-half hours to Mohegan Lake, where Lisa and I had arranged for them to join us at J. P. Morgan's now-century-old Great Camp Uncas. We had also arranged for a tour of nearby Great Camp Sagamore, the historic summer home of Alfred Vanderbilt.

Then Len called. Something had come up while they were at Lake George. They weren't sure what was happening, nor could they talk about it, but they needed to stay for a while. Then they called again and said they were returning to Albany, but might come up later. We called them back that night, and this time they said that there was a serious matter that needed to be tended to. They apologized, but had to decline our invitation.

Within a month or two, the reasons they pulled out were clear to everyone. A coup had been completed. Marino had been ousted as majority leader by his fellow Senate Republicans, a result of Marino having failed to support George Pataki in that year's GOP gubernatorial primary. Pataki had gone on to win the governorship, and Joseph L. Bruno was the new leader of the Senate Republican conference.

It was widely reported that Senator Ron Stafford had played a key role in the so-called Thanksgiving Coup. Bruno elevated Stafford to be deputy majority leader. Marino, stripped of most of his staff, his perks, and his influence, resigned three months later. Len Cutler and Angelo Mangia were cast out of the inner circle of Senate Republicans.

A NEW DAY

Mario Cuomo moved quickly to embrace the new Environmental Protection Fund.

Just weeks after its passage in July 1993, the governor announced his intention to buy much of the 2,000-acre Heurich Estate along Lake Champlain in the Adirondack Park. The property, which included Split Rock Mountain and almost three miles of undeveloped shoreline, was a haven for eagles, falcons, and the endangered eastern rattlesnake. An auction sale of the estate to a private buyer had just been averted by the timely purchase of much of the property by the new Open Space Institute, headed then by Peter Borrelli.

The governor's staff staged a bill-signing ceremony for the fund on the Heurich Estate. Under a tent on a beautiful August day, Cuomo and Stafford, both of whom had resisted the creation of a permanent environmental fund, enthusiastically embraced it. I watched as they cracked jokes with each other and jockeyed to get into photographs. (See figure 1.7.)

Figure 1.7. Bill signing, Environmental Protection Fund. Front row L. to R., Paul Schaefer, Senator Stafford, Governor Cuomo, Gary Heurich. Commissioner Jorling, Peter Borelli are standing behind the governor. *Source*: Nancie Battaglia.

The signing was followed by refreshments provided by Gary Heurich, which included beers brewed in Utica, New York, from the recipes of the defunct family-owned brewery in Washington, DC. The Christian Heurich Brewing Company was once an important presence in the city, sitting until 1956 beside the Potomac River where the John F. Kennedy Center for the Performing Arts is now located.

Gary revived the family business under the name Olde Heurich and sold his New York–made beers in the nation's capital until 2006. But he was never able to realize his dream of reopening a brewery there.

The Olde Heurich brand would become synonymous with the Adirondack Council. Gary became an active Council supporter, a board member and a purveyor of refreshments to Council events over the next few years. It was good beer. I especially liked the Foggy Bottom Ale.

And I liked Gary. He was a handsome young guy who enjoyed life. One of the wags at our Elizabethtown office had made up a story that Gary was the model for the cartoon character Richie Rich. I remember struggling up Capitol Hill in Washington one hot July day a few years after the sale of the Lake Champlain estate. I had a fully loaded briefcase in one hand and a stuffed suitcase in the other. I was sweating through my starched white shirt, marching to the Rayburn House Office Building for a series of meetings. Gary appeared alongside me driving a Mercedes convertible, the top down, his two golden retrievers in the backseat. The dogs wore matching red neckerchiefs. He stopped briefly at a light to shout out to me that he was headed for a beer tasting. For a brief moment, I hated him.

After the bill signing, I would have only one more occasion to meet personally with Mario Cuomo. I was at an environmental conference on the shore of Lake George in the fall of 1994, when word came that the governor would like to address us. The reason given was that the he wanted to award Paul Schaefer, a legendary wilderness advocate in the Adirondacks, with an award for environmental achievement.

Paul deserved it, but it was not an easy offer to accept. It was only days before Election Day. Most of the groups at the conference were non-partisan by law and in practice. Hosting the governor while not offering the same opportunity to his Republican opponent, George Pataki, raised ethical questions. A powwow ensued.

Some said, "He asked us; we did not ask him. What's the problem?" Others said, "Pataki is not going to win, why worry?" Still others said they didn't want to hear a lame last-minute pitch from the governor for our votes.

I said to myself, "Why the hell is Cuomo wasting time days before the election coming to Lake George?"

In the end, the majority agreed that we should accept his offer. So the next day around lunchtime, Governor Cuomo landed on the lawn in the same helicopter that throughout the campaign his opponent had criticized him for using. The copter made an incredible racket that was jarring in the quiet setting along the lake. We watched the noisy thing land and the governor emerge along with his environmental aides and walk slowly up a hill toward us. We followed him like the Pied Piper into a chapel near the conference site.

It turned out to be a most appropriate setting. We were expecting a rah-rah speech extolling the governor's environmental accomplishments and urging us to drive a sea of green voters to the polls. Instead, a humble, thoughtful and seemingly sincere Mario Cuomo told us of how much he appreciated and was inspired by the good work we did. He saw the natural beauty surrounding us in the Adirondacks and around the Empire State as God's gift to us all. He was happy to have the opportunity to protect some of that natural beauty for future generations, and he knew and appreciated that we unselfishly strived to do the same every day. He said it was an honor to be our governor, and if we did not speak again he wanted us to know that. He said not a word about the pending election.

I sat stunned by his tone and demeanor. This is pretty low-key for a campaign speech, I thought. Was he tired? Why did he come? What does he mean, if we do not speak again? Then it hit me.

"My God," I thought, "he knows he is going to lose."

Cuomo had come to say goodbye.

I was touched by his grace that day. I shook his hand before he walked back down the hill, climbed aboard his helicopter and flew off to a different future.

CALL ME GEORGE

I first met George Pataki when he was a young member of the Assembly. He had just been named the minority leader of the Republican members of the Committee on Environmental Conservation. It was routine for me to ask for a meeting with each committee member at the beginning of the state legislative session every year, with the goal of finding common ground with each one and getting a better sense of their interests.

As usual, I was running late for the meeting and bolted into Pataki's outer office a few minutes late. I was checking in with the secretary at the front desk when I saw him in the doorway to his private office. He waved me inside.

I told Pataki what the Adirondack Council's priorities were for the legislative session and he listened attentively, and then cut the meeting short. He said he too was running late and motioned me to follow him out to the main office.

"I don't think you'll have much trouble with me anyway," he said, as he made a sweeping gesture at the office's walls.

The usual decor when legislators decorated their Capitol office included photos of historic sites or pretty views in his or her district, provided on loan from state agencies. The assembly member from Peekskill, however, had lined his walls with professionally mounted large-format photos of the Adirondack Park by famed photographer Nathan Farb. There was not a photo of Peekskill to be seen.

FORGED BY FIRE

When George Pataki became the Republican nominee for governor in 1994 and sought to oust Mario Cuomo after three terms, the vast majority of the environmental community remained loyal to the Cuomo administration heading into the election.

After Pataki's upset victory, the general feeling of uncertainty in the environmental community, given the sea change about to occur in the executive and at state agencies, was tempered by our belief that the governor-elect was a strong environmentalist, fond of quoting Teddy Roosevelt. We scrambled to make new connections with his team and were optimistic about the future.

But things would sour pretty quickly.

In its first months, the Pataki administration waged war on the state agencies charged with promoting conservation; he abolished the State Energy Office, which had coordinated the planning of energy policy statewide and promoted energy conservation.

At the Department of Environmental Conservation, he named a former business lobbyist, who I felt had always been on the wrong side of environmental issues, to a key position. She then directed weekly firings of staffers. Unsuspecting employees were told to box up their personal items under the eyes of supervisors and were marched out of the building as soon as possible. The dismissals were conducted on Friday afternoons to limit media coverage, so we called them the "Friday Afternoon Massacres."

The environmental community quickly lost faith in Pataki.

The Adirondack Council decided to try a tactic we had never used before. We still could not believe that Pataki was personally authorizing this string of antienvironmental actions. It just seemed odd for the guy we had known as a proenvironment legislator. We decided to smoke the governor out.

We assembled a list of pending, upcoming and past actions by the governor or state agencies that we did not like. We gathered enough material for a couple of weeks of news releases that included our negative spin. Then John Sheehan, our communications director, went to work. Every couple of days, we would issue another release attacking the administration. Every infraction was directly linked to the governor.

Newspapers in the North County and farther west in Syracuse, Utica and Rochester regularly wrote stories based on our releases. The papers and radio stations in Albany picked up a few as well.

John had a good relationship with reporters at the *New York Times* during this period. We decided to go for broke and encouraged the *Times* to write a story about the disenchantment in the environmental community with the new governor. As was our practice, we told the governor's office that it was coming ahead of time, and we tried to have our fingerprints all over it. The story ran on page one of the Sunday paper, above the fold. Depending on your perspective, that display was about as good—or as bad—as you can get.

At first we were disappointed that the Council was not more prominently mentioned in the article. But it had the desired effect. On Monday morning, I got a call from Bradford Race Jr., a former law partner of Pataki now serving as secretary to the governor, the number 1 staff position.

I had met Brad for the first time earlier in the year at his office in the Capitol to pitch our agenda for the governor's first legislative session. The meeting was unremarkable. All I remembered were the golf balls strewn around his office that made walking treacherous. Apparently, he dealt with stress by working on his putting.

Now he was sharing his stress.

Brad screamed at me over the phone, "Who you think you are?" He shouted that we would never set foot in the governor's office again.

At first I was startled, but soon I was amused. Brad wasn't very good at playing the Big Bad Wolf. As he continued, he seemed to be losing steam.

I told him that the Adirondack Council had been around for twenty years. "We were here before Pataki," I said, "and we will be here after Pataki."

Brad found his rage again. I decided to change tactics.

I told him that we had shown that we could get the governor bad press, but we preferred to get him good press. Brad fell silent and listened.

I said, "Trust me, we are even better at getting good press. Give us a chance and we will deliver for the governor. Work with us and you will be glad you did."

I continued, "Let me give you a couple of suggestions of what the governor can do. If we don't deliver on our end, then you make your own judgment on whether it was worth the effort."

The call ended cordially. I promised to get back to him the next day.

As I hung up, considering my next move, my thoughts turned to a trip I had taken earlier that year. I was one of several passengers in a DEC helicopter out of the Albany airport. Our flight plan was to take us to view state wilderness lands from the air located in the Adirondack Park. We had flown into an unexpected hailstorm and our pilots had just been given permission to return to the Albany airport. Through our headsets, we could hear the pilot advise that the weather had turned poor. Poor? Hailstones were pinging steadily off the copter like gunshots and the sky ahead was various shades of gray and true black. It was my first helicopter ride, and at one point the aircraft seemed to turn up and over. I reached out for anything I could grab. I had no idea that the machine could do that.

It was the summer of 1995, and we had been flying at the invitation of Michael D. Zagata, commissioner of the Department of Environmental Conservation. He had asked representatives of environmental groups to take a flight over the Adirondack Park to see what nature can do. Only days before, the Park had suffered its most devastating natural disaster since the Great Blowdown of 1950. An unusual line of storms generated straight-line winds of great force that cut through some of the greatest wilderness areas in the western portion of the Park. Tens of thousands of trees had been flattened in oddly orderly rows. The storm had also damaged nearby developed areas and had caused several deaths and injuries in state campgrounds when trees fell onto tents.

The question was, how should the state respond? After the Great Blowdown of 1950, the state attorney general had issued a formal opinion that allowing private timber companies to harvest the downed trees on the state forest preserve did not violate the section of the state Constitution declaring these state forestlands to be "forever wild" and off limits for the removal of timber. Zagata now wanted to do the same thing—to "suspend the Constitution," as he artlessly put it.

Many of the same forces that had influenced the 1950 decision were in play in 1995: the opportunity for industry to make a quick buck, the protective instinct to "clean up the mess" on the forest floor, the need for government to appear decisive, and, most powerfully, the public's fear of fire.

Newspaper articles soon appeared describing what could happen if the fallen timber was allowed to remain on the forest floor. All that "fuel" would feed a fire of "biblical proportions," it was claimed. The towering flames would sweep from west to east across the Adirondacks and eventually "jump the Northway" (four-lane Interstate 87, which runs from Albany to Montreal), burning everything in its path until it reached the shores of Lake George and Lake Champlain.

Fortunately, the environmental community closed ranks on this issue. We devised a common strategy that would keep the trucks and skidders out of the forest preserve: The state Constitution had to be defended.

We knew that once the governor's office got word environmental groups were considering a lawsuit it would first try to head it off. If that didn't work, the executive office would try to isolate the groups and cut them off from information. So we proceeded on two tracks. Green groups that had access to free legal assistance or funding to support a lawsuit formed a coalition and started spreading the word that they were ready to sue the state if necessary. If a lawsuit were filed, the other groups would stay out of the litigation so that the environmental community kept the lines of communication open with state agencies, and in particular with the governor.

In the meantime, everyone worked to get accurate information out to the media, which unfortunately was already hyping the prospect of a fiery end to the Adirondacks. Reporters needed to know that the Constitution prohibited the taking of timber from the forest preserve. But getting that point across was harder than we expected. The interviews were oddly similar.

"Even in an emergency?" a reporter would ask.

"Yes," one of our colleagues would answer.

"Even if the trees aren't standing?"

"Yes."

"Aren't you concerned about fire?"

"Yes, but most of the blowdown is in an area where it rains a lot and where the terrain is full of gravel (called eskers) and surrounded by streams. It is naturally fireproof."

"What about owners of adjacent private property?"

"They are free to take whatever measures on their lands they see as appropriate."

"But didn't they take timber from state land after the 1950 blowdown?"

"Yes. They broke the law."

It turned out that the Council's greatest asset in our media campaign was a member of our board of directors, a former forest ranger named Clarence Petty. Clarence was an Adirondack legend. He had a long history as a wilderness guide. He personally mapped hundreds of miles of rivers for the state, and was one of the oldest flight instructors in the United States. My favorite personal experience with Clarence came when he was attending his first Council board meeting after back surgery. I asked him how he was feeling, and he complained that he should never have had the surgery. Clarence said he had taken his guide boat out the day before and had gotten tired after paddling only five or six miles and had to go back home. Clarence was eighty-six at the time. (See figure 1.8.)

Clarence had worked for the conservation department in the 1950s and had seen firsthand the damage done to the forest by timber harvesting after that blowdown. That made him a well-informed advocate in this campaign, and on top of that he was quite charismatic in a gentle, unassuming way, a talented storyteller, and a passionate defender of the Constitution. We

Figure 1.8. Clarence Petty, Gary Randorf, Greenleaf Chase. *Source*: Nancy Trautmann.

used him in interviews whenever we could, because he charmed the pants off every media person he met.

In the midst of the dispute, the chairman of the Adirondack Park Agency, Gregory Campbell, also appointed by Governor Pataki, was persuaded by the timber industry to take action on his own. The APA, which functions as a giant planning board for the Park, had oversight of the development of millions of acres of private lands. Private landowners had also suffered damage in the blowdown, and commercial timber companies were understandably anxious to recover whatever they could of their lost assets, which had had been standing comfortably in vertical storage but now stood to rot and lose their market value.

But Campbell's proposal overreached. No one would have quibbled with granting emergency permits to specific landowners to recover downed trees. Campbell instead proposed a general permit allowing clear-cutting of privately owned timber virtually anywhere in the six-million-acre Park. The plan went much further than earlier general permits in that landowners didn't even have to notify the state before starting to log, and could wait for months before filing paperwork on their operations. The APA would not even know you were clear-cutting hundreds of acres of your forest. In media interviews, we started called it "mail-order clear-cutting."

Assemblyman Richard Brodsky, a Westchester Democrat, had succeeded Maurice Hinchey, my old boss, as chairman of the Committee on Environmental Conservation. The committee had jurisdiction over most matters directly affecting the Adirondacks, including oversight of the DEC and the APA.

Brodsky was a character. He was outspoken, smart, and often sarcastic. In the Assembly, he was willing to debate virtually any topic with colleagues on the floor, with reporters, or with anyone standing in front of him. Some of my colleagues found Brodsky uncooperative and difficult, and they got frustrated with him to the point that one told me that listening to Brodsky made his teeth hurt. I always thought his confrontational approach, which forced fellow legislators and lobbyists to articulate and defend their ideas, was part of his charm.

Like many other legislators, Brodsky liked to bellow out to his staff from his inner office. One day, I was waiting to meet with him when he roared out, "Tea!" I was not aware that having tea in the early afternoon, after committee meetings but before the full legislature met, was a daily ritual in his office. When Brodsky was informed that day that I was waiting for him, he invited me to join him. It was excellent tea.

I confess that I stopped by his office around that time of day more frequently thereafter, hoping to be invited for tea. I found that during this daily ceremonial session Richard was a much more mellow fellow. It was the best time to raise more challenging matters with him.

Brodsky was no fan of Governor George Pataki, who he sarcastically called the "environmental governor." And I never really knew why, but it was obvious in the governor's office in turn that the collective blood pressure went way up whenever I mentioned Brodsky's name. What I deduced was that each man and his loyal staff were eager to be seen as the better environmentalists, and this presented a lobbyist a clear opportunity to play them off against each other. Game on!

Early in Governor Pataki's first term, I briefed Richard (who insisted I call him by his first name) on our concerns about the clear-cutting of timber in the Adirondack Park. We discussed APA Chairman Campbell's proposal to issue a general permit allowing private landowners to engage in the damaging process without any oversight by the state. In our opinion, any number of abuses could and would occur. We complained to the media and to the governor's office, but I also asked Richard for his help.

Much to my surprise and pleasure, Brodsky said he would like to hold a hearing in Lake Placid on clear-cutting. I said we would definitely help set it up and that the Council would provide expert testimony.

I accompanied the new chairman and his staff member, Louis, to the Adirondacks. The weather cooperated perfectly and it was an interesting drive up from Albany. Richard asked about my family—Russians, Ukrainians, and Poles who had immigrated to America and settled in the cities of Watervliet and Cohoes in Upstate New York. Richard shared stories about his family's arrival and settlement in the Downstate Russian Jewish enclave of Brighton Beach.

Our families had immigrated at about the same time, but for different reasons. My family had been loyal to the czar and had fled the onset of the Russian Revolution. Richard's family fled Russia to avoid persecution as Jews. We realized, as we shared more details, that there was a chance that two of our great-grandfathers had met. In Red Square.

Richard laughed heartily as he concluded that my great-grandfather, a Cossack in the czar's service, probably had beaten his great-grandfather during a protest. We both thought this outlandish but potentially true. What a riot! Richard had insisted on holding a news conference before the hearing on clear-cutting as a way of introducing himself to the region's reporters. He wanted a nifty setting for that event, and we had suggested the top of Whiteface Mountain. It was one of the Adirondack's famed High Peaks, and you could drive right up to the top, from which you could see most of the other High Peaks and all of Lake Placid. It would be perfect. (See figure 1.9.)

As we drove up the final approach to the summit, Richard asked us if he could practice his speech in the car. Then he launched into a heavy Yiddish accent and said, "I am so happy to be here at Whitefish Mountain, where there is so much whitefish they named a mountain after it!" Louis and I laughed and said that should go over well.

When we arrived at the summit, there was a mass of print, radio, and television reporters. The local media was curious about the new environmental chairman from Westchester and eager to meet him.

We piled out of the van and Richard stopped to pull something out of the back. It was a cowboy hat with a feather prominently attached to the band. Richard obviously thought the hat conveyed the impression that he was not a city slicker, or flatlander in Adirondack parlance. It also gave him an opening to talk about his fishing exploits during his annual summer vacation at his wife's family ranch in the Bridger Mountains of Montana.

The reporters were charmed by Richard's performance, and everything went well until a newly arrived reporter asked, "So what's with the hat?"

Figure 1.9. The view from the summit of Whiteface Mountain. *Source*: Nancie Battaglia.

Richard launched into his Montana story.

She interrupted and said, "No, the feather."

"The feather?" Richard said. "I think it looks good with the hat."

"No," she persisted. "What kind of feather is that? It looks like a bald eagle feather."

Richard's face betrayed the slightest appearance of panic. "I really don't know," he said.

"It is against federal law to possess a bald eagle feather," she declared. The Assemblyman-lawyer shot a glance at me. I shrugged. I had no clue.

Richard tried to laugh off the query. "Well, no harm came to a bald eagle in the making of this hat, if that is what you mean." "It doesn't matter," she insisted. "It's like ivory. You can't possess it."

Whether or not it really was an eagle feather in the hatband, the day was lost. Richard could not take the hat off fast enough. The next day, it seemed as though every story about Richard's appearance included the feather controversy. Several television stories led with it. So much for making a good first impression. At least Richard didn't tell the whitefish joke.

~

Clear-cutting, a highly efficient and cost-effective harvesting technique using huge machines, was and remains a controversial practice. The Sierra Club had just released a book titled *Clearcut: The Tragedy of Industrial Forestry*,[6] filled with large format photos from the western United States showing acres upon acres of devastated hillsides that resembled moonscapes. Richard Brodsky did hold the hearing on clear-cutting the next day, and our resident staff ecologist Michael DiNunzio was the star witness. Mike, I had recently learned, had help draft the current restrictive regulations on clear-cutting in the Park. Brodsky ultimately was pleased with the hearing and said, "Where have you been hiding this guy?" He encouraged me to bring Mike down to meet legislators in Albany. The true impact of the hearing remains unknown to me, but it was certainly noticed in the second-floor offices of the governor in the Capitol.

Most New Yorkers, and I wagered that secretary to Governor Brad Race was among them, did not know that clear-cutting of forests, even on private lands, was legally allowed in the Adirondack Park. Subject to a specific permit, and pursuant to a forestry plan, landowners could level a considerable number of acres at one time. But the rules in New York were much tighter than the rules for timber cutting out west. Clear-cutting was rarely used in New York or even contemplated. Until now.

In September, John Sheehan worked to get the *New York Times* to run another article. "State officials, environmentalists, timber companies and landowners are locked in debate over what to do, or not do, with the tens of millions of toppled or tottering trees," it read. "Answering these questions poses a subtle political test for Governor George E. Pataki."

We had our issue of choice. Could the governor step in, Brad?

A second piece would run later in the *Times*. This one noted that the environmental community had reversed course and was praising Pataki after the governor had intervened to order significant modifications to the general permit proposed by the APA chairman. In the article, our executive director called the revised proposal "the governor's redraft."

Brad called me the next morning. "That was great. A great piece. The governor is really happy about it," he said. "What do we do next?"

It was the start of a beautiful political relationship.

In the end, Pataki rejected Commissioner Zagata's proposal to harvest fallen trees in the forest preserve. At the news conference announcing his decision, Clarence Petty joined the governor at the podium.

BOND ACT BOMBSHELL

I had a meeting with P. Nicholas Garlick, one of the legislative counsels to Governor Pataki, on a Friday in early 1996. He had asked me to come by to discuss a specific issue, but he seemed to grow bored with our topic after a few minutes and changed the subject.

"What are you doing this weekend?" he asked.

"Mowing the lawn, nothing much," I answered. "You?"

"I have to work. In fact, I may want to call you. Can I have your home phone?"

I left wondering what that was all about. I found out the next morning. Nick called and urged me to drive to Garrison, a couple of hours south of my home. He said Pataki wanted to meet with me and some other people, but offered no more information.

A summons from the governor was not to be ignored. I drove with haste to Garrison.

The meeting site was in the backyard of a local environmental advocate. A steady trickle of my colleagues was arriving and helping themselves to cold sodas from a cooler set up near two picnic benches.

There was a group of ten or more of us when the governor arrived in a black van, dressed informally, with his counsel Mike Finnegan in tow. Sandwiches were distributed and we chatted informally for what seemed like forever before the governor called the meeting to order.

Finnegan laid out the administration's concern that the environmental needs of the state were not being met, from water quality to hazardous waste control to land acquisition. The defeat of the bond act in 1990 was a big part of the problem, as the state would soon exhaust the funds remaining from previous bond acts. Annual legislative appropriations, and even the new Environmental Protection Fund, would make only a dent in the backlog of projects. So, Finnegan concluded, what did we think about another attempt at passing an environmental bond act? (See figure 1.10)

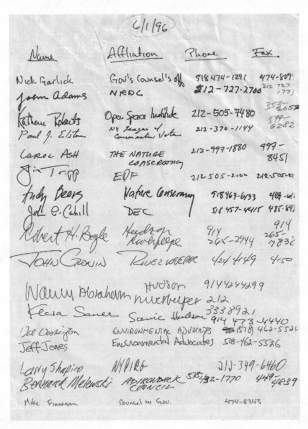

Figure 1.10. Sign-in sheet for the governor's meeting. *Source*: author's own material

The crowd on the picnic benches remained silent. We were stunned. The bond act had lost in 1990 partly because of the lukewarm support of the governor's Republican Party. Could Pataki be serious?

Finnegan went around the tables, asking each person to share his or her reaction.

The initial responses were cautious. "How are you going to get other Republicans to support it?" "Have you talked to the legislative leaders?" "Have you polled for public support?" "How can you go back to the voters so soon?" One person even said, "I pass for now."

Then they got to me. "I think it's brilliant," I said. "I definitely think you could pull it off."

Pataki and Finnegan looked at each other and their faces brightened. A few years later, Finnegan told a cocktail crowd of Adirondack Council supporters in New York City that he would always remember my reaction.

And the notion *was* brilliant. The majority Democrats in the Assembly would never see this coming. They would be caught flat-footed and would have to support it. As for the Republicans, well, the governor had ways to appease them. Most New York residents had always supported environmental protection, but they wanted their support to be won, not assumed. A well-funded campaign for environmental bonds could succeed with the active support of the governor. There was no question about the need for one.

It didn't take long for the others at the meeting to warm to the idea, and in fact to start making wish lists on how to spend the money. After entertaining a few ideas, Pataki said that he would consider all our ideas before the administration made a formal proposal, but it had to include one thing: funding for research on low-emission and electric vehicles. "That is my pet project," the governor said.

The legislature would have to approve a bill to get Pataki's plan onto the November ballot. The leadership in the Democrat-controlled Assembly was indeed taken by surprise when the governor unveiled his proposal with the support of much of the environmental community already in hand. They quickly gathered themselves to punish any known conspirators with the governor.

Opposition to what was dubbed the "governor's proposal" became a litmus test for access. Anyone who publicly declared support for the plan could forget about getting any meetings with Assembly leaders or their staffs for the rest of the legislative session. Some environmental groups whose political effectiveness depended on cooperation with Democratic members of the Assembly immediately buckled.

The Adirondack Council took the opposite tack. We were early and fervent supporters of the Clean Water/Clean Air Bond Act.

The Council had coincidentally been awarded a grant from an entity that sought to improve nonprofit groups' access to the media, and it occurred to us that a well-timed advertisement in the *New York Times* could help persuade the legislature—and especially Downstate Democrats in the Assembly—to have another go at an environmental bond act. With the assistance of our new partners, we designed a full-page ad to run in the *Times*.

The ad's price came as a shock, but we were able to cut the cost substantially by running the ad in black and white and leaving it to the *Times*'s advertising staff to choose when and where in the paper it would appear.

We need not have fretted about the placement. The ad ran on the back page of Friday's Weekend section, meaning it would not only be widely seen but also would stay on every coffee table for a day or two.

The ad featured a huge headline reading "THE ADIRONDACK PARK IS UP FOR GRABS." Its text explained that enormous parcels of private land, among the most precious in the Adirondack Park, were coming up for sale, and the state lacked the funds to acquire them for the public. Governor Pataki had a plan for a new funding, but the legislature needed to approve it. The ad urged the public to contact the leadership in both the Senate and the Assembly to "Save the Adirondack Park."

We were all pleased with the appearance and the placement of the ad. But it was only the following Monday that we became aware of its full impact.

I got a call from my past colleague in the Assembly, Rick Morse. "Now you've done it," he told me. "The Speaker is pissed. You guys are persona non grata."

"Why?" I asked.

"Because of the ad in the *Times*. His office is getting hundreds of phone calls from his constituents. The lines are jammed."

"Wow," is all I could say.

We hadn't intended to target Assembly Speaker Sheldon "Shelly" Silver, but we could not convince his staff of that. We were already in the doghouse with some members and staff of the Assembly's Democratic majority for siding with Pataki when he ambushed the legislature with his surprise bond act announcement. And now, Rick told me, we were "on the top of the shit list."

Still, it was the biggest bang for our advertising buck the Council had ever seen. And by the end of the legislative session we had not exactly been forgiven for our dalliance with the governor, but at least we were getting meetings again with the speaker's aides. (See figure 1.11.)

Figure 1.11. *New York Times* ad, Adirondack Park up for grabs. *Source*: Adirondack Council.

AN ALL-NIGHTER IN THE RED ROOM

As the legislative session progressed in June of 1996, a bill to put the bond act before the voters seemed to be on course for passage. Then my friend and ally, Bill Cooke of the Citizens Campaign for the Environment, stopped by my office.

Trouble was brewing among groups concerned about one of the proposed programs in the bond act, Cooke said. It involved brownfields, the term for polluted and abandoned sites, usually in urban areas, that could be cleaned up and rehabilitated for new industrial or residential use. Because these urban sites already had access to water and sewer, redeveloping brownfields was considered "smart growth" compared to bulldozing green spaces.

I learned that the governor's office had come under pressure to relax the standards it had proposed in its draft bill. It now wanted to allow much more contamination to remain at any cleaned-up brownfield site and still call the site clean and safe. Bill said he was concerned that "brown groups" (as opposed to "green groups" like ours that worked to protect natural areas and generally did not work on pollution issues) were prepared to fight the governor on this point and could possibly sink the bond act legislation.

Bill wanted me to join him at a meeting that was starting soon to discuss how to proceed. I warned him that I had not been following this particular issue very closely.

"I thought you used to be the counsel to the Legislative Commissions on Solid and Hazardous Waste Management," he reminded me. I had to acknowledge that was true.

"Well, then," he said, "you know more than ninety percent of the knuckleheads that will be in the room. I'm asking for a personal favor here. You are coming at my request."

I went with Bill to the meeting and encountered little objection to my presence. Most of the advocates in the room did not know about my past job and thought I might be an asset in the discussion.

I heard that the brown groups were themselves facing pressure from the governor's office to capitulate on the weaker standards. Not only that, but they were supposed to meet with Pataki's aides only an hour later, and they were meeting now to agree on their position. I tried to get up to speed with the issues involved as the groups agreed on their bottom line: The current standard in the bill must be preserved.

It was a good thing I was wearing a suit. The next thing I knew, I was in the Red Room, an ornate former office for the governor on the second floor of the Capitol that was now used for ceremonial occasions.

Mike Finnegan, the governor's counsel, greeted us and made a point of asking why I was there. "He's with me," said Bill.

The brown groups laid out their concerns to Finnegan, other Pataki aides and staffers from state agencies. After some discussion back and forth, Finnegan asked for time to confer with his colleagues and told us to stay in the room until he could get back to us. Before leaving, he warned us several times: "We may not be able to get the Senate on board for the bond act without some changes."

Our group waited for two hours and then, disturbingly, started to break up. Some folks from the Hudson Valley said they had to get back Downstate. One group left, saying they had dinner reservations—and asked us to report back to them.

Bill was beside himself. "Now do you know why I wanted you to come?" he asked.

As the room emptied of our allies, the scene reminded me of a conversation I had overheard in Cafe Capriccio, a fine Italian restaurant in downtown Albany, a favorite hangout for the political crowd. Zenia Mucha, who had left Senator Al D'Amato's office to become Pataki's communications director, was seated in a booth next to the bar, where I sat trying to extract information about a bill from a legislative staffer. The colorful Mucha was holding court with a few reporters. The topic came around to the environment, and she scoffed loudly at the idea that reporters would take environmental lobbyists seriously. I recall her saying, "The tree huggers can't get a job. That's the only reason they work at nonprofits. They don't have the courage to get real jobs. They don't have any balls."

Finnegan finally returned to the Red Room. He had nothing new to offer, pressed us to agree to the governor's new language on brownfields and finally asked us to wait again while he went next door to meet with his colleagues. He told us that for security reasons, we could not wander the Capitol hallways after hours. We might not be able to reenter the Red Room.

This became a pattern. Finnegan and other aides returned from the room next door. We sat and argued. They left again, and we waited some more. This went on for hours.

Finally Bill said to me, "Wait here. You want coffee?" When he returned with a couple of cups, I asked, "Where did you get this?"

"Down the hall," he said. "The secretary showed me how me how to make it before she left. There is nobody here. They are trying to wait us out, get us tired, so that we will cave in."

The evening moved slowly into the early hours of the next day. Bill and I, wired from the coffee he kept making, passed the time by chatting about almost anything. Our remaining colleagues slept in their chairs, waiting for the return of Finnegan.

At around 3:30 a.m., Finnegan reappeared, looking refreshed. We roused our sleeping colleagues. I took the lead in what turned out to be the final round of discussions and insisted that we would not budge. In effect, we were gambling that Finnegan's claim that the Republican members of the state Senate would not back the Republican governor's signature initiative was a bluff.

The governor's aides finally folded their cards and agreed to keep the standard unchanged. Bill and I walked out of the Capitol as the sun came up. The birds were singing. We walked to a nice diner and had breakfast.

The Senate, as we had bet, accepted the original language. It would be several years before another bill would amend the brownfields law to redefine "how clean is clean."

And in November, voters approved the Clean Water/Clean Air Bond Act, making millions of dollars available for land acquisition among other worthy environmental improvements. It was just in time. Huge parcels were coming up for sale inside the Park, many of them owned by timber corporations or private parties who were for the most part financial supporters of the Republican Party.

That had been the last slender reed of credibility for some Democrats seeking to justify their opposition to the bond act. "The governor will just pay off his supporters by buying their land with your tax money," they had told voters. As it turned out, the voters cared more about the Park.

And once the voters had endorsed a bill that had been backed by the governor and both houses of the legislature, the environmental lobbyists were released from our temporary purgatory in the Assembly.

Some months later, I tried to squeeze one more concession out of Governor Pataki. I urged him in a private discussion to issue regulations that would shift new development in the Adirondack Park away from the shorelines and backcountry parcels now going up for sale.

"Why regulate it?" he said. "We'll just buy it all." And so he did.

STORM CLOUDS OVER LITTLE TUPPER

Rumors had been abundant that Marylou Whitney, the widow of Cornelius Vanderbilt "Sonny" Whitney, a key financier of the movie classic *Gone with the Wind* and heir to multiple fortunes, was considering selling some or all of her 56,000-acre estate in the town of Long Lake, in the western part of the Adirondack Park. The holding included the largest privately owned lake in New York state, Little Tupper Lake. It was famous for its genetically unique species of brook trout and for being part of a historic canoe route that once stretched more than 100 miles through the western Adirondacks.

The Whitney estate was on every environmental group's list of private lands they wanted the state to acquire. One of the "Jewels of the Adirondacks."

In October 1997, Whitney, seventy-one, married John Hendrickson, a thirty-two-year-old real estate developer and former aide to Governor Walter J. Hickel of Alaska. The rumors of a land sale increased.

The first real sign that the rumors could be true was an innocuous application to the Adirondack Park Agency for a three-lot subdivision to sell existing cabins to Whitney friends and associates. I routinely reviewed the APA agenda with Joe Moore, who worked in our main office in Elizabethtown. Joe uncovered the fact that several years earlier Whitney Industries, the lumber business that Marylou had inherited, had submitted a smaller subdivision proposal, and the APA board had reserved the right to require a master plan for the business's entire 56,000-acre holding if another subdivision application was submitted.

Master plans for large properties had been an APA focus. Its board had recently required a utility company, Niagara Mohawk, and a hiking and paddling club, the Adirondack Mountain Club, to submit master plans for their properties before it would approve new subdivisions. We decided to demand that the agency now require a master plan for the Whitney estate.

Whitney and her husband resisted. The media knew that anything involving Marylou Whitney was popular and newsworthy, so they carried the story prominently. Fortunately for us, APA Chairman Gregory Campbell exercised his particular talent for putting his foot in his mouth and declared that a master plan was unnecessary because the family was "just moving a few lines around." It was a plumb stupid thing for the chairman of any planning board to say to a reporter, and the issue continued to gather steam.

The APA at the time had a wonderful practice of open committee meetings with public participation. A full agency meeting at the end of three days of deliberations would complete the monthly session with a decision on the Whitney plan.

Much to the consternation of the Whitney family, I received permission to address the APA board on the need for the master plan. Whitney's attorney and I were granted equal time. Their attorney argued that this was a small subdivision on a big property and that Whitney had no intention of further subdividing it. I emphasized the need to fairly apply the agency's policy on master plans and that a plan was especially needed in this case to protect the unique trout in Little Tupper Lake. My arguments failed to sway the board.

The Council believed that any applicant other than Whitney would have been compelled to complete a master plan. Our executive director directed me to contact an environmental law firm about the prospects for a lawsuit. The chances for success were not clear, however, and in the end we accepted an offer from Whitney's attorney to give us advance notice of any new submissions to the APA. I was not sure we had really gained anything until the next shoe fell. John Hendrickson wanted to meet with us.

Only a few months after assuring the APA that Whitney had no development plans, Hendrickson presented a map of a proposed subdivision of 15,000 acres with a large number of townhouses and a hotel on the site of the Whitney Industries headquarters on the shore of Little Tupper Lake. (See figure 1.12.)

Hendrickson had two main points. Whitney was serious about the subdivision and already had potential buyers lining up, he said. But for the right price, Marylou would entertain the idea of selling all 15,000 acres,

Figure 1.12. Political cartoon on Whitney Estate. *Source*: Adirondack Council.

including the entirety of Little Tupper Lake, to the state of New York. A few days later, Whitney submitted its subdivision application to the APA.

We wasted no time. The same day the application was submitted, we issued a news release demanding that the agency immediately require the preparation of a master plan for all 56,000 acres. I imagine the Whitneys expected that. What they did not expect was our demand that the APA revoke their earlier permit. We maintained that by submitting a sophisticated application for a major subdivision only a few months after claiming it had no such plans, Whitney had appeared to have submitted false or misleading information to the agency. That was grounds under APA regulations to revoke the earlier permit.

The agency, forced to finally do something, split the baby. It required them to submit a master plan before the new application could advance, but denied our request to revoke the earlier permit. Chairman Campbell sent me a letter stating that the agency was going to give Whitney a chance to respond to our complaint, in the interest of fairness. He then forbade agency staffers to talk to us. For the first time in APA history, all communications on a pending permit would go solely through the chairman.

We strongly felt that Whitney had intended all along to sell to the state. Applying for the large development did two things for them. First, it jacked up the price of the property by showing what it could be worth on the private market. Hendrickson even had a model home built on one of the previously subdivided parcels on Little Tupper Lake. Second, it protected them if the state took the extraordinary measure of taking the property by eminent domain. A few years before, a Long Island art dealer had argued in the New York State Court of Claims that the value of his waterfront property, which the local government had seized, should be valued according to its development potential as evidenced by a proposed subdivision map and not by any other valuation method. In an out-of-court settlement, the owner of Barcelona Neck was rewarded handsomely. It made sense to me that Hendrickson would similarly hedge his bet. And he had a good attorney.

Local government officials quickly lined up behind Whitney. The supervisor of the town of Long Lake praised the new tax revenue that would come from the luxury estates and from the hotel. Some local residents expressed hope that celebrities would be attracted to the area and bring even more dollars to the community.

Local officials knew that much of the Whitney estate was hardly taxed at all. State law awards a local property tax exemption to private landowners who enroll in a state program to encourage forestry. Whitney Industries was a prominent participant in that program. The majority of their 56,000 acres were enrolled in the tax abatement program.

Years before, Long Lake had adopted a new tax district designed to increase property taxes on valuable waterfront property, and tried to apply it to the Whitney holdings. The Whitney family took the town to court. They argued that if their waterfront property was enrolled in the state forestry program, it should not be subject to the higher town taxes. The courts agreed.

As the Council staff was reviewing the maps of Whitney's large new proposed subdivision, we made an important discovery. The plans called for the lands surrounding virtually every waterfront homestead to remain in the forestry tax abatement program. Only the footprint of the structures would be taxed at a higher rate.

Working closely with Peter Bauer, then executive director of the Residents' Committee to Protect the Adirondacks, we developed a plan to evaluate the true tax benefit of the Whitney subdivision to the town of Long Lake. Lisa M. Genier of our staff was named project director.

She worked with a graduate intern in our Albany office who conducted research and analysis. Peter Bauer had his volunteers comb through tax records to acquire invaluable data. We then compared the future tax benefit to the town from state acquisition of the property to the revenue from homes in the proposed Whitney subdivision. The results were clear. Retaining the forestry tax exemption on most of the property in the subdivision would dramatically reduce the future revenue from the subdivision that was eagerly anticipated by the town. By contrast, state lands in the Adirondack Park are fully taxed by local governments. State acquisition of the Whitney parcel as forest preserve would provide more tax revenue to Long Lake than the subdivision!

What's more, the new revenue would start to flow immediately if the land were purchased by the state. Taxes on the subdivision would phase in as the structures were built, and it would take almost fifteen years for the tax revenue to be even comparable with state acquisition. And state ownership came with no demand for county or town services.

The Council and the Residents' Committee released the tax analysis and publication to the media and to the Town Board of Long Lake. Like a faucet being turned off, all the supportive public chatter from the local government officials vanished.

Now we could get down to business.

The governor announced that he was dispatching his counsel, Michael Finnegan, to negotiate with John Hendrickson and Marylou Whitney. His decision was praised in the *New York Times*, and other editorials surfaced across the state encouraging the state to buy the Whitney property.

It only made Marylou bolder. Marylou Whitney announced to reporters that that she would not sell to the state because it was offering too little. She and Hendrickson would make a number of public statements claiming absurd valuations of the property. Their comments had an effect, but not what they intended.

The inflated claims alarmed the new director of the Open Space Institute, Kim Elliman. The well-funded institute was in the business of acquiring land for preservation and protection up and down the Hudson Valley. The institute was originally chartered to protect lands along the lower Hudson, but this had been reinterpreted by its board to extend its reach to the source of the Hudson River in the High Peaks region of the Adirondacks. Elliman convened a meeting of several land protection groups, including the Council, and top state officials. He argued that the state had to drop the Whitney acquisition if it got too pricey, because the sale could drive up prices for other Adirondack parcels. That would adversely affect the ability of his organization, the Nature Conservancy and others to purchase key properties. We listened in dismay as key players in land protection now made the case against buying the Whitney property.

Marylou Whitney's press outings also attracted the attention of the Sierra Club.

Extremely active in land protection on a national level, the Sierra Club had been oddly passive when it came to the Adirondack Park. Now, like a hummingbird seeking sweet nectar, it flew into the Whitney affair.

First, the Sierra Club produced hundreds of bumper stickers reading "Buy Whitney Park." Then it launched one of its notorious radio advertising campaigns in which it announced a huge purchase of time, released the spot to the media, and sat back as it was widely aired on news broadcasts. The actual media buy was much smaller and narrowly focused than the Sierra Club had implied. However, the Club was careful to buy time in the Capital Region and in Saratoga Springs, where Marylou Whitney owned another large estate. Those were the two places where associates of both Governor Pataki and Whitney would be sure to hear the ads.

The Sierra Club campaign also garnered a lot of unsolicited support. Memorably, a country music station modified the old Ricky Nelson hit "Hello Mary Lou." The lyrics of the new version, which was aired repeatedly, began "Hello Marylou—Goodbye Park!"

But it was only when the Sierra Club threatened to send pickets to Marylou Whitney's annual ball during the thoroughbred racing season in Saratoga Springs that things got rolling. The threat got the immediate attention of an alarmed John Hendrickson, who called the director of the Sierra Club. After their talk, the Whitney ball went on without incident, the public game-playing by both sides stopped, and the family's negotiations with the state resumed.

By the end of 1997, Governor Pataki was able to announce an agreement to buy the 15,000 acres. A news conference was held in the inspiring Adirondack exhibit at the New York State Museum in Albany. Marylou Whitney notoriously upstaged Pataki by whacking him on the backside with a ceremonial canoe paddle. The governor did not seem amused, but the press loved it.

The Whitney purchase began a new era. By the time Pataki left the governor's office at the end of 2006, the state would protect more than a million acres of forest and farmland from development, most of it in the Adirondack Park. But it would not be easy.

CHAMPION SURPRISES

The announcement in October 1997 took us by surprise. Champion International Corporation had decided to sell all 52,000 acres of its holdings inside and just outside the Adirondack Park. The lands included many miles of undeveloped shoreline along wild and scenic rivers.

With the bond act and the Environmental Protection Fund in place, it only took only a day or two before the environmental community was demanding that Governor Pataki buy the property. Recreation enthusiasts, including the Adirondack Mountain Club, were particularly excited about the prospect of the public gaining access to paddle some of the more beautiful and navigable stretches of the Park's rivers. (See figure 1.13.)

The environmental groups coordinated their efforts. Photos were compiled. Media packets were assembled. We even got the New York City Council to pass a resolution, sponsored by Councilman Andrew P. Eristoff, urging the governor to make the purchase. Countless hours were spent with state staffers making the case for acquisition. We proposed state ownership for some parcels and conservation easements, which would restrict development but allow sustainable forestry to protect others. That approach would keep the price down, preserve open space, allow commercial timbering to continue and guarantee public access to the most beautiful tracts.

Figure 1.13. Paddlers on Grasse River. *Source*: Nancie Battaglia.

Still, we kept hearing that the governor was undecided. I decided to make a pitch directly to the new DEC Commissioner, John P. Cahill, who was most likely to have the governor's ear on this issue. The sheer size of the acquisition right in the midst of the Whitney property negotiations was daunting. Cahill told me he was personally in favor, but he was looking out for the governor's interests and for that reason had doubts about the wisdom of moving forward.

I played my best and last card. I told Cahill that if the governor made the purchase, we would tell the media that Governor Pataki had become "the modern architect of the Adirondack Park."

"The modern architect of the Adirondack Park," the commissioner repeated aloud. "I like it! I'll see what I can do."

Soon thereafter, things took a turn I had not anticipated. In order for Champion to sell the large tracts, even to the state, it would need a subdivision permit from the Adirondack Park Agency. I visited the agency's headquarters in Ray Brook, New York, to see the staff. They had just completed a field inspection of the Champion lands, and it was pretty clear from their reaction that something was awry. I asked to see their Champion file, and saw that was chock-full of photographs and field notes documenting a large number of leased hunting and fishing cabins that were illegal. They were either too large, sited too close to a stream, or were in violation of other state regulations.

"What are you guys going to do about this?" I asked. The staffers shrugged. I had seen that reaction before. It would be a political decision. They would be told whether they would be doing anything at all.

The situation posed an enormous dilemma for the Adirondack Council. In the course of pursuing one of the best opportunities for public acquisition in the history of the Park, multiple and serious violations of the law had been unearthed. Not only were dozens of hunting lodges in violation of APA rules, but many cabin owners had also violated the terms of their leases with Champion, which were even tougher than the agency regulations. The failure of the agency to act on these violations resulted either from its lack of enforcement personnel or a false assumption that Champion would police its own leases.

One thing was certain—the situation had to be remedied. Subdivision permits were designed to ensure that the land was not abused and that water quality was preserved. Our staff was unanimous in the view that we had to challenge the illegal cabins, even if it threatened the sale to the state.

In a private meeting, I told the governor's staff about the problems with the hunting cabins and that everything was documented in the APA files. I reminded them that the agency's policy was that no party could receive a subdivision permit if there were unresolved violations on its property. Further, we felt that a hefty fine was appropriate. And I told them that the Council was prepared to go public unless the right thing was done.

The aides were beside themselves at hearing the news. They knew they would face resistance from some local officials and the hunting clubs that would see their cabins removed. But in the end, the staff did the right thing and the governor pushed ahead with both the purchase and the enforcement actions. Champion paid a fine in excess of one million dollars. Hunting cabins on lands to be acquired by the state would be removed immediately. Those on lands that were to be covered by conservation easements, and which would be open to the public for hunting and recreation, would be removed within ten years or so after the terms of the easements were negotiated.

Even after all measures were taken to achieve compliance, about 220 cabins would remain short term, and sustainable timber harvests would continue on large tracts. But the public would gain access to remarkable lands and waters for recreation.

At the news conference announcing the Champion deal, our staff was handing out our news release to the waiting reporters while Commissioner Cahill delivered a few remarks. At the end, he introduced Governor Pataki with a flourish as "the modern architect of the Adirondack Park!"

I blanched. Damn, he stole our phrase!

But I had kept my promise. Our release also called the governor "the modern architect of the Adirondack Park." A reporter walked by and waved our release at me. He said, "You guys are losing your touch. You stole 'modern architect' from Commissioner Cahill!"

THE FIREMAN

A purchase by the state was only the first step in protecting key properties in the Adirondack Park. Equally important was how the state would manage those lands.

In 1972, the New York state legislature required the new Adirondack Park Agency to adopt a State Land Master Plan. Now each new parcel of state lands added to the protected forest preserve in the Park must be classified. A "wild forest" classification meant that motorized equipment for recreation could be used on those lands and snowmobile trails could be created for public use. A "wilderness" classification, however, meant that the land would be free of any motorized vehicle or boat and treated as a truly natural area, with minimal intrusion by human beings. The Adirondack Council was all about wilderness. Our board of directors made that clear to the staff.

The Council had developed its own vision for the future of the Park. It had created a series of glossy publications by the early 1990s identifying and mapping the lands we believed the state should acquire and how those lands should be classified. The series was called 2020 Vision. 2020 Vision was, in effect, the policy guide for our staff.

In the first wave of what would become a flood of state acquisitions, the Whitney purchase and other parcels recently acquired were to be classified for future use and management by the Adirondack Park Agency. The state DEC was responsible for proposing management classifications and then seeking the endorsement and the approval of the park agency. The Whitney property and several other tracts had been targeted in our 2020 Vision series as potential wilderness areas, but it soon became clear that the staff at the state agencies did not always share our vision for some properties.

A behind-the-scenes struggle ensued when the Council and our allies sought changes in the DEC's proposed classifications. We were successful; in the days leading up to the park agency meeting on the issue, the DEC made several changes to its initial classifications to address the Council's concerns. The proposal was now 90 percent of what we were hoping for. But as usual, we continued to lobby up to the moment of the final decision for all the changes we wanted.

The involvement of the Whitney property in the package of classifications guaranteed that interest in the APA meeting would be high. DEC Commissioner Cahill, who like several other agency heads had a seat on the APA board and had a vote on the final decision, made the rare decision to attend himself instead of sending the customary staff surrogate. The significance of the event also led our executive director, Tim Burke, to attend.

Despite our down-to-the wire lobbying, the agency adopted a proposal that still had only 90 percent of what we wanted. One parcel was not classified as wilderness as we had hoped.

After the vote confirming the DEC recommendations and the meeting had adjourned, a buoyant Cahill saw Tim in the hallway and asked him if he was pleased. He clearly expected a positive response.

Tim's pointed answer went something like this: "If you think I am happy that you personally kept all of these lands from becoming wilderness in our lifetime, no, I am not."

Cahill's face flushed crimson. He said nothing, but turned and headed out the door, staff in tow. I turned to Tim and we had a brief conversation about the wisdom of pissing off the Environmental Commissioner. Tim said that Cahill would just have to live with what he said, because it was true.

The crowd dispersed and I headed Downstate to our Albany office. I was on the expressway near Albany when I got a call from Gavin J. Donohue, the Executive Deputy Commissioner of the Department of Environmental Conservation. Many lobbyists called Donohue "the fireman" because it was his job to put out political fires inside the department before they could spread to the governor's office.

"Bernard!" he shouted. "What the hell happened at the park agency? I got a call from my boss and he was crazy angry. He was shouting and cursing. Your boss apparently said something to him that really pissed him off."

"I know," I replied. "I was there."

Then Donohue asked, "Are you on a cell phone?" I said that I was. "How long will it take you to get to a land line?" Ten minutes, I told him.

It was not the first time that I'd been asked those questions. Early in Pataki's first term, cell-phone calls between staffers had been legally intercepted by a third party and leaked to the media. The content of the intercepted calls embarrassed the governor. Donohue thereafter preferred to discuss sensitive matters over a land line, which could not be legally intercepted by amateur radio operators.

Of course, it worked both ways. About a year later I called the department during after–hours, and one of my contacts in the executive offices was still at work. I expressed concern about a new proposal by a specific legislator.

"Don't worry, he is not serious," I was told.

"Why are you so confident?" I asked.

"He called us earlier today and said just the opposite. He told us that he was not serious."

My contact said that he was not on that call, but "You can hear for yourself." The next thing I heard was the legislator's voice saying exactly what had been described to me. After about thirty seconds, the staffer broke back in.

"See? I played part of the call back for you. We record incoming calls that might be important. It is perfectly legal under New York law because only one party to a phone call was required to consent to its being recorded. Of course, the callers don't know they are being recorded. And by the way, you now owe me." Of course, I did. This was another example of a "chit," a universally accepted unit of exchange in Albany political circles. I was given information of value about the existence of the recording system, and now I was obligated to return that chit at some time in the future. And by accepted norms at the Capitol, a chit could be called in at any time by the party to whom it was owed, no questions asked.

In this case, I was not asked to keep the information to myself. I would return the favor for sure, but I also traded that piece of information many times over. It was especially valuable in trade with legislators or their staffers who frequently called the department. Being tipped off that your calls might be recorded (and possibly could then be used to embarrass you or worse) was extremely valuable information in the Capitol. It was very helpful to have legislators feel they "owed me one" in return. Chit for chit.

After ending my own cell-phone call with Donohue and detouring to the Council's Albany office, I called him back and related what had happened at the APA between his boss and mine.

"We can't have this," he said. "Did I tell you he was crazy angry? You and I can't do our jobs if our bosses are mad at each other. How are we going to fix this?"

I told Donahue that I did not think anyone else had witnessed the blowup, and promised to get back to him.

I called Tim and explained the situation. I said that the call from Donahue showed that Cahill had genuinely felt insulted, whether that was justified or not, and that threatened our access to the administration. I recommended, and he agreed, that we would issue a news release praising the classifications, and Cahill's efforts in particular. We also would tell our communications director not to mention any disappointment about the final outcome.

I reported all this to Donahue. He was hoping for more, but I told him that an apology was too much to ask. Tim really meant what he said.

We resolved to try and find opportunities to repair the damage. Gavin and I needed each other.

THE GOVERNOR TAKES A HIKE

For almost ten years, the Open Space Institute (OSI) had been trying to woo NL Industries, formerly named National Lead, to sell them the Tahawus Tract in the High Peaks region of the Adirondack Park. The tract, now abandoned, had been used during World War II to mine titanium dioxide. The mine occupied only a small portion of the tract, and the institute was attracted by its other attributes. The site was adjacent to state-owned lands that were part of the High Peaks Wilderness to the north, and it contained Henderson Lake, recognized as the source of the Hudson River. (The Hudson's waters actually originate in the higher-altitude Lake Tear of the Clouds, but flow through a series of brooks with different names until they reach Henderson Lake.) The Tahawus tract also contained one of the few remaining intact fire towers that used to line the region's peaks, as well as a corporate retreat and boathouse on the lake.

Tahawus was also historically famous. It was where Vice President Theodore Roosevelt learned that President William McKinley had turned for the worse after being been shot while visiting the Pan-American Exposition in Buffalo, New York. Roosevelt left his hunting cabin and took a famous night carriage ride over mountain roads to the nearest rail station, where he learned that he was now President Roosevelt.

It took years for negotiations to close on the purchase. By 2003, the biggest obstacle was the responsibility for any hazardous materials still at the mine site, but this was eventually overcome as NL Industries proved eager to cash in on its asset. The State of New York was the Open Space Institute's silent partner in the deal but it was years before the state acquired most of the Tahawus Tract from OSI, including Henderson Lake.

The October 2003 news conference announcing the state purchase was held on the shore of Henderson Lake. Governor Pataki invited the Council's executive director, Brian Houseal, and me to attend. I also got permission for my legislative assistant in Albany, Scott Lorey, to tag along—a rare and exciting chance for him to attend an event in the Park.

The governor arrived and greeted the crowd of local officials, state employees, and environmentalists. Among the dignitaries was George H. Canon, the longtime supervisor of the host town of Newcomb. Canon had long advocated that the state purchase the property, but when the time came he tried to impose a long list of conditions that he simply seemed to make up. Canon's frequent barbs about "tree huggers," while likely a big hit at the local watering hole, were best loved because they got Canon's quotes in the newspaper. Photographers were covering the Tahawus event, and at one point the Council's own photographer captured Canon, Houseal, and me in the same frame. All three of us look uncomfortable, and Canon whispered to us as we stood posing that if we gave the photo to the local paper, he would kill us both. (See figure 1.14.)

After Pataki's remarks, the plan was for the governor to board one of a flotilla of canoes that had been assembled at the shore so that he could be the first member of the public to paddle on the newest wilderness lake in New York state. The only problem was, nobody had asked the governor.

I heard Pataki say, "Can we go for a hike instead?" Anything you say, Governor! Off went the assemblage up a trail toward a far-off point of land along the shore.

I was wearing a blazer, and Scott was in dress shoes. So as the crowd marched off, we stood there for a minute or two, debating what to do.

Figure 1.14. Brian Houseal, George H. Cannon, and the author. *Source*: Adirondack Council.

Scott pointed to the massed canoes sitting unattended. "Seems a waste to let those canoes just sit there," he said. I agreed immediately, and soon we had separated one from the flotilla and were paddling out toward open water. Ours was the only boat out there.

It was a joy. The scenery was beautiful and we relished the fact that we, and not New York's governor, were the first to paddle the now publicly accessible Henderson Lake. We two pioneers took photos of each other to document the event.

Our dispositions changed when we rounded the point. The wind came up, and suddenly we were battling whitecaps on the water. I urged Scott to dig in harder to help keep the boat aligned, which was the moment he admitted that he did not have a lot of experience paddling a canoe. That was right before he said that we should have taken a life preserver with us, because he could not swim.

We came about. The hikers, including the governor, were still out on the trail when we reached the shore. We secured our canoe and were soon headed back down to Albany.

Thirteen years after leaving the staff of the Assembly to join the Adirondack Council, that day would be the first, last, and most memorable ribbon-cutting event that I would attend in the Adirondack Park.

SO THEN WHAT HAPPENED?

THE MORGAN ESTATE, HEURICH ESTATE, AND FOLLENSBY POND

At a 1994 fundraiser in New York City for the Adirondack Council, Governor Mario Cuomo delighted the crowd by announcing that the State of New York would acquire the first three of the ten Jewels of the Adirondacks identified in 1990 as at risk by Adirondack environmental groups: the Morgan Estate, with a mile of shoreline along Lake George; the Heurich Property with three miles of shoreline along Lake Champlain (from the Open Space Institute, which acquired it in 1993); and Follensby Pond near Tupper Lake. Negotiations by the state with the landowner of Follensby would notoriously break down and it would not be protected until 2008, when the Nature Conservancy announced its purchase of Follensby Pond from the McCormick family. The 14,600-acre property includes the 1,000-acre Follensby Pond and more than ten miles of shoreline on the Raquette River. Follensby Pond was known as the site of the famous "Philosophers Camp," a unique outing in 1858. Ralph Waldo Emerson, the poet and painter William James Stillman were among a group of luminaries from the Boston area who spent a month at the site. Follensby Pond was also chosen as the site for the successful hacking of young bald eagles from Alaska, which was the seminal effort to reintroduce the bald eagle to New York state. (See figure 1.15.)

PRESTON PONDS

In 2003, the Open Space Institute purchased nearly 10,000 acres of the Tahawus Tract, south of the high Peaks, including Henderson Lake and the Preston Ponds and Duck Hole. Much of the property was transferred to the State of New York in 2008. (See figure 1.16.)

INTERNATIONAL PAPER

As part of his "million acre" public lands program, Governor George Pataki, entered into an agreement in 2004 with International Paper, a major landholder in the Adirondack Park. The deal was said to be the largest land protection deal in New York state history. The deal, which was brokered by the Conservation Fund, a Virginia-based environmental nonprofit group,

Figure 1.15. Follensby Pond. *Source*: Nancie Battaglia.

Figure 1.16. Preston Ponds and Duck Hole. *Source*: Nancie Battaglia.

resulted in the state purchasing conservation easements (the development rights) on more than a quarter million acres. As part of the deal, the construction of ninety preapproved subdivisions in the Park did not go forward.

CHAMPION INTERNATIONAL CORPORATION

The controversial 1999 purchase of land from Champion International Corporation was partially undone by Pataki's successor in office, Governor Andrew Cuomo. In 2011, the Adirondack Park Agency approved a swap in which the private Heartwood Forestland Fund donated 2,100 acres in the Park to the state forest preserve in exchange for retaining 220 hunting cabins (and their leases) on former Champion lands for which the state held conservation easements. The cabins had been slated for removal under the terms of the original deal.

FINCH, PRUYN AND COMPANY

The Finch, Pruyn paper company, publicly opposed to any further state land acquisitions, was the last holdout in the Adirondacks. In the end, Finch sold all its land holdings in the region which, in turn, passed to the Nature Conservancy in 2007. The not-for-profit group later sold the State of New York development rights to some parcels and the full title to others.

The Nature Conservancy, in a press release, announced it had purchased 161,000 acres in all, featuring 415 miles of rivers and streams, 300 lakes and ponds, 90 mountain peaks, and 16,000 acres of wetlands. The Conservancy and the state Department of Environmental Conservation agreed to conserve and protect the lands as follows:

- 89,000 acres will continue to be working forests with sustainable logging subject to conservation easements;

- 69,000 acres will be transferred to the state to become part of the forest preserve;

- 1,100 acres will be set aside for community purposes in three towns.

Governor David A. Patterson made the first purchase from the Conservancy. The purchases continued under Governor Andrew Cuomo, including one of the highest waterfalls in the Adirondack Park, OK Slip Falls, and lands adjacent to the upper Hudson River and Hudson River Gorge.

These acquisitions opened the upper Hudson to recreational paddlers and access to the waterfall to the public for the first time in more than 100 years. The Essex Chain of Lakes, included in the purchase, has eleven lakes and ponds that comprise a great paddling opportunity. (See figure 1.17.)

The last in a series of purchases by the state included the Boreas Ponds Tract, about 20,000 acres with scenic views of the High Peaks. Public hearings were held late in 2016 on whether to classify the entire tract as wilderness or whether to allow motor vehicles on its multiple dirt roads. After a public relations and lobbying battle between environmental groups on one side and local government and snowmobile advocates on the other, the Adirondack Park Agency in 2018 recommended a compromise, accepted by most parties to the dispute, allowing multiple uses of the land while preserving the vast majority of it as wilderness. (See figure 1.18.)

THE WHITNEY ESTATE

In July of 2019, May Lou Whitney passed away. Her husband, John Hendrickson, announced a year later that he intended to sell to a private buyer the vast majority of the remaining 36,000 acres of the Whitney estate. Despite strong interest in the conservation community to protect the lands

Figure 1.17. OK Slip Falls. *Source*: Nancie Battaglia.

Figure 1.18. Boreas Ponds. *Source*: Nancie Battaglia.

and waters, and restore a historical canoe route, Hendrickson publicly declared he would not sell to the State of New York due to what he felt was mismanagement of the heritage strain trout waters in the 15,000 acres previously purchased by the state. (See figure 1.19.) A public campaign to

Figure 1.19. The Whitney estate. *Source*: Nancie Battaglia.

convince Governor Andrew Cuomo to buy or protect the remainder of the estate was launched in 2020 by the group Protect the Adirondacks.

All of the "Jewels of the Adirondacks" originally identified by environmental groups at their Blue Mountain Center conference in 1990 are now either part of the public forest preserve or private lands that are subject to conservation easements that will keep the lands as open space.

CHAPTER 2

THE BOWLER BOYS

My first challenge as the new lobbyist for the Adirondack Council in 1990 was to fix a problem that had arisen years before. The issue wasn't on the Council's legislative agenda.

An important tool for land protection is the conservation easement. Instead of owning land outright, a state or conservation group could acquire the development rights from a landowner without purchasing the entire property. Property rights are often described as a "bundle of sticks"—the right to develop, to farm, to timber, to extract minerals below the surface, and so forth. Any single stick can be removed from the bundle and sold.

Landowners can sell or donate their development rights to a conservation easement buyer while continuing to own and use the land for purposes such as timber management, farming, or recreation. Buyers pay substantially less for the easement than they would to buy the property outright. These "sales" also can confer considerable tax benefits to the landowning easement grantor.

Although conservation easements had been available under "common law," our legacy from England, they carried a number of burdensome requirements. New York moved to eliminate many of these by enacting a law in the 1980s to expand the availability of conservation easements and allow the easement holder to enforce it even against the seller on whose land it sits. One significant hurdle New York eliminated was to expand the flexibility of conservation easements so that the holder of the easement need not be an adjacent landowner.

The embrace of the conservation easement was especially useful in the Adirondack Park, where large landowners (many of which were corporations) fell mainly into three categories: old estates, timber companies, and recreational clubs. And it was quite timely, because the Park's large landowners were in transition. With property taxes rising, young inheritors of old estates may have loved the properties' luxury and solitude, but they were no longer thrilled with the cost of ownership. Private clubs, too, became increasingly strapped for cash and new members. And companies with large timber holdings in the Adirondacks were being battered both by worldwide competition and changes in demand for paper products, leading them to increasingly view their slow-growing timber assets as a liability.

I was three months into my tenure at the Council when Frank Clark, an attorney from Syracuse who represented the fledgling Adirondack Land-owners Association, called me. He wanted advice on lobbying the state assembly. Clark specifically asked me if I could get him an entrée to key assembly staffers, and Gary Randorf, our executive director, gave me the go-ahead to help out.

Clark was working mainly on behalf of one of the large landowners in the Association, the Ausable Club, a private institution in St. Huberts, New York, which others had described to me as a playground for wealthy conservative Republicans. The only other thing I knew about the Ausable Club was that it had granted a common-law easement to the state to let hikers cross its very large private holdings to get to the High Peaks of the Park—access it was now threatening to shut down.

The subject of existing common-law easements had been ignored when New York enacted the new law on conservation easements. Now the Ausable Club and other clubs with preexisting arrangements wanted to have their common-law easements receive the same recognition—and the same tax treatment—as conservation easements. The Ausable Club's efforts in recent years to win changes in state law to "look back" and include common-law easements had failed to gain traction. Now it wanted help.

The club's argument seemed fair to me. I had been involved when the state's conservation easement law was first signed in 1983 and amended in 1984. It's true that the topic of existing easements was pushed aside in those discussions, because dealing with them would have added unwelcome baggage to an already complex piece of legislation. The mind-numbing details of property rights law had already exhausted the attention span of many lawmakers. Some advocates of the new law had discussed going back to the legislature to fix such oversights, but for whatever reason, the environmental community had not done so.

I was advised that the Ausable Club had a friend in Senator Ron Stafford. The club, as well as most of the Park, was in his district, and many club members were contributors to his campaigns. But unlike its good access in the state Senate, the club had little or no access in the Downstate-dominated, Democrat-led Assembly.

I arranged for Clark and his associates to meet with Steve Allinger, a key staff member of the Assembly's Ways and Means Committee. That committee was the gatekeeper for all bills that might have fiscal implications for the state, and was also famous for being "where good bills go to die." I had learned that Ways and Means was indeed the club's principal roadblock, having shown no interest in their easement problem. I had a good working relationship with Allinger, an enthusiastic recreational user of the Park, so I asked him to meet with my new friends from the Adirondacks.

Steve called me up the day after their visit. "Was that a joke?" he demanded.

"What do you mean?" I asked.

Steve responded in an irritated tone. "Two dudes showed up in my office wearing bowlers, black pin-striped suits and carrying umbrellas, asking me to give them a tax break. They said you sent them."

I did not know what to say.

"I repeat, was that a joke?"

Apparently Steve thought that I had played some sort of elaborate prank on him. Trying to dig my way out of trouble, I told him that I had not met his guests personally; I had just directed them to the right person in the Assembly staff to talk to.

"And that certainly was you," I said somewhat desperately.

As I struggled to find other ways to apologize, Steve calmed down noticeably. He seemed relieved to learn he had not been the butt of a joke, but he was now even more puzzled by his visitors. I said I would call him back later in the week.

I called Frank Clark in Syracuse. "How did your meeting with Steve Allinger go?" I inquired.

"Hard to say, but I think he was a hard sell," Clark said.

"Steve said your companion was wearing a bowler and carrying an umbrella," I said.

"Well, we both were," he said. "It was raining. Why?"

"You don't see many bowler-style hats in Albany."

"That's too bad. They are fine hats."

A week later, I called Steve back and asked if I could talk to him myself about amending the law to capture the older common-law easements.

"Sure, come on by, as long as you don't wear a bowler," he quipped.

This meeting went much better. Clark had given me more information on the size of the easements held by the Ausable Club and others, and our staff had given me a briefing on the club's history. The Ausable Club had at one time owned most of what is now considered the High Peaks region of the Adirondacks. By the early 1900s it had amassed more than 40,000 acres, including many of the very mountains in that group of the state's forty-six highest peaks. It had sold property to the state twice, most recently in 1978.

As I told Steve, it was the club's easement that allowed the public easy access to Upper and Lower Ausable Lakes, popular entry points to the state lands in the High Peaks region. The club even ran a bus from its lodge to the lower lake.

Something clicked. Steve had hiked those trails. He had taken that bus.

Steve now understood both the importance of the easement and why the members of the club might feel unfairly treated. A rising property tax burden, coupled with the increasing cost of running buses to the lakes and picking up litter on trails and in parking lots, were the reasons that the club was pressing to get tax equity with other easement grantors.

Steve took up the cause, but as the legislative session dragged on he reported that he needed help to get the bill through the legislature. The governor's office was showing little or no interest in the matter, apparently not believing that the Ausable Club would or could shut off legal access to its lands. Just as important, the club's natural ally, Senator Stafford, was not weighing in.

I arranged for Clark and some of the Ausable Club principals to meet with me to discuss strategy. At their suggestion, we met at the Fort Orange Club in Albany. I welcomed the chance to pay my first visit to the private club, known as a place where Republican legislators had business lunches or rented rooms while in town.

I mentioned that Senator Stafford needed to weigh in on the issue and was told flatly that I should leave Ron Stafford to the Ausable Club. He would come around. I was also given the names of several club members who could reach out to Governor Mario Cuomo. One of the names was Lewis E. Lehrman.

That struck me as odd, because Lew Lehrman was the Republican candidate whom Cuomo had defeated in 1982 to become governor. It had been a fairly close contest that I remembered most because the red suspenders that Lehrman liked to wear with his suits became a symbol of his campaign. I had embraced the same style several years before the Lehrman campaign, and red suspenders were my favorite.

During the 1982 campaign, Democrats harassed me constantly about my attire. I toughed it out, but after the third complete stranger asked me, "Who are you trying to be, Lew Lehrman?" I put the suspenders away. For the record, that is not why Lew Lehrman did not get my vote. I was happy to get my suspenders back after the election, though.

Lehrman proved to be an important ally. He took my suggestions to heart, got directly to Cuomo, and kept me informed of his communications with the governor and others. (See figure 2.1.)

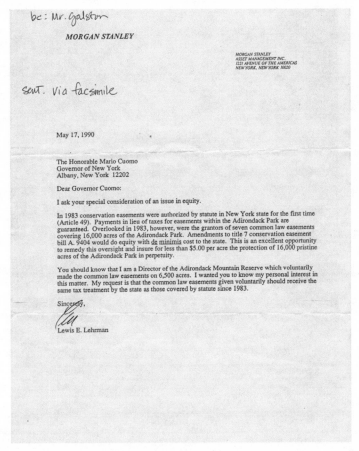

Figure 2.1. Lewis Lehrman's letter to the governor. *Source*: author's own material.

The bill passed the legislature. A month or so later, my family and I were invited to enjoy the High Peaks as guests of the Ausable Club.

We never accepted the offer, although I appreciated it—I had never even seen the Ausable Club. But saving public access, not the club's tax dollars, had been my motivation.

Another year would pass before I saw the club for the first time and realized what we had missed. It boasted an enormous clubhouse, a golf course with incredible views of the unique setting, tennis courts, and many other amenities, all within a short hike of the High Peaks and the Ausable lakes where members could reserve authentic Adirondack guide boats. I had no idea what a perk I had been offered.

CHAPTER 3

NEW YORK'S BIG SECRET

By the time George Pataki was elected governor of New York in 1994, the state had already launched a resoundingly successful tourism campaign called "I ♡ New York." The campaign's ads featured a catchy tune on the radio and fast-paced images on television that convincingly portrayed the state as both a natural and urban playland.

The ads commonly showed the Adirondack Mountains and the region's waters, but never mentioned the existence of the Adirondack Park. Why in the world were we keeping the Park a secret from the rest of the world? I wondered.

A chance encounter while I was on vacation in Colorado drove the point home to me. I had taken my sons on a three-week driving tour of the great national parks of the West. We were in southern Colorado when we decided to take a leisurely raft trip down a local river.

Our companions were two women of college age from Boston who were traveling across the country on a summer-long adventure to visit as many major state and national parks as they could.

When I mentioned that the rafting through the Hudson River Gorge in the Adirondack Park was much more challenging than the little riffles we were gliding through, the women asked me where the Adirondack Park was. They were startled to hear that when they had traveled the New York State Thruway west from Massachusetts to Buffalo, they had driven just south of a six-million-acre state park. They had heard of Lake Placid and Lake George, but they did not know that both were inside the largest state park in the lower forty-eight states.

Lisa Genier, on the Council's lobbying team, and I had been frustrated by a lack of progress on that very topic in the just-concluded state legislative session. Many local government officials, opposed to land-use controls imposed by the state in 1973, adamantly refused to acknowledge that they or their constituents lived in the Park. Working with Assemblyman Pete Grannis, we had tried to overcome that self-defeating perspective, starting with what we thought would be an easy legislative initiative.

Grannis, with our help, tried to reach agreement with Senator Ron Stafford, who represented most of the communities in the Adirondack Park, to establish a temporary commission to promote tourism development in the Park. But Tom Grant, an aide negotiating for Stafford, insisted that the bill could not contain the word *Park* in its title or text. Stafford would accept only the phrase "Adirondack region." Grannis, arguing that such a position missed the entire point of the effort, refused. The effort fell apart.

That debacle came to mind when our Colorado experience revealed again the public ignorance about the Park. I vowed that when I returned to work, I would find a way to get the governor's office to promote it.

I asked Lisa to work with our student interns in both of our offices to research how New York's tourism dollars were being spent. That included a visit with the "I ♡ New York" staff.

Over the years, they found, tourism dollars had been allocated to local tourism boards on a county-by-county basis. Communities inside the Park were encouraged to promote local attractions such as skiing in Lake Placid, boating on Lake George or fishing in the town of Inlet. But we were stunned to learn that none of the dozens of brochures and pamphlets that our staff gathered even acknowledged that these locations were within the Park.

Whether by benign neglect or (as we suspected) by design, not a single state tourism dollar was being used to promote the existence of the Adirondack Park. The largest state park in the continental United States was New York's biggest secret. Now that we had a clear idea of the status quo, I asked for the opportunity to give a presentation to Lynette M. Stark, a top aide to Pataki as deputy secretary for the environment.

Whenever I thought I had something promising, I told the governor's staff that they needed to meet with me and that they would be glad they did. As long as I delivered information that was new or different, it worked like a charm—instant meeting, every time.

I can't say that Lynette was pleased to have me put a new issue on her plate, but to her credit, once she heard my pitch she asked us to give a second presentation to a broader audience, including top staff people from the economic development team and other parts of the governor's operation.

Our message was simple. Why not let a rising tourist tide lift all Adirondack boats? Rather than have communities competing with each other for tourist dollars, they could all benefit by having the state of New York promote both the Park and the towns within it.

To help make my point, we brought along some of the state and local tourism brochures that failed to mention the Park. I related my experience with the two travelers in Colorado who would have visited the Park if they had known it existed.

Finally, I mentioned that my family had spent two days in Jackson, Wyoming, when we visited the nearby Grand Teton and Yellowstone National Parks. The town offered maps of the natural areas, and even paid guides, while visitors to the Adirondacks could not get a map of the entire Park unless they visited the only bookstore in Lake Placid and bought the poster/map produced by my organization, the Adirondack Council.

I assured the governor's aides that millions of tourists would want to visit the Park and bring their dollars to its gateway communities—but only if they knew about it!

We had made our point. Within a year, the Pataki administration had begun to commit real dollars to promote tourism in the Adirondack Park, both in state publications and in its grants to localities. Now, most of the gateway communities promote their location in the Park routinely—even those that formerly believed that their location in the Park hurt their economic prospects. Time and tourist dollars heal all.

SO THEN, WHAT HAPPENED?

Tourism in the Adirondack Park is booming. The State of New York now systematically promotes the Adirondack Park in its budget, as do most of the localities with tourist destinations such as Lake Placid and Lake George. Governor Pataki did much to convince local leaders that the future of the Adirondacks lies with tourism, and his successors have continued to drive grant programs and policies that support tourism, from cell phone and internet service to water and sewer infrastructure and tourist accommodations.

Governor Andrew Cuomo conducted several "Adirondack Challenges" in recent years, drafting members of the state legislature and local officials to participate in events celebrating the Park's recreational resources. The first Adirondack Challenge was a boat race of officials down the Hudson River using public access acquired in the Finch, Pruyn land purchase. Recreational tourism in the Adirondack Park hit an all-time high in 2016.

Success brought its own problems. By 2017, crowds of hikers were overwhelming the High Peaks mountain region, resulting in public calls for the state to divert hikers to other parts of the Park. Paddlers and climbers also surged into the Park to take advantage of its resources. The Park's 330,000 permanent and seasonal residents now face millions of visitors each year. According to the Adirondack Council, 2017 saw 12.4 million visitors, an increase of 500,000 from the year before. The love of the Park continues unabated. During the height of the Covid pandemic in New York state, the surging public interest in access to the open spaces in the Park overwhelmed many parking areas and trailhead access points in the 2020 summer and fall seasons.

CHAPTER 4

THE CANAL CANARY SINGS

It was a day like any other, until we got the phone call. The caller was unwilling to give his name, but he had interesting information. The legislature was about to hold a series of hearings on the future of the New York State Barge Canal, the successor to the fabled Erie Canal. There were things we ought to know, he said.

The Erie Canal, which was ridiculed as "Clinton's Ditch" after Governor DeWitt Clinton, secured its initial funding from the legislature in 1817, was built with an elaborate series of locks to facilitate commerce between the state's western ports and New York City. A century later it was enlarged, improved, and renamed the Barge Canal.

Eventually, most of the functions of this major piece of transportation infrastructure were taken over by the railroads and the Interstate Highway System, leaving the canal little more than a recreational waterway whose limited revenues did not offset its fiscal drain from the state.

The lands adjacent to the canal, however, were a different story. In some places, they offered the potential for prime commercial and residential development if they could be made available to the private sector.

The legislature was moving in 1992, to shift control over the canal from the Department of Transportation to a newly formed Canal Corporation. The powers of the proposed corporation, including the ability to sell off state lands for development, were the subject of upcoming public hearings.

Our mystery caller informed us that to ensure sufficient water would be available in drought periods to float traffic on the Erie Canal, the state had long ago built reservoirs to the north of its path. Six of those reservoirs were inside the Adirondack Park. The reservoirs, according to our informant, were now not used for canal purposes.

According to our snitch, a permit system intended to give landowners temporary access to the reservoirs' shores had been, and was continuing to be, abused. The private landowners were using the state lands lining the reservoirs as their private waterfront retreats.

I was familiar with the state's use of "temporary revocable permits." The NYDEC used a similar system to give private landowners temporary access to state forest preserves that surrounded their holdings, usually for the purpose of timbering. The permits were notorious for being abused.

Our "canal canary" encouraged us to check out the reservoirs for ourselves before the canal hearings convened. He suggested that we might even find private vacation homes built on state land.

The Adirondack Council got calls like this periodically. In most cases, the informant was a neighbor with an ax to grind or a retired state employee who felt that the higher-ups had ignored his good ideas. But this felt different.

I passed the information on to our executive director and added something our caller had not said: The shoreline lands might be part of the state forest preserve that Article 14 of the New York Constitution mandated should be protected as "forever wild." I got the go-ahead to investigate the allegations.

I decided to drive to Herkimer County, spend the day checking out a reservoir or two, and then head back to Albany. I invited Lisa Genier, our legislative assistant, to go along. An Adirondacks native from Mineville who had previously worked for the Democrats in the Assembly, Lisa knew the North Country and Upstate politics. She was also young and smart and personable. She was a terrific presence for the Council at the legislature.

I also thought that this was also a good opportunity for our legislative intern, Doug Gerhardt, to get out of Albany. We always promised our interns that in addition to an enlightening view of how the legislature worked, they would also get a field trip or two to the Adirondack Park. The only trip into the Park that Doug had gotten so far was to our Elizabethtown office ten minutes off Interstate 87.

I told Doug that he should collect maps, binoculars, and a camera with extra film and get a rental car for us. I made it clear that we did not want to draw much attention, but that we would be in the car all day and thus needed a comfortable four-wheel-drive vehicle.

When Lisa and I met the next morning at the office parking lot, our intern was already there, standing by a brand-new, all-white, deluxe Jeep with Florida plates. So much for not drawing attention.

The evening before, I had reviewed the legal status of canal lands in the Park. In 1908, in *People v. Fisher*, the state's highest court had ruled that canal lands within the Adirondack Park were in fact forest preserve lands.

The court had been asked to review a dispute between the state and a landowner who had cleared timber along a canal reservoir from the high-water mark (commonly referred to as the bathtub ring) down to the water. The court ruled that such lands could be managed for legitimate state purposes such as water supply, but not for timbering. Even if the lands were managed by a state agency not usually thought of as a conservation entity, the forestlands in the Park, by virtue of Article 14 of the state Constitution, were protected forest preserve lands. Therefore, "bathtub-ring" lands couldn't be taken, occupied, or used for private purposes.

Until the early 1990s, the state Department of Transportation operated the canal system and issued temporary revocable permits for landowners to install seasonal docks on the reservoirs. The fifteen-dollar permits were valid for only one year and could be revoked without cause.

The practice was common on state-owned lands including the Great Sacandaga Lake, a huge manmade flood-control reservoir elsewhere in the Adirondack Park that was managed by a state authority, the Black River-Black Creek Regulating District.

The first reservoir that Lisa, Doug, and I visited was called North Lake. It took us almost three hours to drive to the northern part of Herkimer County in the southwestern portion of the Park. The road crossed the lake's dam and ran alongside a building marked as a state station. Signs posted at the lake entrance made it clear that we had entered state property.

We drove along the lake for a while, astounded at what we saw. Although the law stipulated that the state owned the "bathtub ring" around the lake, a fish and game club, and numerous landowners had erected what to us appeared to be permanent docks on this land. Elaborate docks also connected several private vacation homes to the water. (See figure 4.1.)

We started taking pictures. Every time we spotted an apparent violation, I drove our "they must be from Florida" vehicle into position, barking out to my photographer in the back seat, "Get that! Get that!"

We were barely halfway along the shore of the first reservoir when Doug admitted, "We only have three more pictures left. I only had one roll, and I forgot to get more film." We high-tailed it into Forestport Station, the nearest hamlet, and found a Stewart's convenience shop to replenish our supply of film before heading back to the reservoir. Only two hours lost.

The result was the same at all three reservoirs we visited. Adjacent landowners had built permanent structures on state lands. We documented docks, boathouses and even vacation homes built over the water.

Figure 4.1. Canal lands political cartoon. *Source*: Adirondack Council.

We drove back to Albany as night fell, knowing that we had found something important.

The next step was to see the permits. The Department of Transportation was very accommodating, although we had to drive to Utica to see their records. The regional supervisor there quizzed us as to why we were interested in seeing the permits, but he accepted our explanation that we were comparing how various agencies ran their programs in the Park (which was the truth, if not the whole truth). He assured us that the permits were all in order, but that he had noticed that the department had not received the $15 seasonal payment from some landowners, and that would be remedied.

The permits were virtually all the same. And yes, some payments were late. In fact, most were in arrears by five to ten years!

When the photos from our trip were developed, we skipped the usual Monday conference call with our staff in Elizabethtown. Instead, the Albany contingent elected to drive two hours north to personally attend the staff meeting. We were eager to show and share what we had.

The staff unanimously agreed that we needed to participate in the legislative hearings in Albany on the future of the state canal system. Lisa and I would reveal our photos for the first time there, and John Sheehan, our communications director, would work the media afterward. We enlarged the most interesting photos for the hearing. As our testimony unfolded, Lisa did her best impression of game show hostess Vanna White. Smiling continuously, she placed the photos on an easel as I described them one by one. She also handed smaller versions of the photos to the legislators on the dais.

I felt we had done well, but felt even better when I was stopped outside the hearing room by a business lobbyist who told me, "You just blew the doors off the place." The *New York Post* published one of our photos the day after the hearing with the screaming headline: "SQUATTERS!"

Governor Cuomo's staff called us in a panic. Are you trying to derail the canal legislation? Are you trying to embarrass us? We assured them that we had no agenda other than protecting the people's interests. The abuse of the permits was obviously a practice allowed by the Transportation Department, and perhaps even predecessor agencies, predating the current governor.

We told Cuomo's staff that we had no idea who owned the private properties and to what extent they were encroaching on state land. But any problem had to be cleaned up, and our advice was that it should happen quickly.

The members of the Assembly and Senate knew a good issue to ride into an election when they saw it. The legislation creating the Canal Corporation was approved, but it included a million-dollar appropriation for a new survey of the public canal reservoirs. It also directed the state agencies to clean up the permitting process and to move any encroaching entities off the forest preserve.

We celebrated.

A year later, the survey began and we found out just who those landowners were. And there were dozens, including the Adirondack League Club.

The club at the time was the largest land-owning private club in the world, with thousands of acres in the vicinity of the canal reservoirs. Just the year before, it had celebrated a major anniversary of its founding by republishing old maps for a commemorative brochure. In a moment of kismet, I had come across the brochure in an antique shop in the hamlet of Old Forge, New York, while on summer vacation.

Unfortunately for the club, the brochure's maps clearly showed that Canachagala Lake in the middle of the club's property was in fact a state-owned reservoir, and that the state also owned a spillway from that reservoir to another one that was easily accessible to the public. In other words, you could walk on state land from one lake to another, right into the heart of the world's largest private club.

The Adirondack League Club wasted no time in hiring attorneys and its own surveying team. The newly formed state Canal Corporation, which appeared intimidated to us, agreed to share information and the proposed protocol of its land survey with the club. Gradually, and with the cooperation of the corporation's staff, the club had inserted itself into every aspect of the corporation's decision making on the issue

The Council publicly decried this as a breach of responsibility to the public. It was quite clear to us that the state corporation would, if left to its own devices, resolve the matter in whatever way was most favorable to the club. The corporation delayed or denied our legally appropriate requests for public documents. Meetings scheduled weeks in advance were canceled at the last minute without notice.

We assumed that the Adirondack League Club was making the most of its connections to the Republican Party and to Governor Pataki's office. Our Democratic friends in the legislature were no help. They had mined the "squatters on state land" issue for its political value and had "solved" the problem with the canal legislation. Now they were content to await the outcome of the survey, refusing to acknowledge that the process could be influenced or corrupted. The Democrats were content to be bystanders as long as they could blast the Republican-led state agencies afterward for doing a poor job. After all, the canal lands were not in their districts.

The key to the entire dispute was one policy principle. Under the newly adopted canal law, if the reservoir lands inside the Adirondack Park were "no longer needed for canal purposes," they would be treated as state forest preserve lands. They would no longer be under the jurisdiction of the Canal Corporation but the Department of Environmental Conservation, which managed most of the preserve.

As I recall, despite the canal's obvious lack of need for most of the reservoirs, only Chub Lake, with little or no development around it, was transferred to Environmental Conservation. To the surprise of no one, the Canal Corporation determined that Canachagala Lake was "essential" to canal operations and retained control of it. Public access was not allowed.

CHAPTER 5

THE PRISON IN THE PARK

I received a call from our executive director, Tim Burke.

"Did you know that a new state prison had been proposed for Tupper Lake?" he asked.

I had heard the rumor.

Tim said that a number of our top contributors from the Tupper Lake area were concerned. They had created an informal group and had approached him about whether the Council would oppose the new prison. Tim had told them that it was unlikely that our board would go on record as opposing the prison in the Park.

I asked what exactly our position was on the prison. "Are we opposing it?"

"Certainly not without a vote of our board," Tim said. "See what you can find out about it. I'd still like be helpful without getting entangled in the thing."

It wasn't hard to get the details. The legislature in 1997 had approved Governor Pataki's request to add 1,550 maximum-security cells to the state prison system, and the rumored new prison was to be a type known as "maxi-maxi." The worst of the worst offenders from prisons around the state would be placed in two-person prison cells. They would be given one hour of exposure to daylight per day, exercising in what amounted to a dog run. To my mind, these cellmates were sure to marry each other, kill each other, or watch each other go mad.

The public was being told that "an exhaustive site search was being conducted." But Albany insiders told me that the decision of where to place the prison had been made. The New York State Department of Corrections and Community Supervision had already secured an option on property inside the Adirondack Park near the town of Tupper Lake, my sources said.

The department was claiming that this was just one of many potential sites under consideration, but virtually every Upstate Republican senator had "speculated" in conversations with me that the new prison was going to be in the district of Senator Ron Stafford, chairman of the Finance Committee. Only one of the potential sites was both in Stafford's sprawling district and inside the Park: Tupper Lake.

I drove to Tupper Lake in the company of Bill Cooke, a fellow lobbyist for the Citizens Campaign for the Environment.

We drove around the area, but couldn't determine where the new prison was to be sited. Bill suggested that we drive to the town landfill because, he said, "In small towns, the guys at the landfill always know what's going on. All the gossip is exchanged there."

I agreed, and within moments we knew exactly where the proposed prison was to be.

We drove there and saw that a construction access route had been cut into the property. As we entered, another car was leaving. We had no idea who it was, but we waved as if we belonged there. The occupants of the other car hesitated a moment, then waved back and drove off.

We found that a bulldozer had cleared the exact perimeter of the proposed prison. Bags of soil samples were everywhere, as were surveyor's flags. Far from looking like a potential site, this looked to be a prison under construction.

Bill asked if I could open my car trunk. He grabbed one of the bags of soil and stuffed it in. "They're not just looking at this site," he said, "and you'll need to prove it."

At a Council staff meeting a few days later, I related what we had seen. Our staff photographer, Gary Randorf, said he was taking a flight that weekend over the Park and suggested that he could go over the site. As it happened, a late spring snow fell the night before Gary's flight, leaving a dusting everywhere. Gary's aerial photos showed that the perimeter had been bulldozed into a clear outline of the proposed prison exactly matching the one in an "artist's concept" sketch released by the corrections department.

The next regular meeting of our board took place shortly thereafter, and as usual I presented my report.

I showed the photographs to our directors and for dramatic effect, pulled the bag of soil from beneath my chair and dropped it with a thud on the table. Gary's photos, I said, show that the corrections department has settled on the Tupper Lake site for the new prison. This soil sample is another piece of evidence, I said. The board members shook their heads, but no one asked me how I got the bag of dirt. They probably did not want to know.

Weeks went by, and as the controversy about the prison site grew in the media, I grew nervous about the bag of soil, now next to my desk. There were indications that meeting attendees were telling folks in other organizations about what they had heard and seen at my presentation. It had been good theater, after all.

The soil proved to be the perfect medium for growing tomatoes in a small planter behind the office. Problem solved.

Bill Cooke called me the next day with news about the Tupper Lake site.

"This thing is going down the drain," he said. "Corrections has messed this up. You and I have to go to Senator Stafford and tell him what you found. And we have to do it in Plattsburgh," where Stafford's law offices were located.

Bill's instinct was right on. There was no need to make an enemy of the senator who represented most of the Adirondack Park. And I liked the idea of going to Stafford's law office. It was hours away from Albany, and the sheer effort of our attending a meeting there showed that we had an important message to deliver on a serious matter.

We were warmly received in Plattsburgh. I told Stafford that the corrections department had made serious mistakes and possibly had violated state laws. These mistakes made it likely, I said, that a protracted legal fight would take place and delay any prison for quite a while.

I added that prison opponents were well funded and committed to stopping a new facility inside the Adirondack Park. The senator surprised us by saying he knew exactly who was involved in the opposition and that they had already visited him.

Bill and I acknowledged that prisons were an important industry in the North Country and in Stafford's district, providing good-paying jobs with minimal use of resources. I made it clear that the Council would not oppose a prison at another site. The corrections department had already identified the town of Malone, which already had several prisons, as a secondary site. Malone, while outside the Adirondack Park, was still in Stafford's district.

The senator then spoke at length about his background and upbringing. He grew up an orphan in the shadow of the Clinton Correctional Facility, a maximum-security prison in Dannemora, New York. He understood the North County communities, he understood the people, and he understood the importance of the prison to the local economy.

We repeated that we were not opposed to a prison, just that location inside the Adirondack Park. The senator said that it would be difficult to disappoint the local leaders in Tupper Lake, who were looking forward to the economic boost of the prison.

A week later I got a call from Peter Repas, one of the senator's senior staff members. He offered to arrange a meeting with the corrections department to go over the prospects of the prison in Tupper Lake. Could send him a letter with a list of our concerns?

I was disappointed. It sounded like Stafford had decided to try to save the Tupper Lake site. A fight seemed to be brewing, and I was under clear orders not to drag the Council into the fray publicly.

Maybe I could get some concessions, I thought. I sent Repas a list of concerns, including traffic, nighttime lighting, and other topics related to the environmental review.

Peter called back the next day, asking me to join him in a meeting two days hence with corrections officials. As the meeting approached, I grew concerned about its purpose. If this was a meeting to save the Tupper Lake location, I already knew that my bosses did not want me to facilitate the siting of a prison in the Park.

There can be only be two outcomes, I thought. One was that the corrections department would offer enough concessions for the Tupper Lake prison to proceed. The other was that the department would offer no compromises and open conflict would erupt. In that case, I decided, I would ask our board to get publicly involved.

Just in case, I prepared a request for documents under New York's Freedom of Information Law (FOIL) The manner in which someone made a request could indicate long-term intentions, so I intentionally drafted my request in a way that it appeared to be the foundation of a long-term court fight.

At the meeting, I found Repas and two corrections officials. Everything was very cordial until I asked for concessions. My every request was deflected or denied outright. I felt foolish to have come. Letting my temper get the best of me near the end of the meeting, I declared that we were getting nowhere and pulled a large envelope out of my briefcase.

"Here is a FOIL request for documents. I expect to hear from you within five days," I said. And that was the end of the meeting.

I had barely gotten back to my office when the phone rang. It was Repas, and he was furious. He said that I had violated basic meeting etiquette and had embarrassed him.

"You could not have met with those key officials without me being there, and you abused the privilege," he said. He concluded by saying he was shocked by my behavior, had thought I was wiser than that, and that he would have to tell Stafford what I had done.

Then he hung up on me.

He was right, of course. I acted inappropriately. I could be disappointed in the outcome of the meeting, but I should not have embarrassed my host.

Several weeks of silence followed. I became concerned. Perhaps my stealth campaign was not going to work, but we could not go public. It was clearer now than ever that the Council's board did not want to take a public position.

Then opportunity literally knocked. The chairman of the Sierra Club's Adirondack Committee, Tom Kligerman, stopped by my office. Tom told me he had heard that there were problems with a potential prison in the Park. His level of knowledge only helped confirm my suspicion that our council members were yakking it up with people outside the Council. Tom added that the Sierra Club was trying to become more active in the Adirondacks and that the prison issue sounded like an opportunity for it to get involved.

I quickly saw that we had a new drum major to lead our parade. I explained that my board was reluctant to get involved, but if the Sierra Club took the lead, we might follow. I offered to tell him as much as I knew about the prison.

The Sierra Club took the mace in hand and marched with it. With our staff helping a bit behind the scenes, the Sierra Club held a news conference, complete with maps and charts, condemning the proposal for a "prison in the park."

The reaction was almost instantaneous. Tupper Lake business and political leaders excoriated the Sierra Club. Within days, bumper stickers trashing the club appeared on cars, and signs were erected on lawns declaring "Sierra Club Not Welcome."

The Adirondack Council had tried to stay neutral, but we could no longer hide in the weeds. Our board adopted a lengthy resolution, which we made public, calling for a thorough environmental review of the project and expressing a strong preference that the new prison be sited outside the Adirondack Park. But the board stopped short of declaring outright opposition.

I decided to open yet another front. The Sierra Club's active opposition had stimulated media interest in the prison issue. The Council had not yet gone public with Gary Randorf's aerial photographs, so I took them to Governor Pataki's office to meet with his assistant director for state operations, Lynette Stark.

Stark, through sheer competence, had worked her way up the Republican ladder in the state Senate and into a demanding but influential job with Pataki. Over the years we had gotten comfortable speaking directly and honestly with each other. Actually, Lynette had always been comfortable telling me what she thought.

The first time I met her, she was the brand new assistant to the legendary Ronald Pedersen, the environmental and energy policy director for the Republican Senate majority. I had arrived late at a large meeting, so I approached her afterward.

"Hi," I said. "I wanted to introduce myself."

"I know who you are," Lynette said, "and I already know everything I need to know about you." Then she walked off down the hall.

I stared after her with my mouth agape, unable to summon a comeback.

Our relationship had improved since those days. I was visiting her office now without an appointment, and Lynette's secretary was not at her desk. Just then Lynette walked out of her office.

"Lynette," I said, "I need ten minutes—and trust me, you will be glad that you met with me."

She gave me five minutes.

I told her of the trip to Tupper Lake. I pulled out Gary's photographs and said that we were prepared to distribute them to the media, but wanted to show them to the governor's office first as a courtesy. She looked them over but was noncommittal.

Later that afternoon I got a call from Lynette. "Can you share the photographs? Just overnight?" I had our intern walk them over to her office.

I picked them up the next day and asked Lynette, "What did you do with them?"

"The governor wanted to see them," she said. "It was very helpful. Thank you."

Soon, a curious thing happened. The Associated Press news agency obtained an internal memo to the DEC Commissioner from his legal staff. It said there was a strong likelihood that construction of the prison at the Tupper Lake site would contaminate a water aquifer and a nearby wetland complex.

The very next day, the Corrections Department announced that it had decided to build the new prison near the existing prisons in Malone. Senator Stafford issued a news release saying he was disappointed that the prison would not be in Tupper Lake, but noting that it would be built in his district and would benefit his constituents.

I never discussed the topic again with the senator, his staff, or the governor's office.

In what might appear as a coincidence, soon thereafter a group of prominent Tupper Lake summer residents announced that they were forming a group to support economic initiatives there. They proposed a new tourist attraction: a natural history museum focusing on wildlife of the Adirondacks. The group raised an enormous amount of private money within a few years. The Adirondack Council endorsed the project, and I was directed to lobby in Albany and Washington for state and federal funds to support the museum's construction.

SO THEN WHAT HAPPENED?

The new museum thrives to this day. (See figure 5.1.)

On May 17, 2021, the *Adirondack Daily Enterprise*, calling the museum the foremost attraction in Tupper Lake, reported that the site had welcomed more than one million visitors.

Figure 5.1. Wild Center in Tupper Lake. *Source*: Nancie Battaglia.

The Natural History Museum of the Adirondacks, renamed the Wild Center, continues to grow, with new facilities and program development. It is now 115 acres with live displays and features a treetop walkway.

CHAPTER 6

MARY-ARTHUR AND ME

Mary-Arthur Beebe walked up the aisle. She stopped, looked me in the eye, and declared in a loud voice and in no uncertain terms: "You are a terrible person."

She leaned in farther. Her face contorted with anger as she hissed, "We will win. You can count on that!" Then she stomped off.

I had never met her before.

Mary-Arthur was executive director of the Lake George Association—a private group seeking a state permit to dump toxic chemicals into Lake George to kill a troublesome weed. I was leading the opposition.

Mary-Arthur and her fellow boaters on the "Queen of American Lakes" were being increasingly inconvenienced by the presence in some smaller harbors of Eurasian watermilfoil. The invasive plant grew on the lake floor in shallow waters and its long tendrils reached the surface. The plant, usually called milfoil, could readily foul a boat propeller, and swimming through a milfoil patch was difficult and unpleasant.

The milfoil had spread noticeably in the lake in recent years. The weed could be controlled by placing solid mats on the lake floor or by pulling it up by hand. Both these methods required divers and were time-consuming and expensive. The chemical treatment sought by the lake association promised a "one and done" approach.

As the Adirondack Council saw it, the problem with this option was that Sonar, the aquatic herbicide to be used, was not particularly selective in what vegetation it killed. It might have an unanticipated impact on beneficial flora in the lake, even damaging rare or state-protected species. So we intervened in the permitting process.

We were successful in persuading the governing board of the Adirondack Park Agency to require two public hearings. Anyone could testify at the first, while the second was a formal and lengthy administrative hearing with expert testimony. The Council and the Lake George Association would participate in the formal hearing, after which the agency would decide whether to grant the permit the association was seeking.

The first hearing, called a legislative hearing, offered an opportunity for any member of the public to make a comment without being challenged. That is where I first encountered Mary-Arthur Beebe. She had just finished reading her statement and was on her way back up the aisle when she paused just long enough to tell me off.

She was wrong about me being a terrible person, of course. But Mary-Arthur's predication of the outcome did look prophetic at the time.

The Council had launched an array of news releases attacking the project, none of which seemed to get traction. We argued that the environmental impact statement was not comprehensive; that swimmers might be exposed to the chemical; that many residences still took drinking water directly from the lake (even though that was now illegal) and might be exposed to chemical contaminants; that the dumping of the chemicals could not be properly controlled and a drift of the toxin down the lake was inevitable. But nothing seemed to slow the formidable Lake George Association flotilla and its battleship, Mary-Arthur Beebe.

Then one night, after state offices were closed, I got a call from a fellow who worked in the Capitol.

"Can I stop by?" he asked. Sure, I told him, and asked what was going on. All he would say was, "Tell you when I get there."

My visitor arrived with a briefcase full of maps. When he laid them out, I could see they were maps of Lake George, but they were very different from the maps I was used to. These were maps of the vegetation underneath the lake's surface. As it turned out, this fellow had studied the lake in college and was very familiar with its flora. He explained that very tall vegetation grew like a spine down the middle of the lake, invisible from the surface. He said these enormous plants were largely responsible for the legendary clarity of Lake George, cleansing the water and also providing shelter for fish.

The chemical Sonar would kill not only the invasive milfoil, he asserted, but also had the potential to damage the most critical and beneficial vegetation in the lake.

My guest also pointed out that because the State of New York owned the bottom of the lake, the state had to give permission for the herbicide to be applied. By law, he added, that permission could be given only if the natural resources of the state would not be harmed.

The visitor said we could not use his name, and he took his maps with him. He said he talked to us because he could not stand by and watch the lake be ruined.

The information was a godsend. Now we were on the offensive again, pushing hard in public for the state to protect the lake's vegetation.

However, we were startled to learn that the state Office of General Services had already given its permission for the chemical treatment. But it became clear that the signature on the letter granting that permission came from a rank-and-file worker who had been directed by a superior to send it. The person who signed the letter knew nothing about the lake's resources, and the agency had conducted no research, investigation, or inquiry. There had just been an order from on high.

Under the rules of the formal hearing, the presiding administrative law judge issued a subpoena that we requested, commanding Office of General Services officials to appear at the hearing. We wanted them to provide testimony under cross-examination about their actions. The agency simply ignored the subpoena, a refusal that made newspaper headlines. It was actually better for our side that they did not show up.

Fortune then smiled on us again.

A new revelation came from the Darrin Freshwater Institute at Rensselaer Polytechnic Institute, a private research university in Troy, New York. (The institute's facilities on the shore of Lake George included a research vessel, so the professors had no shortage of student volunteers and interns every summer.)

The institute issued an annual report on the lake's water quality that included careful mapping of the milfoil infestation. The reports had been used by the Lake George Association to document the milfoil problem and to justify the need for chemical treatment.

Late in the hearing process, we noticed that the most recent institute report was not among the documents submitted by the association for the hearing. In fact, the public release of the latest report had been delayed.

One of the guiding maxims at our lobbying office was, "If it seems strange, it is strange." We soon understood why the latest report had been delayed. It showed a marked slowing of milfoil growth throughout the lake, and even a population decline in some of the areas proposed to be treated. The new research showed that the milfoil problem was the result of a natural cycle and was going away on its own!

In the last stage of a Spanish bullfight, when the bull is tired and wounded, the matador finishes off the beast with a deft thrust of his sword between the shoulder blades and through the heart. Our attorney, Thomas A. Ulasewicz, displayed similar skill at the end of the administrative hearing as he cross-examined the final witness for the Lake George Association, the out-of-state expert who would supervise the actual chemical treatment of the lake.

In his prepared testimony, the expert had claimed extensive personal knowledge of Lake George, including its seasonal patterns. He testified that he was both a frequent visitor to the region and a regular collaborator with the academics at the Freshwater Institute. Tom asked the expert when the lake usually froze over, and he responded with an approximate date.

"What about this year?" Tom asked.

"About the same time as last year," the expert replied.

"It froze completely over around the same time, then?"

"Yes."

Tom paused before he asked, "Would it surprise you, then, that this year the lake did not freeze over at all?"

Right through the heart. Olé!

The expert sputtered and looked vainly around the room for help as we presented the judge with several news articles reporting the unusual circumstances of the previous winter. For the first time in recent memory, ice fishing had been banned on Lake George because the ice was very thin, and in some places nonexistent.

"No more questions, your honor," Tom said. With his credibility shot, the association's expert witness stepped down.

The permit was denied, and the vote wasn't close. One day later, the state announced new funding for nonchemical treatments of the invasive milfoil. There would be more money to place mats on the lake bottom and new funding for divers to remove the plant by hand. This nonchemical control program has been a success.

CHAPTER 7

WELL, I'LL BE DAMMED

Peter Skinner was a fast-talking, hyperactive guy. His title was chief scientist in the Environmental Bureau of the New York Attorney General's Office, but he seemed to have his spoon in a lot of pots.

Skinner was a dedicated kayaker well before kayaks became a common person's toy. I could always tell if he was in Albany during the warm months because his car would be parked near the Capitol complex with his kayak atop it. His license plate read "IKAYAK."

He was usually a source of good information about what was happening in various state agencies, so I always took his call. He was also the brother-in-law of one of our board members.

One early spring day, Pete called with an unusual request. Could I meet with somebody the next afternoon? He could not tell me who or why, but he did say that I should block out two hours. I hesitated, even though my calendar was open, and then Pete used my own tried-and-true formula for getting a meeting: "You will be glad you did." How could I resist? On that promise, I went to meet the mystery man.

Pete was there with a fellow he introduced as Bruce Carpenter. Bruce had just formed an organization called New York Rivers United that was based in Utica, New York. I asked, probably impolitely, why Utica? Because, he replied, that is where he lived, and he was the only staff member.

Over the next two hours, Bruce explained why he was had come to Albany. The federal government licensed every major dam on every major river in Upstate New York, including many of rivers in the Adirondack Park. Those licenses had been issued fifteen to twenty years ago. Many of these licenses were about to expire, and if not renewed, those dams would have to be removed and the rivers restored to their original wild state.

Bruce and Skinner, who was active in the recreation group American Whitewater, planned to participate in the federal relicensing process controlled by the Federal Energy Regulatory Commission. The two of them wanted and needed a sympathetic ally.

Bruce said he believed that Niagara Mohawk Power Corporation, the utility company holding most of the dam licenses in the Adirondack Park, was eager to renew them and did not want to go through a long, expensive hearing process. The company would prefer to reach a settlement with any parties involved in the proceeding, which they hoped the Federal Energy Regulatory Commission would approve and adopt.

Under federal law, parties to the relicensing process could include affected Native American tribes, state resource agencies such as the New York Department of Environmental Conservation, the US Fish and Wildlife Service, local government officials, recreational users of the river such as American Whitewater, and private organizations that had a clear environmental interest or represented citizens who did—such as the Adirondack Council.

The idea sounded attractive, but I was wary of committing the Council to a multiyear, highly technical process that could consume a lot of our resources.

That is when Bruce closed the deal. He laid out maps showing that Niagara Mohawk owned considerable property along the major rivers in the Park. The lands had been purchased forty years ago in anticipation of a major spate of new hydroelectric dam-building. That construction was no longer going to happen, and now Niagara Mohawk was taking a beating from local governments who levied taxes on that waterfront property. Bruce did not think that any dam inside the Park would actually be removed, but challenging them would help move the settlement process along.

He saw an opportunity, he said, for stretches of the rivers that had been diverted and dewatered by the construction of the dams many years ago to once again receive regular flows of water, restoring natural wetlands and historic fisheries in the Park. And then Bruce reminded me that the terms of the new licenses would dictate the future of river basins for at least the next twenty-five years.

That sold me. The Council was in.

I would find out later that Carpenter had left his previous occupation to take this project on. He had been a used-car salesman. Good closer, that Bruce.

The extremely complicated federal relicensing process was quite an education. All-day meetings were spent poring over data on water flow and maps of property ownership, plus listening to statements and responses from every party at the table. At other times, we went on field visits managed by

Niagara Mohawk. We hiked along each river bank looking at prospective spots for canoe launches and takeouts. We observed planned water releases at predetermined flow rates to document which downstream areas would be flooded or simply restored. Documents and proposals were exchanged by the hundredweight.

We examined historic documents on vanished trout fisheries. We studied scientific analyses of the potential both for reestablishing those fisheries and for stocking other fishing areas. Campsites were scoped out. Trails to waterfalls and visitor observation areas were considered and mapped. We planned for communication systems to advise whitewater enthusiasts of water releases, both planned and natural. We tried to anticipate how to promote future tourism for both the able-bodied and disabled. We heard the concerns of Native American tribes. We came to appreciate how the hydroelectric system on each river was managed and how much water was needed to operate it efficiently and return a profit. We sought out the needs and wish lists of downstream users, including flood control.

And we made some interesting discoveries.

No official field trip was organized to the Beaver River in the central Adirondacks, so Lisa Genier and I took a multiday trip that included several lakes, among them the Moshier Reservoir on the Beaver.

Driving the dirt roads along one lake, we saw a curved concrete ramp that buttressed one hydroelectric dam. The structure was the bane of Niagara Mohawk because more than one local daredevil had tried, and failed, to climb it in his all-terrain vehicle. One, injured in the attempt, naturally sued the company.

Another attractive nuisance we viewed was a large rock wall reachable only from the water that had become a mecca for local climbers. Niagara Mohawk wanted to offload that site to the state forest preserve to remove the threat of future liability to the company. When I expressed doubt in a meeting that the utility would have any liability for simply owning the rock wall, I was in for a real-world surprise. The company agreed that the courts would eventually find it was not liable for any injury suffered by trespassers. But mounting a legal defense would be so expensive that the company simply settled any lawsuits without fault being declared one way or another. Now the word was out among plaintiff's lawyers, and the utility feared a wave of new suits. Its new posture was, get rid of the damn rock wall!

In a meeting to discuss the fisheries of Moshier Reservoir on the Beaver, we were surprised to learn that the state Department of Environmental Conservation (DEC) had been stocking tiger muskellunge. The tiger muskie is a voracious predator that can grow to thirty pounds. The DEC's stocking of muskies in the St. Lawrence River was popular with anglers, but it seemed out of place in this relatively small body of water.

Again, when things seem odd in New York government, a good assumption is that they are odd for a reason. The movie *Jurassic Park* was a big hit at that time, and I asked the state fisheries representatives whether they were concerned about creating a "Jurassic reservoir" by stocking the monster muskies. The US Fish and Wildlife folks roared at the joke, but the state employees just looked embarrassed and sat there steaming.

They felt they had to give an explanation: The stocking of tiger muskies had been at the request of the local fish and game club. So what? I asked. I wagered that any fish and game club in New York would like to have the huge fish in their lake, but the department certainly wouldn't have to accommodate them. Well, they said, the area's representative in the state Assembly belonged to the local club, and their bosses had ordered them to put the fish into the reservoir.

Okay then! Moving right along. But once it was out in the open, the stocking program was terminated. They say sunshine is the best disinfectant.

That wasn't the only time an elected official was involved in the future of the federal licenses.

The Ausable River is dammed by the Rainbow Falls hydroelectric facility owned by New York State Electric and Gas. The dam lies just above Ausable Chasm, a deep rock cut near Keeseville, New York, that is a spectacular tourist attraction in the northeast portion of the Adirondack Park. For many years, Ausable Chasm, a private company, has operated guided boat trips down the gorge in addition to its popular trails and overlooks. Whitewater enthusiasts were questioning whether the federally regulated waters of the river could legally be used exclusively for the benefit of the tour operator. The kayakers claimed that the public had the right to access those waters as well.

The operators of the tourist boats were understandably worried. They had operated exclusively for many years and owned the neighboring lands. They feared both that the paddlers would interfere with their operation and that a tragedy could take place in the Chasm's swift waters. They certainly wanted no obligation to rescue any kayaker in trouble.

Word of this development soon reached the local state senator, who happened to be on the board of directors of the Ausable Chasm, and soon his staff was at every relicensing meeting for the hydroelectric facility.

If an effort to demonstrate that qualified kayakers could competently navigate the waters of Ausable Chasm, a test run was organized. Volunteer paddlers were recruited and a contingency rescue plan developed. Under the scrutiny of many interested parties and a video team, the kayakers set out down the gorge. Some ran the route with aplomb, but more than one had to be hauled out before completing the run. Thus the heavyweight fight ended with no decision, and it would be years before federal regulators approved the use of the Ausable for recreation by the public.

The dam relicensing process attracted the participation of many groups besides the Council, including New York Rivers United, Trout Unlimited, the National Audubon Society, the Association for the Protection of the Adirondacks, the Adirondack Mountain Club, and others. It resulted in a series of federally approved settlements. On behalf of the Council, I signed off on agreements on the Raquette, Sacandaga, and Beaver Rivers that dramatically improved the ecological health and recreational use of these water systems.

On the Beaver River, the settlement resulted in the reopening of a historic canoe route and the expansion of an adjacent state wilderness area. It proposed the reestablishment of a trout fishery that, until the natural river bed had been dewatered, had been celebrated as one of the greatest trout fishing streams in the East. Agreements were struck for new whitewater opportunities, with scheduled water releases and new access to the river both inside and outside the Park boundary.

On the Raquette River, recreational improvements were made, minimum water flows were restored to original natural parts of the river, and significant lands were scheduled for donation to the state of New York. In a decision important for the ecology of the river system, reservoir fluctuations would be minimized, allowing for better protection of wildlife. Five thousand acres of land would be forever protected by a state conservation easement and more than thirteen miles of the river would be opened for public recreation.

For the Upper Hudson/Sacandaga River a legally significant settlement was reached among twenty-nine signatories that all lands to the high-water mark of Great Sacandaga Lake were part of the Adirondack Park forest preserve. The settlement also attempted to address the ongoing conflict between the use of the lake for recreation and its primary purpose, flood control, with better management of the water levels. As was the case in all the settlements, new recreational opportunities, including canoe access and a scenic overlook, were part of the package.

A two-hour sales pitch by a guy from Utica, New York, would lead to some of the most long-lasting and significant improvements in recreation and ecological protection along the major waterways of the Adirondack Park. We all owe a debt to that great closer, Bruce Carpenter.

CHAPTER 8

TIMBER RUSTLERS

In 1997, if you were caught cutting down a beautiful tree in an old-growth forest in the Adirondack Park, you would be subject to a harsh state fine: ten dollars.

That had been state law for more than ninety years. In the early twentieth century, ten dollars was a hefty sum, but no longer. If you picked the right size and species, a single tree might be worth hundreds of dollars.

As timbering progressed on private lands in the Adirondacks, it was harder and harder to find mature trees, especially those in demand for high-end furniture and flooring such as walnut, oak, and cherry. Market prices for timber were on the rise throughout New York and New England.

There had always been timber theft in the region. Cutting well over the property line into the neighbor's woods, taking out the oaks when you contracted only to take out the hemlocks, or just plain understating your actual harvest to the landowner—those timber thefts occurred every year.

But by the early 1990s, being caught with an illegally harvested tree was well worth the risk of a ten-dollar fine, if you were caught at all. The state's force of forest rangers had been diminished by budget cuts to a historic low, even as timber rustling in the state forest preserve was becoming rampant.

State forest rangers in the Adirondacks approached our staff. They were frustrated, telling us that their call for new police action on timber theft was not making it up the conservation department's chain of command. We appreciated that the rangers thought we could help them and set out to put the matter on lawmakers' agenda in Albany.

It seemed like a pretty simple thing to fix: increase the fine to an appropriate level. But it was too simple. Contrary to what you might think, the simpler the legislative bill, the harder it can be to pass. Unlike many complex issues that came before the legislature, this one was so straightforward that everyone felt safe to have a firm (and often uninformed) opinion. That being the case, any number we proposed as the new maximum fine for timber rustling would be subjected to extensive wrangling by outlaw lobbyists and by certain cowboys and cowgirls on the legislative staff.

So we decided instead to propose a floor. Let everyone fight over how much higher the fine should go (and who should get credit). We settled on a fine of $180, which was, by our reckoning, the equivalent of 10 dollars adjusted for inflation over the years.

Our first pitch to legislators was kind of fun. Timber rustlers in our greatest park! They are hauling away the people's trees from land that was purchased with tax dollars! Tax dollars pulled from the pockets of your constituents!

Then we would add the kicker: Assemblyman, even if our trusty rangers catch the rustlers, we can't string 'em up. All we can do is fine them ten dollars a tree!

Jaws would drop and heads would shake. Some lawmakers just would not believe it. "That can't be true," they said. "Come back after you do your research."

But we assured them we had done the research and it was true.

We thought we should bring in another official player to support us. Concerned about the rangers' lack of support from higher-ups at the Environmental Conservation Department, we approached the state attorney general's office. Officials there were quite enthusiastic, and Attorney General Dennis C. Vacco made timber theft part of the formal package of legislative proposals he submitted to state legislators.

The reception in the Democratic-led state Assembly was very good. In both 1997 and 1998, bills to curb timber theft passed overwhelmingly, despite the fact that the attorney general was from the opposing party.

The Senate, however, was another matter. We met with Fred Anderson, the chief staff person for the chairman of the Senate Environmental Committee, Carl L. Marcellino, to ask if the senator might sponsor the bill. Anderson, a former ski guide in the Adirondacks, was usually helpful, but this time he told us that the only thing his boss and the rest of the Senate Republican conference would want to know is what Senator Ron Stafford thought.

Not only did Stafford represent most of the Adirondack Park, but as chairman of the Finance Committee, he had a big say on member items—special pork barrel appropriations for just one district—in the state budget. It was reasonable that any senator would hesitate to take action that affected Stafford's district without consulting him first, for fear of reprisal.

With that advice, we met with the senator's assistant, Tom Grant. It was hard to fathom that he was serious when he told us that Stafford would not support any bill unless it included a Christmas tree exemption.

"A what?"

"A Christmas tree exemption," he explained. "Any resident inside the Adirondack Park could take up to three Christmas trees per year per household from state land."

From the constitutionally protected, timber-cutting-banned, "forever wild" state forest preserve? We asked.

"Yes," Grant said. "It is widely known that it is a tradition in the North Country to go onto state land and cut down three Christmas trees."

I pause now only to give credit where credit is due. Tom Grant never cracked a smile while saying this.

Okay, I'll bite, I thought. "Why three?"

Grant answered with great certainty. "One for my family, one for my wife's family, and one for my parents' house."

We left that meeting with our heads spinning. Was that really a tradition in the North Country? I asked Lisa Genier of our staff, who grew up inside the Park. While she did not doubt that Christmas tree theft was common, she said, it certainly did not amount to an honored tradition.

And three trees? Was Grant setting down a starting negotiating position, or was he just screwing with us? And if so, why?

We dutifully reported to senior staffers in the Assembly and the sponsor of that chamber's timber-rustling bill what we had heard. They all agreed that it was too bizarre to be real. What was the real reason the senator did not want a bill to pass they wondered?

We finally figured out that Stafford would not take any action that might harm any of his constituents if he could avoid it, and he had a broader definition of who might be affected by the bill than we did.

Stafford himself then introduced the first bill on timber rustling in the Senate. The reasons that lawmakers introduce bills are often misunderstood. They might introduce a bill just to solicit campaign contributions. Or they might introduce a bill just to control the issue. In almost all cases, first in time was first in right—especially when a senator from the majority, with seniority, was involved.

Over time, the senator's staff would slowly back away from the Christmas tree exemption—one tree at a time.

Meanwhile, the problem of timber rustling began to draw more attention. The headline on a piece in the *New York Times* summed things up: "As timber prices rise, so do thefts of trees."

Now some new parties weighed in too. Vacco lost his reelection bid and newly elected Democrat Attorney General Eliot Spitzer submitted his own proposal, with penalties much more severe than what were previously on the table. Spitzer proposed that any prosecutor should have the latitude to demand a wide array of fines and criminal charges. The Empire State Forest Products Association, which represents timber owners, loggers, and manufacturers of wood products, argued that these proposed penalties were too high, the burden of proof for prosecution was too low, and the means of calculating the value of the stolen timber was too arbitrary.

We organized several negotiating sessions between the interested parties, to no avail. The Forest Products Association remained opposed, and so the Senate sat on any action for another year.

One of the sticky issues for the forest product trade group was the innocent or accidental theft of timber, although it never really proposed a solution. The next year, we pressured its president and chief executive, Kevin King, to explain how one of its members could innocently run afoul of the proposed new law. In response, he arranged for a meeting with representatives of Finch, Pruyn and Company, which owned vast timber holdings in the Adirondack Park.

We learned that Finch, Pruyn properties often shared a border with state lands in the Adirondacks. The boundaries were not marked, and in some places both sides still used maps drawn in the 1880s.

Mistakes can happen, we were told. Finch demanded that the state not be allowed to prosecute any theft of timber off state land by an adjacent landowner if the state itself had not clearly marked the common property boundary. Finch said that requiring their company to mark the boundaries would be an unacceptable financial burden. I came away with the impression that mistakes had already happened.

We felt that such a provision in a new law, however well intended, amounted to a written invitation to steal from state land. The attorney general's office felt the same way. We were stalled again.

It did not help that Peter J. Bruno, a senior executive at Finch, was the brother of Joseph Bruno, the majority leader of the Senate. That was the first thing "Uncle Joe" told us when we met with him in his new capacity as Senate leader—after asking if we wanted to have a picture taken with him.

Soon the Adirondack Landowners Association raised another policy concern. It demanded that thefts of timber from private landowners by harvesters also be addressed in the bill.

At first, we hated the idea. Making the measure more complex was not what we had in mind. But we soon realized that including theft on private lands would ultimately attract more legislative support. The scope of the bill would now be statewide, because timber theft and chicanery by harvesters had become a widespread problem. Also, the Landowners Association, which was comprised of private clubs and large estates in the Park, had influence in the Senate, and with Senator Stafford in particular.

The Forest Products Association raised yet another issue that Stafford promptly agreed to address in a rider to the Senate bill. In downstate communities, within commuting distance of New York City, new housing developments were being built on lands adjacent to large forested tracts. The new homeowners were startled to learn that the beautiful wooded vistas from their picture windows could rapidly disappear when the forest's owner decided to harvest the mature trees.

Campaigns led by these new local voters were under way in several downstate towns, seeking to change local zoning laws in order to keep wooded areas from being heavily harvested. The timber industry responded by seeking new state protections for the besieged woodlot owners.

The collision of these two issues, timber theft and forestry rights, now threatened the prospect of any action at the Capitol. The Association of Towns of the State of New York strongly opposed a forestry rights rider in the timber theft bill, while the forest products industry demanded it. It was a tug-of-war that brought the bill to a standstill.

Inside the Park, we were making more progress. Finch was isolated when the other remaining major timber company in the Park, International Paper, acknowledged that it had already taken the initiative to mark the boundaries it shared with state land.

In the 2001 legislative session, Assemblyman William Parment, who was sponsoring our legislation, and Senator Stafford finally reached an accord. The bill now included a provision allowing the Commissioner of the Department of Environmental Conservation to intervene at the request of an aggrieved forest landowner. If necessary, the Commissioner could force changes to any local zoning law that he found to be detrimental to or inconsistent with sound forestry by private landowners. Despite this, the legislative session ended without a new law. A frustrated Parment put the blame on the attorney general's office, whose memo to legislators opined that the accord "unduly restricted" local government ordinances, which promptly sapped the bill's support in the Assembly chamber. The Senate passed the compromise bill as the Assembly sat on its hands and watched another year go by.

It became a dark joke in our office that all we had accomplished over the previous several years was to inform the public that anyone could steal a tree from the forest preserve and risk only a ten-dollar fine.

Finally, after the Legislative Commission on Rural Resources held statewide hearings and the governor's office became actively involved, a bill addressing timber thefts on private and public lands was enacted in 2003.

The new law made timber theft a Class A misdemeanor, punishable by a fine of $250 a tree, three times the stumpage value, or both. The cost of restoring land to repair any damage from the theft could also be imposed on the offender. As for the issue of forestry rights, the new law merely required the state environmental conservation Commissioner to comment on any proposed local ordinance at the request of an affected forest landowner. That compromise apparently satisfied both the towns and the timber industry.

Governor Pataki signed the bill into law at a Syracuse hotel run by the owners of L. & J. G. Stickley, Inc., a famed furniture manufacturer and a member of the Empire State Forest Products Association.

It had taken us six years, but we had succeeded. (See figure 8.1.)

Figure 8.1. Timber theft bill signing. Author at center rear. *Source*: author's own material.

CHAPTER 9

THE NEW CHAIRMAN

We occasionally did favors for other organizations whose work we supported. A portion of our lobbying time was dedicated to work on issues or projects that would benefit the Park but were not necessarily a high priority for the Adirondack Council. Usually, it was a request for help to secure funding.

Sometimes the request was from the governor's office. We traveled to Washington more than once to lobby for the Forest Legacy program, an annual appropriation to the states for specific land protection projects.

More than once, we helped the Clean Air Markets Division of the federal Environmental Protection Agency win budgeting struggles over funding for air-monitoring stations located in the Northeast.

Securing new sources of funding for scientists working on acid rain and loon research in New York state was also a regular assignment. We helped secure state and federal funding for the new Wild Center museum in Tupper Lake. We even helped secure funding to upgrade the sewage treatment plant in the village of Lake Placid.

One day the Adirondack chapter of the Nature Conservancy called. It wanted our help in getting the state to help buy land in the Clintonville Pine Barrens in the northeastern part of the Park. The Conservancy's request resulted in one of the strangest lobbying visits of my career.

Like the Albany Pine Barrens, home to the Karner blue butterfly, the Clintonville barrens provided habitat for the pine pinion moth (*Lithophane lepida lepida*) and another rare nocturnal species, the Acadian swordgrass moth. Both were rapidly disappearing due to their sensitivity to artificial light, which disrupted their behavior. The Clintonville Pine Barrens were the only known location of *Lithophane lepida lepida* in the United States, and a proposed housing development now threatened to eliminate its sole remaining habitat. The Conservancy was seeking a line in the state budget to help purchase the core of this habitat.

So my task was to save *Lithophane lepida lepida*! It did not have the public appeal of, say, a rare white bear, but it certainly was worth the effort and was part of our core mission.

I set up a meeting with state Senator Owen H. Johnson, a Republican from Long Island who had just become chairman of the Senate Environmental Conservation Committee. Johnson would have to sign off if any new funds were to be added to the state budget. The governor had already submitted his proposed budget without specifying funds for the project.

I did not know Johnson well. Lobbying his office on issues important to the environmental community usually fell to Long Island groups. He was politically conservative, and it was a surprise that the Senate leadership had given him the chairmanship of the environmental committee. It seemed to be a consolation prize for not getting the chairmanship of a committee that he would have preferred.

Still, we were reasonably confident that we had a good shot at the project. Long Island already had a history of efforts to save its own pine barrens, one of only three such large, sandy landforms in the entire state. The senator had yet to make his mark as a statewide player in protecting New York's natural resources, and this project of both state and national significance would be a gift of positive publicity for the new chairman, we thought.

More importantly, we already had "Senator Dominic" on our side. Dominic Jacangelo was a senior staff aide to Johnson, and our experience was that when Dom liked an idea, he could almost always persuade Johnson to go along. Senator Dom had already expressed his interest in helping to save *Lithophane lepida lepida*.

So with some optimism, we assembled the lobbyists for other groups that supported the effort and headed to our meeting. The Nature Conservancy had provided photos of the moth in question and of the pine barrens. Our pitch? Senator Johnson could save the species from extinction in the continental United States!

We explained to the senator that the state itself could not buy the pine barrens. Any state-owned land in the Adirondack Park fell under the New York constitution's requirement to be treated as "forever wild." The endangered moths depended on pitch pines in the barrens to survive, and the pines' health required periodic fires, including human-made events called "planned burns." So we needed a state grant to help the Nature Conservancy buy the land, and it could take the actions necessary to manage the habitat into the future.

We made a point of noting that the state's other two pine barrens—one of which was in the senator's district—were already protected, so the new funds would allow the preservation of the last pine barren complex in the state. It would be a historic move in the environmental history of New York, a fitting action by the new chairman of the committee on the environment. Finally, if Johnson led his Republican colleagues in taking action that the governor and the Democrats in the Assembly had ignored, they alone would get the credit for saving a threatened species.

We finished our pitch, and everyone looked to the senator for his response.

"Well, I appreciate that you want to save this, this, moth," Johnson said haltingly. "But you know as well as I do that we can't save everything," he continued.

"Species come and species go."

His last remark echoed around the room as the environmental lobbyists sat silently staring at the senator, some with mouths agape.

After an uncomfortable minute, the senator thanked us for coming, got up and left the room.

We filed silently into the hallway. We had gone only a dozen yards when his aide Dominic Jacangelo came running after us.

"I don't know what happened," he said. "But it's not over. I will speak to him."

But apparently it was over. Jacangelo reported no progress in swaying his boss.

Then help arrived. A member of the Adirondack Council from Buffalo contacted our offices shortly after our debacle with the senator. Her family wanted to make a major financial contribution to the protection of the Adirondack Park landscape and asked our communications director if we had any ideas. The next thing we knew, the Nature Conservancy got the seed money it needed to buy the 200 core acres of the pine barrens to protect the habitat of *Lithopane lepida lepida* and the Acadian swordgrass moth.

Chairmen come and chairmen go.

CHAPTER 10

YEAR OF THE MOOSE

The attraction of the national parks in the American West lies not only in their enthralling vistas, but also their abundant wildlife. Observing wildlife in the Adirondack Park also attracts tourists to New York. For years, visitors and summer residents looked forward to watching black bears. Of course, the sightings usually occurred at night when the bears were feeding at the local dump. But even after the smaller town garbage dumps were closed forever, bear sightings remained a source of comfortable conversation between the mountain residents and the visiting flatlanders.

Loons were another big attraction. People loved the call of the loon so much that local retail outlets were able to sell virtually anything that had a picture of a loon or a recording of its call. That included classical music with loon calls interrupting the melody. Liszt with loons!

But a moose sighting was the hottest ticket. *Everybody* wanted to see a moose. In the natural resource world, moose were among a group of animals known as charismatic megafauna. The Adirondack Council had long raised funds by using these animals in our promotional materials. We often looked for opportunities to promote wildlife protection in the Park, since to protect wildlife you need to protect its habitat, which requires attention to water quality and the preservation of wetlands and forests.

The problem was that the native moose population in the Adirondacks had disappeared. The animals did not simply wander away; they were hunted down and extirpated. So the Council was enthusiastic when we learned in 1992 that the State Department of Environmental Conservation (DEC) had quietly been developing a program to reintroduce the moose to the Adirondacks. The western part of the Adirondack Park, with its many wetlands and ponds, was once ideal moose habitat. It could be again.

We knew that reintroduction of the moose would help justify protecting the large expanses of private timberlands in the western part of the Park.

The moose would also be a boon to tourism and local economies and thus would help calm the tensions that always existed between local residents and seasonal visitors.

While occasional moose were spotted inside the Park, they were for the most part wandering bachelors. Young males looking for new territory would drift in from Vermont or down from Canada. Left to its instincts, a moose population would slowly establish itself in the Park, but it would take decades.

The DEC wanted to accelerate that timeline. It had entered into a cooperative program with the Canadian government in which at least one family of moose in Algonquin Provincial Park in Ontario had been radio-collared and was being tracked for possible relocation into the Adirondacks. The idea was that the introduction of a stable family unit into the Park would form the nucleus of a native population of moose.

We wanted to help this program succeed. And we had a terrific idea. The Council would promote the reintroduction of the moose into the Adirondack Park with a media campaign. The heart of the campaign would be a contest to name the members of the moose family when they were released in the Park. The name-that-moose campaign would be, as I liked to call it, "cheesy but effective."

Before that could happen, though, we had to whet the public appetite in order to boost to the state's plans. After the close of the 1992 legislative session, we proclaimed the "Year of the Moose," much like some cultures name the lunar New Year. We ordered stickers and labels to put on every piece of our correspondence. I even made a point of pinning a button proclaiming the Year of the Moose on the lapel of every guest at our annual dinner, including DEC Commissioner Tom Jorling.

Eager to assess the progress of the reintroduction program, I made an appointment to see Alan Hicks, the DEC's wildlife biologist who was in charge of the reintroduction program, at his office at the Five Rivers Environmental Education Center near my home.

It was clear right off the bat that Hicks had no interest in the promotional possibilities of reintroducing the moose. He was focused on actually getting it done. In addition to coordinating with the Canadians to obtain and transport the moose family, he also had to get the new program through the usual New York regulatory gantlet. That required the preparation of an environmental impact statement and a series of public hearings inside and outside the Adirondacks to receive comments.

Hicks preferred to be in the field. The hearings were outside his comfort zone. I offered our assistance, including getting our member groups to the hearings to express enthusiasm for the project.

Environmental impact statements are public documents designed to identify ahead of time the likely effects of any project on natural or human-made resources. In the case of the moose reintroduction program, the statement did a fine job of discussing the historic presence of moose in the Adirondacks and their sad elimination at the hands of humans. Positive outcomes of reintroduction such as increased tourism were highlighted. In an effort to win the support of sportsmen's groups, the document also projected a future hunting season for moose in New York—a plan that I thought would surely draw some opposition, but was probably good politics. The analysis also gave a fair estimate of the cost of the reintroduction program and the risks of more collisions between motor vehicles and moose as the population grew. Overall, it was a competent job.

Just before the start of the public hearings, I visited Hicks one more time and found him a completely different man. He told me that perhaps the reintroduction of moose was a poor use of state money. He said the moose were likely to establish themselves over time anyway. And he didn't want to have blood on his hands.

Startled, I asked him, "What do you mean blood on your hands?"

"I had dinner last night with some friends," Hicks said. "My friend's wife asked me about collisions between wandering moose and cars. She wanted to know what we would do about that. I said we would put up signs on the road to warn people. She asked, 'With more moose, will there be more collisions?' and I had to say that was probably true. She then said that since I was the guy bringing the moose into the Park, my actions would directly lead to more moose-car collisions and more people getting injured or killed."

"Then she asked me if I was 'prepared to have the blood of those people on my hands,'" Hicks said. He turned to me and said, "I don't think I am."

I was at a loss for words. We sat without speaking for a moment or two. Then I tried to buck him up. "Sure, there is some risk," I said. "You even discuss the potential for highway collisions in the environmental impact statement. But that would be true whether the moose are brought in by you or wander in by themselves."

"If they wander in its one thing, but if . . ." Al's voice trailed off and he looked down at the table. Boy, did he look troubled.

I tried again to rally him. "I think it was unfair of her to pin that on you," I said.

"Maybe so," he replied. But he sounded unconvinced.

I ended the meeting and called the Commissioner's office the next day. I didn't mention Hicks, but said that I was calling because I had heard that the moose introduction program had stalled. No, they assured me, the program was full speed ahead. They had no idea why I might have heard otherwise, and the schedule for public hearings would be announced shortly.

I had Council staffers attend the first two hearings, held in the evening at community halls in the Park. At both, Hicks began with a short presentation on the project, complete with slides. That went fine. But in his remarks, and especially in his response to questions, he went out of his way to emphasize the potential for more collisions with moose on the highways. He made it clear to the residents that since they were doing most of the local driving, they had to decide whether it was worth the risk to their friends and relatives to have moose in their midst.

Hicks proceeded to scare the shit out of half the people at each hearing. Local newspapers began reporting that the state was deliberately planning to wreak havoc on the highways.

The comfortable public relations sweater with a moose on the front that we were knitting began to unravel. Alarmed, I brought our concern about Hicks's over-the-top remarks to his superiors. "*Everybody* loves moose," they said. "Don't worry!"

By the end of the public hearings, local officials inside the park communities were clamoring for the governor to stop the impending massacre by moose of their fellow Adirondackers. They pounded on their state senators and assembly members to intervene. Political support for the program quickly collapsed, and the governor's office directed the department to quietly abandon the moose reintroduction program.

SO THEN WHAT HAPPENED?

Moose are now on the loose. In 2015 the state Department of Environmental Conservation, in cooperation with several universities and the Wildlife Conservation Society, a nonprofit group, launched a two-year survey of the moose population in New York state. Its goal is to gather data to be used to create a moose management plan. Twenty-one moose were captured by helicopter and outfitted with radio collars to track their movements. In 2016, the department estimated there were 400 resident moose in the Park.

More than two decades after the aborted attempt to reintroduce moose to the Adirondacks, signs have been erected along some roadways warning motorists of the risk of collisions with them. However, according to the DEC, motor vehicle collisions with moose have generally declined even as their population has increased.[1]

Although Hamilton County in the central Adirondacks was once the center of opposition to the moose reintroduction plan in the 1990s, the Town of Indian Lake hosted its tenth annual Great Adirondack Moose Festival in 2019. (See figure 10.1.)

Figure 10.1. Indian Lake Moose Festival. *Source*: Bill Herrick.

CHAPTER 11

THE AIR CAMPAIGN

April 22, 2002. Earth Day. I was on the road by 6:00 a.m. The trip to Wilmington, New York, in the Adirondack Mountains near Lake Placid, would take three hours.

I checked the weather report before I left the house. Mother Nature had been acting weirdly in the North Country. The week before, the temperature had hit the eighty-degree mark. Two days ago, Au Sable Forks, not that far from Wilmington, had suffered considerable property damage in an earthquake registering over 5.1 on the Richter scale.

But for this trip, things looked good, if not great. The weather report called for a 30 percent chance of snow showers in the high elevations. I grabbed my wool baseball hat and fleece vest just in case.

The skies were clear for the drive up Interstate 87, the Adirondack Northway, and the road was dry. The view, as usual, was spectacular. With the cruise control set at seventy miles per hour, I just held onto the steering wheel for two hours and watched the North Country go by.

Near Lake George, I spotted the sign on the Northway that pumped me up every time I saw it: "Entering Adirondack Park." I had spent much of my professional career working to protect the integrity of the park from threats of all kinds and the views grew increasingly awesome as you continued the drive into the park.

This was my sixth year as general counsel and legislative director of the Adirondack Council, whose members, registered Republicans and Democrats alike, shared a common vision of the park as a model for wilderness protection and biological diversity.

I was also wearing a third hat—acting executive director. Our former executive director, Timothy J. Burke, had resigned the previous July. The morning after the Council's annual membership meeting in Wadhams, New

York, at which we all had a lovely time celebrating the past year's successes, I got a call from board chairman David Skovron. Burke had informed him in the parking lot on the way out that he was resigning—effective immediately.

David said he would talk to members of the executive committee and get back to me. I got off the phone and told my wife, Mollie, that the last time a board chairman said that to me, I was asked to fill in as acting executive director "temporarily."

Most nonprofit groups in trying to meet professional standards, prefer to conduct an open search for qualified candidates. You establish a search committee. You hire a headhunter. You advertise. You narrow the choices. You check résumés. You choose the final few candidates. You interview. You ask the favorites back for a second interview. All of this takes time.

I ended up serving as acting executive director for over a year the last time. Sure enough, I was soon asked to "temporarily" replace Tim.

So, nine months after that July night in Wadhams, I was still the acting executive director, general counsel, and chief lobbyist, and it was beginning to wear on me. I felt that I did not have enough time to do justice to any of my three jobs in the organization.

But as I headed up the Northway, none of that mattered. What a great day today would be!

The president of the United States was coming to the Adirondack Park this morning. At my suggestion! And he would promise to end the scourge of acid rain that had been damaging the lakes and streams and killing the wildlife of the park for over thirty years.

I drove along in a beautiful daydream about the event and its live national media coverage.

And to think, it all started in a bar five years earlier in Portland, Maine.

1997: BORN IN PORTLAND

It was February 1997, and David Greenwood, the Adirondack Council's office manager and part-time policy analyst, and I were in Portland, Maine, attending a conference of air-quality officials from the northeastern states and Canada. We were there to urge them as a group to issue an appeal to Congress for action on acid rain. Notwithstanding a recent report from the US Environmental Protection Agency (EPA) to Congress and ongoing lake sampling in the Adirondacks indicating that acid rain was continuing to harm lakes, streams, and wildlife, there was no momentum in Congress for action.

We did not make a dent in their agenda. We tried everything, even sneaking back into the conference room during lunch and placing flyers on everyone's seat. The proceedings were highly scripted, and we came away empty-handed.

David and I shared our frustration over drinks that night.

We were on our second round when David lamented, "We are just not just grabbing people. We need a new approach."

That was apparent to both of us. It had been two years since we first learned from a report by the EPA that the pollution controls on power plants mandated by Congress in 1990 were too weak to solve the acid rain problem in the Adirondacks.

The Council had celebrated the passage by Congress of the 1990 Acid Rain Amendments to the Clean Air Act. Signed into law by President George H. W. Bush, the new law required power plants to significantly cut their emissions of sulfur dioxide and nitrogen oxides, precursors to acid rain. The Council had worked hard to get it passed and we even had a staff member, Dan Plumley, appointed to an advisory committee on the regulations issued by the EPA that would implement the new law. (See figure 11.1.)

Figure 11.1. The mechanics of acid rain. *Source*: New York State Department of Environmental Conservation.

The 1990 Amendments, thanks to the efforts of Senator Daniel Patrick Moynihan (D-NY), also provided for the regular collection of air-monitoring data in the Northeast so we could tell exactly how well the law was working. That information was supposed to be reported to Congress on a regular basis.

President Bush, in signing the amendments into law, like the rest of us, no doubt had anticipated that the new federal law would solve the acid rain problem. Power plants' emissions of the main pollutants contributing to acid rain were to be cut by 50 percent or more. Better yet, an innovative system for achieving the cuts was put into place.

The system was called "cap and trade." The EPA would assign emission credits to each power plant. One credit equaled the right to emit one ton of pollutants. Over time, the EPA would reduce the total number of these credits—the "cap." Power plants could buy, sell, or trade the credits to achieve their emission goals. For example, if a plant installed effective emission-control equipment on its smokestacks, it could sell its excess pollution credits to another utility that needed additional credits to legally pollute.

There were predictions that this market-based approach would bring large reductions in emissions a very low cost, compared to the usual ways of regulating utilities.

Congress had mandated progress reports from federal agencies on the implementation of the cap-and-trade program. Like most Adirondack advocates, the Adirondack Council was eager to learn how effective the new regulatory program was in fact. But under President Bill Clinton and Vice President Al Gore, the administration delayed the release of those reports. We never did learn the reason for the foot-dragging.

When it became apparent that the target date for the first report due in November 1993 would not be met, the Adirondack Council filed a lawsuit, along with Thomas C. Jorling, Commissioner of the New York Department of Environmental Conservation, and Attorney General Robert Abrams of New York. The goal was to force the EPA to issue the report and to address several weaknesses in the program's regulations, including their failure to propose any circumstances where trading might be restricted. In a separate lawsuit, the Natural Resources Defense Council and the Adirondack Council claimed that the EPA had issued too many emission credits from the outset, making it inexpensive and easy for polluters to avoid reductions in emissions.

Our dealings with the EPA just before we filed the lawsuit were memorable. We met with Brian J. McLean, director of the EPA's Office of Atmospheric Programs, which ran the agency's new clean air markets unit, formed to implement the acid rain program. We were hoping that our persuasion and hints of legal action would be enough to win concessions. Instead, we were met with the rudest response that I had ever received from a federal official.

"Go ahead and sue us," McLean said. "And just so you know, we will ask for another year to complete the report, and the court will agree, and you will not see a thing until we are ready to release it. Period."

McLean also predicted that the lawsuit would eventually be settled and that the State of New York would be the first to withdraw.

He would turn out to be correct on every point.

The month after this exchange, the State of New York withdrew from the lawsuit, after winning some concessions from the EPA, including a date for the release of its report to Congress.

The Adirondack Council and NRDC soon reached our own settlement with the agency. In our settlement, the EPA agreed to lower the cap and substantially cut the total number of pollution credits that would be issued. That would reduce by hundreds of thousands of tons the pollutants that might fall on the Adirondack Park in the form of acid rain. A good outcome.

The target date set by New York and the EPA for release of the report was January 1995. But as the new 104th Congress convened that month, the EPA stated that it would be May before a draft for public comment would be released.

May arrived, but not the report we were waiting for. Instead, the EPA issued only a news release and an executive summary of the draft report that painted the acid rain problem as limited in its impact. The national media read it, saw a nonstory and collectively yawned.

Within twenty-four hours, two scientists who had contributed to the research called us to warn that the executive summary (which is all most legislators and their staff would ever read) was misleading and wildly inconsistent with the body of the report. Participating scientists had not seen the summary before it was released, and the ones who called us were furious at what they said was a political attempt to obscure a problem that was severe and getting worse.

The oft-delayed full EPA report on the cap-and-trade program, the *Acid Deposition Standard Feasibility Study Report to Congress*, was finally issued in October 1995, nearly two years late. (It was dated February 1995.)

Much to his credit, our communications director, John F. Sheehan, quickly absorbed the full EPA report and called the media's attention to important findings that were not mentioned in the executive summary.

The report said that the cap-and-trade program was being well received by industry and was proving to be a very economical approach.

Unfortunately, it also confirmed that without substantial new cuts in power plant emissions beyond those already imposed by Congress, up to 43 percent of the lakes and ponds in the Adirondack Park would be biologically dead by the year 2040.

The EPA report also cited for the first time the existence of "episodic acidification." The EPA said that nitrogen emissions deposited in the form of snow over the course of the winter were released with the melt of the snowpack in the spring. The result was an acidic "spring shock" to streams, rivers, and lakes. The surrounding soils were also being acidified, and acids migrated through the soils, releasing a toxic form of aluminum to the waterways. We were rapidly losing trout and other fish sensitive to acidic waters that could not survive such conditions

We had a lot of science to back us up now, but no political impetus to address the problems being exposed. We repeatedly heard from staff at the Capitol in Washington that it was "too early" to reopen the Clean Air Act and pass new legislation to solve the problem.

A SOLOMON STORY

The alarming news of the dire threat to the Park contained in the 1995 EPA report meant that the time was ripe for a new lobbying assault in Congress. We knew we had to go for help to Capitol Hill and we knew where we had to start.

John Sheehan and I sought a meeting in Washington with the director of air-quality policy for the politically savvy and influential national environmental advocacy group, the Natural Resources Defense Council (NRDC). The NRDC's executive director, Frances Beinecke, had served as chair of the Adirondack Council's board for five years. The group would be a natural ally—and better yet, NRDC staffers were Washington insiders.

We asked in advance for a meeting with David Hawkins, the NRDC staffer in charge of air issues. David was not going to be available at that time, but he suggested another staffer working on legislative affairs. Despite our daily phone calls leading up to the trip, that fellow consented to a meeting only at the last minute on our last day in town. He then kept us waiting for some time before informing us that he only had ten minutes to spend with us.

We shared our plans to ramp up a campaign to get Congress to once again amend the Clean Air Act and finally end the scourge of acid rain. We excitedly told him of our meetings with Senator Moynihan's staff, which had been very promising, and staffers from other offices on the Hill.

I told him that we thought we could get Representative Gerald Solomon, who represented an Upstate New York district that included part of the Adirondack Park, as the bill's lead sponsor in the House.

"He's a conservative Republican and the chairman of the Rules Committee!" he snorted. "You'll never get him. You should leave the lobbying to people who know what they are doing on the Hill."

That ended our meeting. I never had the chance to tell him that Congressman Gerald "Gerry" Solomon was my own congressman. Gerry told me later in a phone call that he would indeed sponsor an acid rain bill.

∾

Back at the Portland bar in 1997, two frustrating years after the EPA report revealed that the acid rain problem had not yet been solved, David blurted, "What about loons?"

"What about them?"

"Acid rain is leaching mercury from the soil, and the mercury is getting into the loons, right?"

"Sure." We both had seen the studies.

We also knew about the power of loons to mesmerize visitors to the Adirondack Park. Whenever we escorted politically important visitors on an overnight visit, we made sure to stay at one of the lakes with a large loon population. When our guests first heard a loon call—often described as "haunting"—they were entranced, and likely to forever consider the Adirondacks a magical place.

In fact, the loon was the Adirondack Council's symbol because it embodied our message: The Adirondack Park is a special place that deserves special attention.

"We've got loons all over our literature," I observed.

"What if the loons were dead?" David asked. "That would grab people."

"Dead loons? Who wants to see that?" I objected.

"Exactly," he replied.

For the next two hours, over dinner, we resolved to change the theme of our acid rain lobbying campaign. We would abandon our traditional approach of "See the pretty places. Let's keep them pretty." Our new approach would be, "All that you hold dear in the Adirondack Park—the birds, the water, the trees, the soil itself—is being destroyed."

We headed back to Albany determined to make something happen on both the state and federal level. We need not have worried.

NO REGRETS

Congressman Solomon would indeed introduce an acid rain bill just prior to the 1996 session of the House of Representatives. The Adirondack Council now was looking to get New York's two Senators, Alfonse D'Amato and Moynihan, to introduce the same bill. We expected Moynihan, who had long been active on the issue, would eventually be on board. D'Amato, a Republican who was not seen as a champion of the environment, would be tougher.

We had unexpected help—from another Republican.

The recent organizing by the Council on acid rain and by fellow environmental groups on other air-pollution issues had gotten the attention of faculty members at the Pace University School of Law in White Plains, New York. They organized a one-day symposium on air-pollution policy. The Northern Forest Alliance, an interstate coalition in the Northeast of twenty-five national, regional, and local environmental groups concerned with forest health and protection, had just endorsed the Solomon bill.

I was taking part in the symposium when I got a pleasant surprise. The keynote speaker, Michael C. Finnegan, recently appointed counsel to Governor George Pataki, surprised the audience by calling on New York's two senators, Pat Moynihan and Al D'Amato, to cosponsor the Senate version of Congressman Solomon's legislation on acid rain. (See figure 11.2.)

The governor had to know and approve of this, I thought. This is a good sign.

I made a note to myself redouble our efforts to get Senator D'Amato involved in the acid rain effort.

But another moment at the Pace symposium had a much greater impact on me. After my panel had concluded its session, several people came up to chat. One fellow was a little older than the rest.

He mentioned the acid rain damage in the Adirondack Park that I had just described in detail and announced that he felt he was to blame.

Taken aback, I assured him, "It's not any one person's fault."

"No, you don't understand," he said. "I *am* responsible."

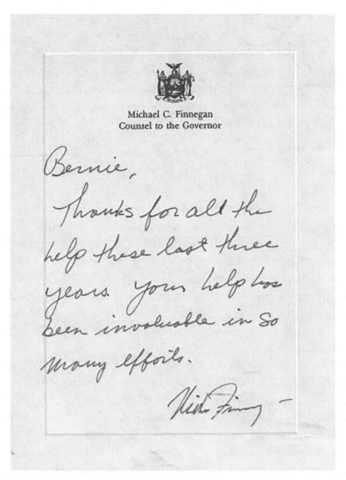

Figure 11.2. Mike Finnegan's note to the author. *Source*: author's own material.

He went onto to say that he was retired from the federal Environmental Protection Agency. He had been part of a team many years earlier when the EPA was trying to figure out how to keep smog and haze from power plants in the Ohio Valley from threatening the health of residents there. He said that it was his idea to require the plants to build tall smokestacks that would let the wind carry the emissions away and disperse them.

"We had no idea that we would be creating another problem elsewhere," he said with a truly pained expression. It was clear he really was taking it personally.

Nobody knew that his idea would contribute to a new problem, I tried to reassure him. "Your task was to protect the health of people who were breathing dirty air every day. You solved the problem and you should be proud of that. You saved many lives." Handing him a Council brochure, I told him, "Now you can help solve our problem by donating and getting active with our acid rain campaign." He brightened and walked away. I hope he believed what I said. I meant it.

SENATOR POTHOLE

Alfonse D'Amato was the junior senator from New York. He came out of the Nassau County Republican organization on Long Island. The press dubbed him "Senator Pothole" for the attention his office paid to what is now reverently called "constituent services," a style in considerable contrast to that of his senior colleague, Moynihan.

D'Amato was Hempstead town supervisor when he challenged Senator Jacob K. Javits, who had first been elected in 1956, in the 1980 Republican primary. In an upset, due in great part to the incumbent's ill health, Javits lost to the newcomer.

With Javits remaining on the November ballot as the Liberal Party candidate, D'Amato defeated both him and Elizabeth Holtzman, the Democrat, despite winning less than 45 percent of the votes.

In the 1992 election, Senator D'Amato unexpectedly managed to hang on to his seat, and win another six-year term, garnering more votes than the popular sitting attorney general of New York, Robert Abrams.

The Senator got on board. He and Governor Pataki would hold a news conference to announce his intention to cosponsor what would later become the Moynihan/D'Amato Acid Deposition Control Act of 1997. Gerald Solomon would carry the bill in the House.

SANTA FE

I learned that in late spring in 1997, my wife, Mollie, would be attending the first ever National Energy Deregulation Conference sponsored by the US Department of Energy in Santa Fe, New Mexico, one of my favorite places. I had become fond of New Mexico while serving as a VISTA volunteer for the Legal Aid Society of Albuquerque following my graduation from law school.

By a happy coincidence, Senator Al D'Amato was scheduled to speak at the conference, and we already had been thinking how we could involve him further in the acid rain fight.

D'Amato was chairman of the Senate Committee on Banking, Housing and Urban Affairs. The Committee was considering the repeal of a law despised by utility and coal companies—the Public Utility Holding Company Act (PUHCA). The law was adopted in 1935 amid the antitrust sentiment sweeping Congress during the Great Depression. It broke up the large holding companies that controlled the majority of the nation's electric utilities and their ability to avoid most state regulation. In the 1990s, PUHCA remained an impediment to utility mergers across state lines, much to the frustration of expansion-minded power companies.

National environmental groups, concerned that repealing the law would lead to the expanded use of dirty coal, started to speak out in opposition. But our discussions with those groups and Senate staffers led us to the conclusion that repeal was likely. So we shifted our approach: Why not try to link the repeal of PUHCA with something positive for the environment?

In a meeting with D'Amato's staff, we made the pitch that repeal of PUHCA should be tied to legislation placing new limitations on acid rain, hopefully the bill he sponsored with Senator Moynihan. For us, it was a divide-and-conquer strategy. We were hoping that utility companies whose main goal was the repeal of PUHCA would see the acid rain limits as an acceptable price, breaking with others in their industry whose top priority was blocking new limits. In other words, splitting the opposition.

What we emphasized to D'Amato's staff was that we were offering the senator a rare opportunity to help his state by limiting acid rain—and it would be a shame if he passed it up. In the New York state legislature, it is a common tactic for a legislator, especially a leader, to get what he or she wants by holding up passage of an unrelated bill. This is known as "taking hostages." It is similar to "back scratching," the practice of one legislator doing a favor in exchange for another, except in this case, just one back gets scratched.

His staff reported back to us that the senator loved the idea of taking a hostage. I suggested that a good place to announce his support was the energy conference in Santa Fe.

I was disappointed when D'Amato's office called later to say that the senator had decided not to attend the conference, but would issue a press release to announce his support.

Recovering quickly, I pointed out that the conference was the perfect venue for D'Amato's announcement, and since I was attending myself, I would be glad to distribute it for him. After some internal discussions, his office agreed.

I then told our executive director, Tim Burke, that D'Amato was going to make a significant announcement benefiting us—but it would require me to travel to Santa Fe.

Tim seemed skeptical, and even more so when he found out Mollie was also going to the conference, but he saw that the payoff was worth the travel expenses. My colleagues, on the other hand, were on to me from the outset, and one of them teased me for an entire day by working the words *junket* or *junk it* into every possible conversation.

Our hotel in Santa Fe was near the central plaza, because the conference hotel across town had filled up quickly. The short drive would be no problem, I thought—until we awoke the next morning to find a foot of snow on the ground and the streets unplowed.

On most days, I imagine, it was a long but comfortable walk across town to the conference center. On this day, I made the long slog through knee-high snow to register, and then headed back to our hotel in my soaked shoes and pants to await the fax of D'Amato's announcement from his office in Washington. After a few nervous hours it arrived, and I asked the hotel staff to make fifty copies.

The hotel, I was told, did not have a copier. But yes, there was a copy center in Santa Fe. It turned out to be in still another part of town, equally distant from our hotel and the conference site.

I plunged back into the snow and trudged to the copy center. In no time, fifty copies were in my hand and I hiked back to the conference.

D'Amato's statement was just what we had hoped for. It was an ultimatum: The senator would not allow any utility legislation out of his committee unless the problem of the acid rain damaging the Adirondacks was addressed. Better yet, Representative Solomon of New York, who had great power over House bills as chairman of the Rules Committee, joined him in the statement.

I dropped off the copies at the conference's press table. At the next break, I overheard two attendees discussing the press release.

"Did you hear about D'Amato's statement?" one asked.

"Yeah, Bob told me that I should grab one, but there aren't any left."

I knew what I needed to do. The bright New Mexico sun was melting the snow, and I waded through slush to and from the copy center. This time I had 300 copies made.

My feet were soaked again by the time I returned to the conference, but the new copies flew off the press table, and I could see groups of attendees huddled to read them. It was the talk of the conference, and reporters bombarded D'Amato's office with calls to confirm its substance.

I savored the experience as Mollie and I extended our New Mexico stay into a minivacation. D'Amato's staff reported that the senator was happy. My boss was happy. I was happy. Mollie was happy. We were all happy.

Bill Cooke once said of D'Amato, "Every six years, he's an environmentalist." That's how often senators have to run for a new term. So I took the D'Amato's new enthusiasm on acid rain with a grain of salt. But there was no denying that he was engaged and speaking out on our top issue. We had invested our time and energy wisely.

EATING THEIR OWN

Because the Adirondack Park was an early victim of acid rain, the Council had been active on this issue, both at the state and national level, since the early 1980s. Working with our allies, including the NRDC, and many other organizations, our staffers Gary Randorf, Dan Plumley, and others won a significant victory in Congress with the passage of the Clean Air Act amendments of 1990. Now the Council was pretty much alone in reviving the issue. We had been instrumental in pulling out of the federal government several scientific reports that documented the continuing damage. We had also worked tirelessly to get the news media, crucially including the *New York Times*, to publicize the breadth and depth of the problem. We had even succeeded in rallying New York's congressional delegation and others behind new legislation that would significantly cut pollution in the Park.

We were all grateful, nonetheless, that these efforts had won the support of everyone who loved the Adirondacks, residents and visitors, Democrats and Republicans alike. I can't tell you how often park residents said something like, "I hate you land-grabbers, but I have to admit, you are doing a dang good job on acid rain." Having the unqualified support of Park residents was politically potent in New York.

After years of lobbying experience, I developed the precept of "stay with what you know." Acid rain was important to our supporters and donors, but other aspects of air pollution were not. The Adirondack Council was not a clean-air group, we were defenders of the Adirondack Park. I tried hard to keep our work confined to issues that resonated inside the Blue Line, and our board generally agreed. Stopping acid rain was integral to our history and our mission.

So at first, we didn't pay much attention when the Clean Air Task Force announced its formation in Washington in 1996. It looked like another broad coalition of national and regional groups focusing on air quality. The first major subject they tackled was the smoglike haze hanging over eastern national parks such as Shenandoah and Great Smoky Mountains in the southern Appalachians. Since the source of the pollution was the same power plants that contributed to acid rain, we supported the effort, although haze wasn't a big issue in the Adirondacks.

The Clean Air Task Force introduced the ideas behind the clean-air issue to more folks, which was a good thing. But the Adirondack Council was not about to give up the direction and control of our acid rain campaign to national groups outside New York state, which is typical of how big environmental campaigns operate. National groups oversee the broad strategy and tactics, while local and regional groups provide the foot soldiers and recruit talking heads for local media. Following was not our thing. Leading was.

We at the Council thought we were on parallel paths with the national groups. But our relationship started to fray almost immediately.

Tensions kept building as we competed for press attention inside the narrow band of air-quality issues within the spectrum of environmental stories that the media covered.

The increasingly inconsistent public messaging started to concern some of the foundation funders and large donors who supported both efforts. We met with some of the Albany-based groups who had joined the Clean Air Task Force. We all agreed that nobody wanted to freak out the donors and that we all could be more prudent in our remarks. Self-preservation is the strongest urge in the nonprofit world.

But the detente did not last. I repeatedly cautioned our interns and my younger colleagues who took great offense when other groups excluded us from meetings or tried to catch a free ride on one of our media events. Maintain a calm and professional demeanor at all times, I advised. It is best for all concerned. The last thing the Council or the cause needs is a news story about the groups squabbling. So of course, I was the first one to lose it.

We had learned that the Albany-based arm of the Clean Air Task Force was organizing a news conference the next day on a topic related to acid rain. We had not been approached and were in the dark.

Then we got a fax. An intern from Environmental Advocates of New York had sent a draft news release on the coalition's topic. He personally apologized for the "oversight" in failing to inform us, but would like to talk about it. Could he come over?

The release was a stunner. The Adirondack Council had months before scored a coup by getting two powerful New York legislators, Representative Gerald Solomon and Senator Al D'Amato, to jointly call for linkage between energy deregulation (PUCHA reform), which was extremely popular in Congress, and new controls on sulfur and nitrogen oxides. The coalition's draft news release urged two other Republican members of the New York delegation who were members of the House Commerce Committee to oppose that link in an upcoming vote, and instead demand that deregulation be linked to reductions in four pollutants, including mercury and carbon dioxide.

Our staff quickly huddled and came to several conclusions:

New York's Republican members in Congress knew that Representative Gerry Solomon chaired the House Rules Committee. Why would any sane member of the delegation oppose a key leader of the same party on this issue? So politically this request of the two members made no sense.

We did not believe that it was an oversight that our colleagues had neglected to tell us about the event. Sending us the release at the last minute would minimize our ability to react, while retaining their ability to tell their donors that they had asked us to participate.

The stark reality was that rather than help us get something passed in Congress that would actually stop air pollution, they were complicating matters and putting our good work in jeopardy. They were eating their own.

I told our staff to have the young intern come right over. It was my mistake. When he arrived, he maintained that the delay in informing us about the news conference had been his own fault. The event had not yet been scheduled, he claimed, and we could take our time getting back to them. We knew better. The more he talked, the longer his nose appeared to grow. I had heard enough. I stood up, extended my arm, and with a flourish summoned from some half-forgotten piece of bad theater, declared: "Leave us! And don't ever darken our door again."

I felt bad every time I encountered the poor fellow after that, since I had attacked the mere messenger. Sadly, he would move to the other side of the hallway when he saw me coming at the Capitol.

Every two years is another session of Congress. All bills have to be reintroduced in the new session. D'Amato did eventually hold an Earth Day press conference in May of 1997, announcing his intent to sponsor a new acid rain bill with Senator Moynihan, which was introduced at the end of July in that year.

But as the primary Republican sponsor of acid rain legislation in the US Senate and as a member of the controlling majority in the US Senate, we needed him to be an active sponsor. We made the usual forays to his office, trying to speak with the senator directly. We talked with his staff and gave them advance notice of events but were without success in meeting with the Senator directly. It clearly was not working for us.

The solution came from our ally Bill Cooke, lobbyist for Citizens Campaign for the Environment. The nonprofit group was thriving under the then-novel approach of door-to-door campaigning. It sent teams of young activists door to door to ask residents to contact their elected representatives in support of CCE's causes. Then they would circle back to pick up the letters and then deliver them directly to the district office of a state assembly member or state senator. Nothing makes a politician pay attention faster than a mass of letters or telephone calls from constituents.

Bill's flash of inspiration regarding D'Amato came when he received an invitation to a fundraiser for Governor Pataki at the Saratoga Race Course, where D'Amato was to be a guest of honor. Bill signed me up without my knowledge and then overcame my reluctance to go along.

The event was the least expensive fundraiser for Pataki that year. It turned out to be a bargain for donors. The flat track had begun placing a tent near the horses' paddock for parties. For the price of your donation to the governor's campaign, you got a day at the track, a nice buffet lunch, drinks, and your own betting windows. Just outside the tent, you could watch as the thoroughbreds paraded right by you to the post. Sweet.

I got a lot of stares from the business lobbyists and Republican legislators. Weren't all environmentalists Democrats? Actually, I didn't feel out of place among the Republican faithful in Saratoga Springs. The Adirondack Council's board of directors was evenly divided between Democrats and Republicans. When it came to policy, whoever helped us achieve our goals was our best friend.

The governor came into the party tent and began working the room. He seemed pleasantly surprised to see me. Then D'Amato arrived. He barely moved beyond the front of the tent, choosing instead to make the supplicants come to him. Bill and I got in line.

Everyone got two minutes to shake the senator's hand and have a photograph taken. Bill took full advantage of the opportunity. In a voice loud enough for many others to hear, he explained to the senator that we had been trying to get a meeting with him for months. D'Amato looked like a deer in headlights, momentarily frozen in the glare of Bill's accusation.

But he recovered quickly and said, "Why, of course I'll meet with you. But it will have to be in DC!" To D'Amato's clear disappointment, Bill accepted immediately and got the senator to publicly direct his assistant to take our business cards. We thanked him, had our photo taken, shook his hand, and left the tent.

Bill, for his own amusement, had our photo signed by D'Amato and sent directly to him. He then cropped himself out of the picture, leaving just the conservative Republican senator and me. Bill showed the photo to Democratic-leaning lobbyists for a week before he gave it to me. Funny. Thanks Bill. (See figure 11.3.)

It took a while, but we got our meeting in Washington. The meeting was odd in two ways. First, the furniture in the D'Amato's office was laid out strangely. There was a curious lack of seating in front of his desk. He directed us to sit down, waving from behind his desk, and all I could find was an ottoman. An uncomfortable ottoman.

Just as we were about to speak, the senator motioned for us to shush.

Figure 11.3. Senator Alfonse D'Amato with the author. *Source*: author's own material.

The phone on D'Amato's desk rang, and he said, "I gotta take this." We sat there and listened to his side of the conversation.

"Chuckie!"

It took a while, but I realized that D'Amato was talking to his Democratic opponent in the upcoming 1998 senatorial election, Representative Charles E. Schumer.

"Yeah, he talked to me too," D'Amato continued.

"What's the point of that?"

"Hey, fuck 'em. What if neither of us shows up?"

"Yeah, exactly."

"Naw, I won't say a word."

D'Amato hung up and dismissed us a few minutes later, telling us to work out the details of new actions with his staff. As we departed, he shouted for a female staffer to bring him a pastry.

I was impressed by the fact that D'Amato and Schumer, locked in a statewide election battle, were talking directly, and that he let us sit there while they spoke. But what they were talking about remained a mystery until a week or two later, when the *New York Times* reported that neither D'Amato nor Schumer had attended the annual dinner of the AFL-CIO union confederation in New York City.

D'Amato later told a reporter in more polite terms that the two candidates had agreed that there was no point in showing up at the dinner if the labor bosses were not going to endorse either of them.

D'Amato would lose his Senate reelection bid to Chuck Schumer that year. He would leave the Senate and his chairmanship, and our PUCHA strategy followed him out the door.

FOULING OUR OWN NEST

Our efforts to gain momentum for action on acid rain got a fresh boost from revelations that drew allies into the battle from inside and outside New York state.

As early as 1993, it was known that the Long Island Lighting Company (LILCO), the gas and electric utility that was serving millions of customers on the island, had become the first major power company to sell pollution credits under the new federal cap-and-trade system.

The buyer was not identified, but it was later revealed that LILCO had in fact sold the credits to a Midwestern utility. Pollution that likely would have drifted out to sea from Long Island might now instead be used to justify emissions upwind, threatening New York from the west.

Environmental Conservation Commissioner Tom Jorling and the Adirondack Council both asked the State Public Service Commission to investigate whether it could intervene in trades by New York utilities to upwind polluters.

In the short term, nothing came of the effort. But in an early 1997 comment to the *New York Times* about the controversy, our executive director Tim Burke noted that because the cost of pollution credits was artificially low in the early years of the cap-and-trade program, it might be a good idea for environmental groups to buy them up and permanently retire them.

A fellow named William E. Davis apparently was paying attention.

Davis was the chairman and chief executive of Niagara Mohawk Power Corporation, which generated and distributed electricity to much of Upstate New York. Sensing a public relations opportunity, the company donated 5,000 of the pollution credits it had been awarded by the federal acid rain program to the Adirondack Council, each one representing the legal right to emit one ton of sulfur dioxide, a major component of acid rain. The Council agreed to permanently retire the credits and turned the company's donated credits into a major publicity and fund-raising campaign.

Anyone donating fifty dollars to the Council would receive a certificate (suitable for framing) stating that one ton of the pollutant was being retired in his or her name.

Governor George Pataki presented Tim Burke with a personal check to buy the first certificate. For weeks after that, state legislators and other politicians lined up to have their photo taken while purchasing a certificate. They sold like hotcakes to the public as well. All proceeds went to the Council's dedicated acid rain campaign. (See figure 11.4.)

Just months later, a broker with Cantor Fitzgerald, in the emerging business of trading pollution credits, informed us—perhaps inadvertently—of an alarming practice by a major mining firm, Amax Coal Company. Amax was taking advantage of the early low price for pollution credits and was giving buyers of its high-sulfur coal one free credit for every ton purchased. It was like a "get out of jail free" card for polluters.

That led to another discovery that we never could have imagined. One of the founders of Amax and still major stockholders were the Hochschild family. In 1904, Berthold Hochschild had purchased Eagle Nest, one of the grand compounds known as Adirondack Great Camps, and the family still owned it.

Figure 11.4. John Sheehan, Tim Burke, and Author present Senator Joseph Bruno with a certificate. *Source*: author's own material.

Harold K. Hochschild, his son, was the chairman of the Rockefeller Temporary Study Commission on the Future of the Adirondacks, whose 1970 report led to the first strong controls on development within the Park. Harold was also among the greatest benefactors of the Adirondack Park in its history, who provided the intellectual framework and major financial support for the Adirondack Museum at Blue Mountain Lake.

To its credit, the Hochschild family, which had been unaware of Amax's pollution-credit scheme, intervened and confronted the company. The practice was halted.

Amax's dealings actually turned out to be a boon to our fight against acid rain. They prompted David Greenwood, who had become a full-time policy analyst for the Council, to call a staffer for the EPA's new Clean Air Markets regulatory programs to find out how the agency kept track of trading in pollution credits.

David was surprised to learn that the EPA monitored the program not with a large staff, but by logging the computerized data that every power plant and broker or trader of pollution credits was required to transmit directly to the agency. What's more, the staffer informed him, every transaction had a unique code. Anyone with a modern desktop computer and access to the internet could learn the identity of each buyer and seller of every ton of sulfur and nitrogen oxides traded under the law. It was public information.

Best of all, David learned that the EPA was not yet tracking or analyzing the data. Recognizing that we were handed a tremendous political opportunity, he excitedly brought me the news.

Now, if we only had a modern desktop computer.

Fortunately, that was easily remedied, and we also found a local start-up company, part of an incubator program at the nearby Rensselaer Polytechnic Institute, that could create color maps from the data.

Our analysis focused on New York. Not only was the Council's mission centered on the Adirondack Park, but we also suspected that the state was a hotbed of credits trading. New York had instituted tight air-pollution controls years before the federal government, so its power plants were already producing less in emissions than what the EPA had calculated as their fair share. That meant the state's utilities had more pollution credits than they could use.

The maps would dramatically show the flow of pollution credits and who was using them, from Maine and the rest of the northeast states all the way to the Ohio Valley. We could show which plants were using credits, which were selling credits and to whom. There was a developing brokerage aspect to the acid rain program led by the firm Cantor Fitzgerald, and we could even track to whom the brokers were selling credits.

We were stunned by what we discovered. Our press release and maps would show that in New York, LILCO alone in the previous two years time had sold almost 80,000 tons of pollution credits to the Midwest and another 115,000 to brokers. Overall, our computer-generated color maps showed a vast migration of credits from New York to the Midwest. In turn, those legal smokestack emissions were coming directly back to New York in the form of sulfur- and nitrogen-laden acid rain. We were fouling our own nest.

We knew that this information was a gold mine in terms of media coverage.

We made one other move. David was overwhelmed getting the data into good order. We decided to organize the data first into credits sold or traded directly from utility to utility. Then we separately analyzed credits sent from a utility to a broker and on to another utility. To manage our time, especially David's, we released the two sets of information to the media weeks apart. In an accidental stroke of perfect public relations timing, Governor Pataki on July 15, 1997, issued a news release promoting his own legislative proposal. The governor sought to require New York utilities to offer to sell their excess pollution credits to a state authority before selling them elsewhere. With this boost, our second wave of publicity caught fire with the media.

The state's politicians knew a good thing when they saw it. From the governor on down, elected officials jumped on the opportunity to defend our priceless wilderness by publicly condemning the villainous utility companies, especially LILCO.

The company rapidly retreated. In a joint announcement with the governor, the company pledged that not another one of their allowances would be used upwind of the state of New York. It announced that it would impose a contractual covenant on the sale and use of its pollution credits, even when purchased by brokers. LILCO even gave 500 credits to the Adirondack Council to retire.

Our acid rain campaign again took off. Donations and media attention poured in, thanks largely to the forthrightness and helpfulness of that one EPA employee.

EPA's top management, however, reacted to our revelations with horror. They saw that their own data might undermine the notion of a free and open market for credits by inducing other state regulators to intervene to prevent pollution hot spots.

In their effort to dispel our claims, the EPA dutifully mapped all the credit trading that was taking place. Its analysis emphasized that the majority of pollution credits traveled only a few hundred miles from their point of origin, but the damage was done. The data clearly showed that acid rain was not a problem just in New York, but had become an issue throughout New England and down the coast to Florida.

State legislators up and down the East Coast jumped all over the news, and they jumped highest in New York. In the Assembly, Richard L. Brodsky, from Westchester County, the Democratic chairman of the Committee on Environmental Conservation, announced his intention to pass legislation requiring every power plant operator in New York to ensure that their unused federal pollution credits would not be used upwind of the Adirondacks or Catskills.

Next came the surprising news that Senator Ronald B. Stafford, a Republican whose district covered most of the Adirondack Park, together with Senator Carl L. Marcellino, of Long Island, who chaired the environmental committee in the state Senate, would work with Brodsky on a bill. Most lobbyists and reporters could not imagine the liberal Brodsky and conservative Stafford cooperating on anything!

1998: OUR CAMPAIGN TAKES SHAPE

On the way back to Albany from the disappointing meeting with air officials in Portland, David and I had agreed to push the Adirondack Council's staffers and board members to produce a color brochure making the case that acid rain was causing damage up and down the East Coast, including to the loon population that migrated along those waters

Our communications director, John F. Sheehan, embraced the idea with enthusiasm and added elements that would appeal to the print and electronic media. It would take us almost a year to find the funding and produce the brochure, but it was effective.

David actually found a color picture of a loon chick that had died of mercury poisoning. We included it in the new color brochure titled "Acid Rain: a Continuing National Tragedy." (See figure 11.5.)

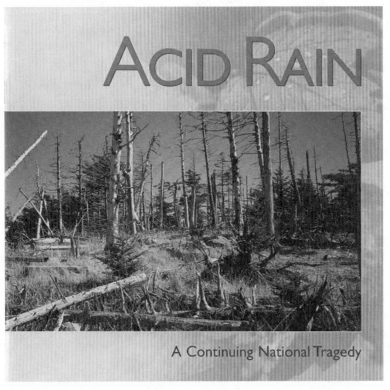

Figure 11.5. Cover of the acid rain brochure. *Source*: Adirondack Council.

The brochure turned out to be the spark for an effective public-relations campaign. That was largely because Sheehan, in what turned out to be a brilliant move, suggested that we include the human-interest story of C. V. "Major" Bowes. Bowes's story had been included in our first major acid rain publication, "Beside the Stilled Waters," in 1987. But repeated ten years later, it resonated with the media.

Major Bowes (he got his nickname from a radio host famous in the 1930s and '40s) operated the Covewood Lodge on Big Moose Lake in the Adirondack Park along with his wife, Diane, and two daughters. The lodge drew its water from a well near the lake. When one daughter began to have stomach problems, Bowes had the water tested, and it was found to contain elevated levels of lead and copper. The rising acidity of the lake's water was leaching the lead out of the family's water pipes into its drinking water.

In 1996, tests by the New York State Department of Health found widespread acidity in drinking water sources in the western Adirondack and Catskill Mountains, where acid precipitation was the most severe.

That same year, the Department of Health also issued advisories warning women of child-bearing age and young children to limit their consumption of fish taken from some of the lakes in the Park. Not only was mercury deposited directly from smokestack pollution, acidic precipitation was causing mercury to convert to its toxic derivative methylmercury, which had in turn begun bioaccumulating in fish and up the food chain. By 2005, the consumption warnings would expand to thirty-nine lakes and ponds in the Adirondack Park.

Bowes became an effective spokesman for the campaign to stop acid rain. He gave interviews to any print, radio, and TV reporter who made the pilgrimage to Big Moose Lake.

WE PRY OUT THE NEXT REPORT

Congress had ordered the National Acid Precipitation Assessment Program to issue a second report that was due after the EPA's cap-and-trade assessment. This NAPAP report, prepared with contributions from multiple federal agencies, was widely expected be a more accurate assessment of the effects of the 1990 law's limits on pollution and of current conditions in the nation's forests and waterways.

Concerned about the possibility of the same kind of delays that had plagued the EPA report, we stayed in contact with the scientists who were engaged in the NAPAP research, and learned to our relief that the work was progressing—but slowly.

By July 1998, the NAPAP report was more than two years late. With our encouragement, Senators Moynihan and D'Amato sent a joint letter to the executive director of NAPAP expressing concern about the timeliness of the report and its data. Taking it one step further, New York's new attorney general, Dennis C. Vacco, declared publicly that if the report was not forthcoming soon "they will see me in Court." (See figure 11.6.)

The EPA did issue a news release with a brief summary less than a month later, identifying a website that the public could access for the full report. The only problem: The website was not functioning.

We contacted the executive director of the program, who told us that the report was completed, but because of a lack of funds to print the document, it might not appear for another six months or more. In March 1999, members of our congressional delegation had still not seen the report.

Then, unexpectedly, we caught a break. We were tipped that the NAPAP report had been inadvertently posted on another government

Figure 11.6. Press conference on acid rain report. New York attorney general Dennis Vacco with the author. *Source*: author's own material.

website. Before it was removed, we downloaded our own copy. But we did nothing with it immediately; because the scientific advisory committee for the various federal agencies that composed NAPAP was scheduled to hold its final meeting in Washington. Out of respect for these scientists, we would not jump the gun.

We were then startled to learn that the committee's members from New York had been told that the NAPAP report was not yet complete and would not be shared with the advisory committee.

The advisory committee's meeting in the conference room of a Capitol Hill hotel was scheduled to start at 2:00 p.m. At 1:35, John Sheehan and I were waiting outside the door with William Cooke, the director of government relations for the Citizens Campaign for the Environment.

Beside us were boxes of the NAPAP report that we had printed ourselves. As the committee members filed in, we handed each member a copy. In their eagerness to join their colleagues, each one politely took a document (even NAPAP's executive director) and quickly entered the room without pausing to see what we had handed them. The staff closed the door to the conference room. Our work was done.

Miraculously, the federal funds to print the report were found shortly thereafter and the NAPAP report to Congress was released.

As we had anticipated, it confirmed the findings of the EPA report and our worst fears. If nothing more were done to stop acid rain, important parts of Adirondack Park would be lost. (See figure 11.7.)

In October of 1998, the sponsors were able to get a hearing for the Moynihan/D'Amato Acid Deposition Control Act before the Senate subcommittee on clean air, wetlands, private property, and nuclear safety. Senator James M. Inhofe (R-OK) chaired the hearing, which was notable for the presence of EPA staff providing testimony on behalf of that agency, including, you guessed it, that very unhelpful EPA staffer we had met in 1993, Brian McLean.

In surprise testimony, the EPA acknowledged that deeper emissions cuts would be necessary to give the Adirondacks and other sensitive areas a chance to recover from acid rain, and declared the Moynihan bill to be a workable solution.

Moynihan was reportedly down with the flu, but Congressman Solomon testified, declaring that the bill now had the support in his house of the entire New York delegation and Democrats and Republicans alike throughout New England.

Figure 11.7. *National Acid Precipitation Assessment Program Report* cover. *Source*: public domain.

Senator D'Amato cited the recent NAPAP report and a recent study of the acidification of trout streams in Virginia. A year after David Greenwood and I had left their meeting in Maine empty-handed, D'Amato also mentioned a new resolution calling for action on acid rain had been issued by the Coalition of New England Governors and Eastern Canadian Premiers.

Senator D'Amato would best be remembered that day for famously declaring the pollution from upwind sources falling on New York's Adirondacks to be "Airborne Terrorism." (See figure 11.8.)

JOHN H. CHAFEE, RHODE ISLAND, CHAIRMAN

JOHN W. WARNER, VIRGINIA
ROBERT SMITH, NEW HAMPSHIRE
DIRK KEMPTHORNE, IDAHO
JAMES M. INHOFE, OKLAHOMA
CRAIG THOMAS, WYOMING
CHRISTOPHER S. BOND, MISSOURI
TIM HUTCHINSON, ARKANSAS
WAYNE ALLARD, COLORADO
JEFF SESSIONS, ALABAMA

MAX BAUCUS, MONTANA
DANIEL PATRICK MOYNIHAN, NEW YORK
FRANK R. LAUTENBERG, NEW JERSEY
HARRY REID, NEVADA
BOB GRAHAM, FLORIDA
JOSEPH I. LIEBERMAN, CONNECTICUT
BARBARA BOXER, CALIFORNIA
RON WYDEN, OREGON

JIMMIE POWELL, STAFF DIRECTOR
J. THOMAS SLITER, MINORITY STAFF DIRECTOR

United States Senate

COMMITTEE ON ENVIRONMENT AND PUBLIC WORKS

WASHINGTON, DC 20510-6175

October 2, 1998

Mr. Bernard Mileuski
Counsel and Legislative Director
The Adirondack Council
342 Hamilton Street
Albany, New York 12210

Dear Mr. Mileuski:

On behalf of the Subcommittee on Clean Air, Wetlands, Private Property and Nuclear Safety, Committee on Environment and Public Works, we would like to invite you to testify on Tuesday, October 6, 1998, at a Subcommittee hearing. The purpose of this hearing is to receive testimony on S. 1097, the Acid Deposition Control Act. The hearing will be held in room 406 of the Dirksen Senate Office Building, and will begin at 9:30 a.m.

In order to maximize the opportunity for Members of the Committee to discuss these matters with you and other witnesses, we are asking that your oral testimony be limited to five minutes. Your written testimony can be comprehensive, and it will be included in the printed record in its entirety, together with any other materials you would like to submit.

To comply with Committee rules, please provide one hundred copies of your testimony forty-eight hours in advance of the hearing. Testimony should be sent to the attention of Patrick D. Mara, Senate Committee on Environment and Public Works, 415 Hart Senate Office Building, Washington, D.C. 20510. If possible, please provide the Committee with a copy of your testimony on a 3.5 inch disk in a WordPerfect file.

If you have any charts, graphs, diagrams, photos, maps, slides, models or other exhibits that you intend to utilize at the hearing, please provide one identical copy of such material(s), as well as one hundred reduced copies of such materials, to the Committee no later than 48 hours prior to the hearing. Exhibits or other materials described above that are not provided to the Committee within 48 hours cannot be used for the purpose of presenting testimony to the Committee.

If you have any further questions or comments, please feel free to contact Andrew Wheeler (202) 224-0146 or Barbara Roberts (202) 224-2969.

Sincerely,

Bob Graham
Ranking Minority Member

James M. Inhofe
Chairman

PRINTED ON RECYCLED PAPER

Figure 11.8. An invitation to testify. *Source*: author's own material.

1999: MOMENTUM BUILDS

We knew we needed to continue to build the momentum for action on the federal acid rain legislation but to ensure that the effort would not siphon funds from other goals of the organization, the Adirondack Council board provided money only for an initial round of publicity. The board did agree to a plan to ask the public to contribute to a dedicated fund that would become the campaign's only source of support.

And the public responded.

Starting with the board's seed money, and the sale of clean-air certificates, the campaign quickly snowballed to attract many new donors. Among our tools were the new brochure, print ads in the *New York Times* and the *Washington Post*, posters in key Metro stations in the nation's capital, a short video, and radio spots. In the full-page ads in the *Times* and the *Post*, we were joined by national groups, including the Natural Resources Defense Council, Environmental Defense Fund, the Wilderness Society, National Audubon Society, Trout Unlimited, and even the National Trust for Historic Preservation. (See figure 11.9.)

The posters in the Washington subway system were patterned on one of the most popular public service announcements ever produced, a TV ad supposedly featuring a noble Indian shedding a tear at the sight of a heavily littered landscape. Our posters, concentrated in the Metro stations, most likely to be used by members of Congress and their staffs, emphasized acid rain's damage to historic buildings around Capitol Hill, including the Lincoln Memorial. (See figure 11.10.)

Our staffer David Greenwood obtained an archived report written by the Department of the Interior that featured photo documentation of the damage done by acid rain to the Washington Monument, the Lincoln Memorial, and the Capitol building itself, among other iconic federal buildings. The report even featured a walking tour of the affected buildings.

What a find! We could now encourage legislators and key staffers to walk home after work and view the erosion of carved figures and other architectural features for themselves. The people we contacted seemed startled by both the damage and that staff of a federal agency had researched and documented it.

I asked David to order more copies of the Interior Department report from the national publication center. But he came into my office later that day to tell me that it was no longer available.

"You mean it's out of print?" I asked him. (See figure 11.11.)

Figure 11.9. *New York Times* acid rain ad. *Source*: Adirondack Council.

Figure 11.10. Congressman Sherwood Boehlert with D. C. Metro Station Ad. *Source*: Adirondack Council.

"Nope. Gone. Like it never existed. Not on the website. I even called, and they don't have it in their system."

We never did learn what happened. It was much later on before it became available again. We just reprinted our copy of the document, and continued distributing it for years.

In the same vein, we also found a study of the Gettysburg battlefield documenting that many of the stone memorials honoring the Civil War soldiers from both northern and southern states had seriously deteriorated because of acid rain.

We had similar good fortune with our radio public service announcements, thanks to the initiative of our communications director, John

Figure 11.11. Cover of the Department of the Interior brochure. *Source*: public domain.

Sheehan. One day he came into my office to let me know that Grammy Award–winning musician Bonnie Raitt, who had just released some new hit songs, had volunteered to record the voice-over for several radio spots urging listeners to join her in supporting our acid rain campaign.

"Holy crap, John! How did you get her to agree?"

"I asked."

Few people knew that Raitt had spent several summers as a young camper in the Adirondacks. In the following year, John Sheehan would approach another popular singer with ties to Upstate New York, Natalie Merchant of the band Ten Thousand Maniacs. Natalie, a native of James-town, New York, would record more radio spots for the campaign. I still think John just wanted to meet her, but she was a great addition to the campaign. With this star power and the help of our student interns, John was able to target major pop stations from Maine to Georgia that eagerly played the free ads. The calls into our toll-free telephone number proved to be a good indicator of which station in which state was currently playing the public service announcements.

Momentum was building for our campaign as our new focus on acid rain's impacts on historic structures, water sources, wildlife, and forests along the Eastern Seaboard was attracting allies.

In June 1999, we held a press conference at the US Capitol, along with several other groups, where New York Senator Chuck Schumer and Upstate New York Congress members John Sweeney and Sherwood "Sherry" Boehlert spoke, all of whom now sponsored the Moynihan bill.

CLEAN HANDS

We had built our campaign on spreading the word that the 1995 EPA report to Congress and the NAPAP report, which followed, had documented that the Clean Air Act amendments of 1990 would fall short of the national goal of ending acid rain. We repeated the mantra in every venue we could find—that without new controls, we might lose much of Adirondacks' natural resources to pollution.

This included a continued push on this point with members of Congress from both sides of the aisle and a separate personalized campaign to unite our own state's delegation. Subcommittee hearings on the bill were continuing and we were given the opportunity to participate in both Senate and House hearings.

At a hearing held by the Clean Air Subcommittee of the Senate Committee on Environment and Public Works in mid-1999, the chairman, Senator Inhofe, delivered a pointed series of remarks directed at me in the witness chair.

He noted that according to earlier testimony, "Even if the Midwest eliminates all emissions, the Northeast will still not comply with the ozone standard."

I allowed that this was true.

Good staff work there, I thought. They gave him an out.

Inhofe then said, "It would seem to me that the Northeast is trying to blame everybody else for their problems."

I answered that the acid rain program is a national one, and that New York had passed the first law in the nation on acid rain, well before Congress took action.

But Inhofe had made his point. We were asking out-of-state utilities and Midwest residents to accept higher costs. New York needed to show a willingness to do the same.

That was easier said than done. But with the help of Commissioner John P. Cahill of the New York Department of Environmental Conservation and the governor's counsel, Michael Finnegan, I was able to return with a surprise for the senator from Oklahoma.

That fall, on October 14, 1999, I sat at a table facing the members of the same Senate subcommittee for another hearing.

In my opening statement, I made a point of responding to the point that Inhofe had raised earlier. After summarizing the damning EPA and NAPAP reports and laying out the Council's case for lowering the national caps on acid rain pollutants, I looked at the senator and said: "I would like to advise you that in a matter of just hours the Republican Governor of New York, George Pataki, will announce that he is directing his commissioner to develop state regulations along the lines recommended by these two reports to make cuts in both sulfur and nitrogen to address acid rain in the next several years." I continued, "The announcement that New York is going to unilaterally call for severe reductions in sulfur dioxide and in nitrogen oxides year-round in New York now gives New York clean hands, so to speak."

This surprise announcement clearly had an effect on Senator George V. Voinovich (R-OH), a subcommittee member who had been a strong advocate for Midwestern interests in the acid rain debate. "Well, I want to say that I congratulate Governor Pataki," he said later in the hearing. "Governor Pataki and I have had differences of opinion on this issue for a long time. I have said to him, 'You're asking us to solve your problem. What are you doing in your state to be a good citizen?' And I think this is a positive step on his part. And you're right, I think it puts him in a much better position in terms of when he is at the table with some of us who have said it's your problem and not ours, and have said you're not doing anything in your own state."

It was a hell of a thing. It was apparent that Voinovich and the other senators were impressed that we could coordinate events like that. So was I, frankly.

It definitely left the impression that the Adirondack Council was an organization that could make things happen. One message was also crystal-clear—we had a full partner in the acid rain fight in Governor Pataki.

The Pataki administration had wanted the shock effect of a surprise announcement, and they got it. National and state environmental groups literally lined up behind Pataki as he made his formal public announcement back in New York and praised his initiative.

2000: CANDIDATES JUMP IN OUR BOAT BUT ROW IN OPPOSITE DIRECTIONS

It was no coincidence that when Hillary Rodham Clinton began her 2000 campaign for a US Senate seat in New York, her first stop in the Adirondack Park was at Major Bowe's Covewood Lodge.

The first lady had surprised the nation by establishing residence in the Empire State and announcing her campaign for the seat of Senator Moynihan, who was retiring at the end of his fourth term.

As was our practice, the Adirondack Council sent a questionnaire to Hillary Clinton and her Republican opponent, Rick Lazio. We asked for their thoughts on environmental issues in New York, and in particular whether they would support legislation to amend the Clean Air Act to further reduce emissions of the pollutants causing acid rain from power plants upwind of the Adirondack Park.

To my recollection, Lazio never responded. But to our surprise, Clinton's staff contacted us to ask if we could arrange a visit by the candidate to Big Moose Lake. The centerpiece of the event was to be a speech in which Clinton would pledge to address the acid rain problem.

For me, the speech was just one of the highlights. I had the honor of serving as the event's host and introducing the First Lady.

But I was also able to bring my younger son Dan to the event. His older brother Matt had met Governor Pataki at one or two events I attended, but Dan had never seen me do a public presentation, much less had the chance to observe me with such a famous figure. Afterward, I asked about his impressions.

"Some of the younger Secret Service guys, with the long raincoats, had automatic weapons on slings beneath their coats," he informed me. He offered no opinion about Hillary Clinton's performance, or mine. (See figure 11.12.)

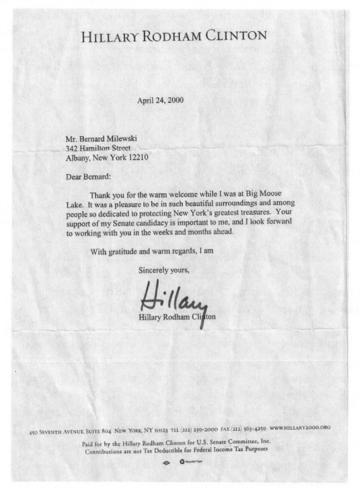

Figure 11.12. Hillary Clinton thank you letter. *Source:* author's own material.

The event was a boost for the public image of the Adirondack Council and brought attention to our top issue. After her election, Clinton would cosponsor the acid rain bill previously introduced by Moynihan and take a seat on the US Senate Environment and Public Works Committee, which had jurisdiction over environmental issues.

Before the 2000 election, the Adirondack Council had approached both major presidential campaigns seeking their endorsement of new acid rain legislation. As a nonprofit group, the Council could not endorse any candidate, but we could share with our members and the public the stated positions of political candidates on issues we cared about.

The Bush campaign answered fairly quickly that they could support new controls on acid rain. That was a pleasant surprise. The response from the Gore campaign was quite a different matter.

I had met Katie McGinty, the chief environmental strategist for the Gore campaign, when she was director of the Council on Environmental Quality in the Clinton administration. Environmental leaders from across the country had come to Washington for a conference on air-quality issues, and a session with Katie, as McGinty asked us to call her, in her West Wing office in the White House was promoted as a highlight. The leaders pressed her on the need for action on clean air, and while she was polite, nobody heard the commitment they had hoped for.

Our executive director, Tim Burke, tried several times in the months leading up to the 2000 election to arrange a phone conference with Katie. When we finally connected, it was the first time that I would hear the term *4P* to describe legislation meant to address a four-pollutant approach to air-quality problems.

Katie declared that Gore would refuse to endorse any legislation, including any bill that would solve the sulfur- and nitrogen oxides–caused acid rain problem in the Northeast, unless it also addressed emissions of mercury and carbon dioxide. It must be 4P (four pollutants)

I marshaled our arguments against that approach. Legislation to further cut emissions of sulfur and nitrogen oxides had already won the backing of most Congress members from the Northeast, thanks partly to our success in shaking loose the scientific studies proving that current laws were not solving the acid rain problem. Moreover, we now knew that acid rain was endangering wildlife by leaching toxic methylmercury into Adirondack waters, where it was bioaccumulating up the food chain, contaminating both the fish and the humans and the birds that ate them. I assured her that the Council was ready to push for better mercury controls as well.

We also understood the growing scientific consensus that human-made contributions to greenhouse gas emissions and global warming were real and posed a looming threat to the world's climate, but the public just was not moved yet by such a seemingly distant and vague danger.

I noted that in contrast to the growing consensus on acid rain, the Kyoto Protocol, a treaty committing nations to reduce greenhouse gas emissions, had been the subject of a nonbinding resolution vote of 95 to 0 in the US Senate just a short time earlier. The Byrd-Hagel resolution expressed disapproval of any international agreement that did not require developing nations to also make emission reductions. The Kyoto Protocol did not.

The Clinton administration had signed the protocol anyway but had not submitted it to the Senate for ratification. It was clear that the Senate was unlikely to even consider ratifying the treaty. I argued that it would take far longer for Congress to reach consensus on controlling greenhouse gases like carbon dioxide (the fourth P) than to approve new steps to address acid rain. I shared our fear that insistence on an all or nothing approach at this time would unnecessarily delay positive action that would benefit both the environment and public health.

I don't know if it was what I said or how I said it, but Katie started shouting into the phone. The conversation deteriorated, and soon it ended.

I seemed clear to me later on that Katie had already been in discussions with the national groups about a new push for legislation to address global warming, in the form of a four-pollutant bill. The groups would in fact launch their campaign, but as it happened there would be no President Gore to support it.

NEW YORK TAKES ACTION

As previously mentioned, much to everyone's surprise, state legislators Assembly member Brodsky and Senator Stafford, had announced in 1997 that they would work together on a bill to curb the upwind flow of pollution credits that contributed to acid rain. Most lobbyists and reporters could not imagine the sponsors cooperating on anything. In a way, the disbelief among the lobbyists and reporters was justified. The two legislators squabbled over the details for years, failing to reach agreement despite the goodwill they had initially expressed. What finally brought them together was yet another federal report issued early in 2000.

In response to requests the year before by Representative John E. Sweeney (R-NY), and Senator Patrick Leahy (D-VT), the General Accounting
Office had conducted a study of emission trading. The GAO confirmed the
basic findings of the earlier Adirondack Council report on emissions trading.
Eastern states were net sellers of allowances and the Midwestern utilities
upwind of them were the primary buyers. (See figure 11.13.)

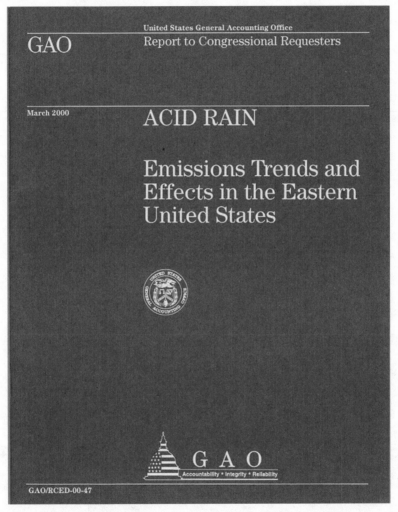

Figure 11.13. Cover of Government Accountability Office report. *Source*: public
domain.

Propelled by the GAO findings, the New York legislature finally passed a bill, which Governor Pataki signed into law on May 24, 2000, mandating that all New York power plants embrace the contractual restraints in interstate trading that LILCO had already voluntarily adopted. (See figure 11.14.)

As the bill had wound its way through the legislative process, many thought that it would not survive a federal legal challenge. There was a strong argument that because the federal government had previously established a program for trading pollution credits, New York's law was a hindrance to interstate commerce.

We recognized this weakness, and the Adirondack Council did its best to help craft the text of the new law and create a record that could help New York's attorney general combat a legal challenge. Nevertheless, a coalition of traders, power plant operators, and coal companies eventually succeeded in the federal courts in getting the law overturned.

Despite that setback, the controversy over the legislation had kept the trading issue alive in the media and helped the acid rain campaign gain strength not only in New York, but all along the Eastern Seaboard—and especially in Washington, DC.

Figure 11.14. George Pataki signs bill restricting pollution trading. Author at center rear. *Source*: author's own material.

2001: THE WORM TURNS

Needless to say, the 2000 presidential election upset the environmental apple cart.

With the near universal support from the environmental community that Vice President Al Gore had garnered, we were optimistic about our chances of addressing acid rain in his first term as President Gore. Now we were in uncertain times.

Yes, we now had three reports from federal agencies that made the case for new acid rain controls. We could already count as supporters or sponsors both senators from New York and Maine and at least one senator from every other Northeastern state. We had almost the entire New York delegation to the House of Representatives. But as we knew, from sad experience, many in Congress continued to portray the problem as one that the Northeast should solve for itself.

It was a whole new ball game in Washington, and we had to pivot.

While the new theme we had adopted after drinks in that Portland bar in 1997 had served us well, garnering new legislative support and funding for our efforts, we found ourselves again in need of a makeover. We once more needed a new strategy in order to get Congress to act on acid rain. At a Council staff meeting in Albany not long after the 2000 election, a new idea surfaced.

"We need a push from the Executive Branch," someone suggested. We recalled that during the campaign, George W. Bush had responded to a Council survey by suggesting he was open to legislation to reduce acid rain.

I pointed out doubtfully, "Bush is getting trashed for coming into office and reversing Bill Clinton's environmental initiatives and stopping regulations that were in the works. The national environmental groups already hate his administration."

"That all is true," another staffer replied, "but he is the president. He can do stuff."

"You know," I recalled, "his dad signed the original acid rain legislation in 1990. His dad lives in Maine, and acid rain is a problem there too. Maybe his dad already knows that the cuts in acid rain emissions from the law he signed were not deep enough to stop the damage. Maybe we can ask Dad to talk to his boy."

Of course, we had no idea how to get the attention of the elder Bush. But I did note that the new president talks about his dad all the time, and about finishing things his dad started.

"There you go," someone said. "George can finish what Dad started, and we can get a better program with deeper cuts in acid rain."

Like psychologists at a cocktail party, we spent the next hour analyzing what might motivate President Bush. Soon we had his psyche nailed. We would try to persuade the elder Bush to talk to his son, if possible, but in the meantime we would sell the president on the idea of completing his father's legacy.

Now, all we had to do was talk to the president of the United Sates. It was a plan.

COALITION FOR SALE

The Adirondack Council had enjoyed a long, albeit fragile relationship with groups such as the American Lung Association (NRDC), and the Sierra Club because our various areas of interest sometimes overlapped. That cooperation simply evaporated after George W. Bush was elected. The national groups just hated the Bush administration from day one. It's true that the new administration gave them plenty of reasons to be angry, starting with dismantling several environmental regulations soon after taking office. And when the White House started to work with us on acid rain, it was more than the national groups could bear. They took their anger out on us.

We tried several times to make the case to our fellow green groups that having someone with entrée to the administration could help the cause strategically. No sale. We were "providing cover" for an antienvironmental administration and were obviously naive dupes of the White House. Or worse.

The Pew Charitable Trusts, together with NRDC and the American Lung Association, had launched, postelection, a national campaign to solidify support for a four-pollutant bill in Congress. Their objective was to create a massive structure in which local and state environmental organizations would work hand-in-hand with a Washington-based lobbying and coordinating effort to establish a grassroots call for action.

This was not an unusual model. Many of the same groups had worked in the same way to form and operate the Clean Air Task Force several years earlier. What made this effort different was that the local and state groups would be paid to participate. While some national groups had long supplied stipends for activists (including me) to travel to Washington for lobby days or issue conferences, this level of underwriting by Pew was new to me.

Our colleague Bill Cooke, was the first to bring our attention to the new, heavily funded campaign. Bill was of the opinion that the folks at Pew had a distorted opinion of the Council's goals and offered to set up a meeting the next time we were in DC.

The trip was unforgettable, not only for the Pew meeting but for the Keystone Cops way we got to it.

To save money, we had made elaborate travel plans. From Albany, we would take a budget airline to the Baltimore airport, about twenty-five miles northeast of Washington. We would then take a free shuttle to the commuter rail station at the airport, ride to Washington's Union Station and hop on the city's Metro transit system to our meeting with PEW.

From the beginning, events conspired against me. I got a late start for the airport and encountered first heavy traffic and then a full parking garage. I was in dire jeopardy of missing the flight. As I entered the airport, I heard the PA system. "Passenger Bernard Malouski, would you please . . ." Although my name has a *w* in it and is pronounced "Muh-LESS-key," the page was surely for me. But I couldn't make out the rest of the announcement.

I was right across from my airline's main check-in area. I rushed straight for the desk, ignoring the glares of all the passengers waiting in line.

"I'm Mr. Melewski," I told the agent. "Was there just an announcement with my name?"

"No, they were calling for a Malouski."

"There are only two Bernard Melewskis in the world. I'm one of them."

She picked up the phone. "I have a passenger here who says he is Mr. Malewski. Did you call for Malewski or Malouski?"

She turned to me and said, "They said they called for Bernard Malouski, not Maleski."

Frustrated, I nearly shouted: "It is a silent *w*!"

"*What* is a silent *w*?"

"My name is pronounced with a silent *w*," I said slowly and deliberately. "They are mispronouncing the name. Here. This is my driver's license."

"Oh. Hold on," she said. "I have the gentleman's driver's license here," she told the airport worker on the other end of the line. "It is spelled Melewski, but pronounced Malouski." She then hung up and said, "Yes, apparently it was you."

"But what was the message?" I asked. "I did not hear all of it."

"Oh," she said. "That was a last call. Your flight is leaving."

"What? Can you tell them I am on the way? Can they hold the plane?"

"No, I can't do that, sir. But maybe if you hurry . . ."

Her voice trailed off as I ran toward the security check. I blew through in record time and ran toward my gate. Too late. They had just closed the door to the ramp. The bizarre linguistic exercise at the desk had cost me my chance of making the flight.

I rebooked for the next flight. While I waited, my colleagues arrived in Baltimore and returned my phone message. They told me our only chance of making the meeting with Pew was to drive directly to their office from the Baltimore airport.

I told my colleague, Scott Lorey, that the Council would pay for the transportation. A taxi was expensive, I thought, but it would just have to do.

Scott met me as I left the secure area of the Baltimore airport.

"Do we have a cab?" I asked him.

"Um, kind of," he said.

We walked out of the terminal and I stopped, mouth agape, at the sight of Bill Cooke standing next to a stretch limousine.

"Get in," Bill said, "we're late."

We got to Pew only half an hour late. It could have been worse, I thought. And soon it was.

Our reception was cold, and the Pew folks were clearly unhappy at the delay. They checked their watches often and went out of their way to make clear that they had more important things to do than to discuss our strategy on acid rain. Like lunch. I sat there wondering why they agreed to the meeting in the first place.

The import of the Pew relationship weighed more and more heavily as we observed the strong effects of the new national campaign they were funding. A clear sign came from Appalachian Voices, a nonprofit group based in North Carolina that had started a regional campaign on air quality focusing on acid rain and the haze that sometimes obscured the Blue Ridge Mountains region. I had met the group's director at an educational workshop in Washington, and over a dinner of Thai food we had agreed to support each other's efforts. The Council saw the alliance as an important part of its effort to gain legislative support along the Eastern Seaboard for new acid rain limits.

So it came as a surprise one day when the director of Appalachian Voices called to say that his group no longer supported our acid rain bills in Washington. His explanation was simple.

"We still support what y'all are doin'," he said. "But we are getting money from Pew now, and it is a condition of the grant that we only support a 4P bill. And for us, it's a lot of money. We will still talk about acid rain in our meetings, but that is as far as we can go."

As it turned out, that was only one example of the power of Pew's purse. Our acid rain campaign had long benefited from good working relationships with the scientific community, particularly with the Hubbard Brook Ecosystem Study in New Hampshire; with Gene E. Likens at the Cary Institute of Ecosystem Studies in Millbrook, New York; and with the Adirondack Lakes Survey Corporation, whose monthly water samples provided invaluable early documentation of acid rain damage in the Adirondack Park.

Whether we were citing these scientists' research or simply referring a reporter to an authoritative source to quote in a story, the relationship was symbiotic. We gained credibility and they gained visibility, which helped with future funding for their work, which we advocated for.

During our meeting at Pew, Hubbard Brook came up in the discussion.

"You can forget about using Hubbard Brook anymore," we were told. "We are funding them. We own them now."

Own them? I wrote the remark off as weird but irrelevant.

We should have paid more attention. Hubbard Brook was soon to release a report on their research into water quality and forest ecology. Our connections in the environmental community informed us that the groups participating in the Pew coalition would get access to the findings a week in advance via the Hubbard Brook website.

An elaborate rollout of the findings had been planned for the media at the National Press Club in Washington. Soon afterward, Professor Charles T. Driscoll, director of the Center for Environmental Systems Engineering at Syracuse University and a longtime Hubbard Brook collaborator, would be on Capitol Hill to share the scientific findings with legislators. Driscoll was a significant researcher who had spent many years studying the effects of acid rain in the Adirondacks, and his work was well respected. We did what we could over the years to motivate state legislators to provide financial support for his work.

I called Kathy Fallon Lambert, executive director of the Hubbard Brook Research Foundation. The word on the street was that they had some dynamic findings coming out, and could we please get a copy in advance? We would do what we could to help them get publicity for the report.

Lambert said she could not do that. I said I had been told that groups could get the report from the Hubbard Brook website a week in advance. That's true, she said, but only for groups supporting the 4P bill. And you don't. Then, in what seemed to me a smartass remark, Lambert said she would mail us a copy—after she returned to New Hampshire from the Washington news conference.

We now realized that the national groups had purchased exclusive first rights to groundbreaking research from one of the Council's major sources. And it was clear they intended to seize the acid rain issue as their own and render us irrelevant. We were little fish in their minds. Now they intended to swallow us whole.

We had to admit that there was certain logic to this power play. Nothing else the other groups had tried was getting them traction in Washington. Why not organize around acid rain, the only air-quality issue that was making any headway in Congress?

We had previously scheduled a lobbying trip to Washington a few days before the Pew press conference. A trip to Washington usually included back-to-back-to-back meetings for two days with legislators and/or their staff at the Capitol. Just before we departed for DC, we got word that some groups had downloaded the Hubbard Brook report. It would be good to know what was in it before our meetings with House and Senate staffers.

Scott Lorey in our Albany office checked the Hubbard Brook website and found nothing. He made a few calls and learned that the Pew-affiliated groups had been given an additional code to access the report. Obviously, we did not have that code.

Scott was undeterred. He tried the simplest thing. He went to the website's site map, and there was a link to the report.

The Hubbard Brook study, "Acid Rain Revisited," was powerful stuff. It documented that the impacts of acid rain went well beyond bodies of water and was affecting the viability of forest soils as well. It forecast bad news for the timber and maple sugar industries as well as for long-term forest health. The report also made the case that the negative impacts extended well down the East Coast.

The Council staff debated how to use this new information. We all regarded this new move by the national groups as a threat to the goals of our organization. It was potentially the end of all the progress we had made on the acid rain issue. We also were in agreement that nothing could be gained by getting into a public shoving match with the other groups. We decided instead to praise them.

We devised a plan. John Sheehan would prepare a news release in which the Council cited the Hubbard Brook report as dynamic new evidence of the need to curb acid rain. I would go to Washington as planned, but my mission would be to run ahead of the visits by Professor Driscoll and company. I would privately brief legislative staffers on the report's contents and how it supported our call for immediate action on acid rain by Congress. Our executive director, Tim Burke, would handle the inevitable blowback from Hubbard Brook and the national groups.

Our news release was issued on a Friday, as I was returning from Washington after telling the staffers in various offices what was in the yet-to-be-released report. Making my rounds, I learned that virtually every office I visited had already booked meetings with Driscoll and others the following week. I was quite familiar over the years with Driscoll's stick-to-the-data presentation style, and the congressional staffers would find my predictions of "here is what Driscoll is going to say when you meet with him" to be pretty accurate.

As usual, one of my stops was at the office of Congressman Sherwood "Sherry" Boehlert. Sherry was an Upstate Republican whose district included Cooperstown, home of the Baseball Hall of Fame. Sherry, along with California Congressman Henry Waxman, had played a critical role in gaining passage of the 1990 Clean Air Act Amendments, which we all had hoped would solve the acid rain problem. Sherry was chairman of the House Science Committee and had actively kept the acid rain issue alive thru his sponsorship of conferences and committee hearings on the topic. The Adirondack Council, along with over fifty national, state, and regional groups, would cosponsor the first major acid rain conference in over a decade in Washington, DC, in May of 2001. A hearing chaired by Congressman Boehlert of the House Science Committee followed the conference. The Congressman had outstanding staff members working in his office and serving on the committee he chaired. It was a pleasure to discuss both the politics and the science of the acid rain issue with Sherry and his staff.

Foolishly, the national groups had violated the first rule of lobbying with the Hubbard Brook report: Politicians want to be the first to know. Instead, they had teased them with invitations to the big reveal on Monday at the National Press Club.

Reporters, meanwhile, fell ravenously on our news release citing the Hubbard Brook report as dynamic new evidence of the need to curb acid rain. They called Hubbard Brook. Kathy Lambert called John Sheehan. John called me.

"Kathy went nuts," John said. "She's out of her mind angry. She has called ten times. She's threatening to sue us."

"What did you tell her?" I asked.

"To talk to Bernard."

When I reminded John that the plan was for Tim Burke to deal with the fallout from our release, he said, "I know. She has called Tim several times."

"What did he tell her?"

"He won't take her call," John said. "In fact, he is not taking any calls."

That was puzzling, but I just told John, "I'll come to the office when I get off the plane. You can tell her when I'll be available."

When I arrived in our Albany office, I found that John was now upset.

"They had an exclusive with the *New York Times* for Sunday" on the report's findings, John told me.

We should have realized that was the case. Of course they did. It was part of their plan. Big and splashy. You gave the *New York Times* an early look at the information, and it appeared in a prominent article in the Sunday paper. The rest of the media then had to attend the Monday news conference in which all the details are revealed.

The Council's release, we now saw, could lead the *Times* to drop its plans for a major Sunday story because it no longer had an exclusive. We had seen the paper do it before. That would hurt the overall cause of fighting acid rain.

John suggested that he issue another release, telling the media that our information was "embargoed" and should not be printed until Monday. Although news organizations are under no obligation to honor retroactive embargoes after they have received the information, they complied with John's request. The *Times*'s Sunday exclusive was saved.

But when Kathy Lambert did call me back, she was still plenty angry.

"You hacked us. You hired a hacker! I'm going to talk to a lawyer. We will sue you!"

"No, we did not hire a hacker," I told her. "And we are praising your report. You have our release, right?"

Kathy was not appeased. She called me twice more that same night, once solely to complain that Tim had not taken her calls.

9/11

In June 2001, the Democrats had taken control of the Senate after one member—James M. Jeffords of Vermont—switched his party affiliation from Republican to Independent. Jeffords had been rewarded with the chairmanship of the Environment and Public Works Committee. I was happy that the Adirondack Council was one of only ten environmental organizations nationwide that Jeffords had invited to a two-day "stakeholders meeting" on air quality in September.

The morning of the meeting in Washington, John Sheehan and I met up and headed down to the Rayburn Senate Office Building. The guards at the security checkpoint became very animated just as we were coming through. We heard one of them mention that they were now on an increased level of alert because a plane had struck a building in New York City. The guards shrugged, not knowing what connection that could have to them. Neither did we.

Soon we were waiting expectantly in the meeting room. Senator Jeffords's aides had begun the meeting and distributed documents, including the policy position papers all of the invitees had been asked to prepare; Jeffords then entered the room. The senator said there had been an airplane crash in New York City and that it was uncertain what that meant, but his judgment was that we should adjourn for now. He suggested that we might reconvene in the afternoon or the next day and said his staff would contact all the attendees.

Confused, we walked into the hallway. Just then, the door of a nearby office was flung open and a fellow shouted to no one in particular, "They've bombed the Pentagon!"

Alarms started sounding, and someone rushing by us turned and yelled, "They are evacuating the building!"

We jumped into a nearby elevator and headed down to the main floor. The elevator door opened to the sight of a huge stream of people heading for the exits. Once outside, we could see hundreds more pouring out of adjacent buildings and into the streets.

Because the less-expensive hotels had been booked, John and I were staying at a hotel away from the Capitol, but within walking distance of the Capitol across the green spaces of the National Mall.

We heard sirens, stopped at a corner, and watched as a convoy of vehicles and motorcycles came careening up Pennsylvania Avenue away from the Capitol. It certainly looked official. There were motorcycles followed by a van, a limousine and a second van.

I watched in complete awe as the first lady, Laura Bush, zoomed past us, alone in the backseat of the limo. Both of her hands were firmly gripping a handhold in front of her. Before I could say a word, the second van—which we now realized was a Secret Service security vehicle—passed us, and we were startled to see men with automatic weapons hanging out the back in harnesses. It was especially startling because they were ten feet away and the barrels were pointed at us.

We stood there stunned for a moment. Then I turned to John and said, "She looked scared as hell. This isn't good."

We moved swiftly onto the mall along with hundreds of other people, all walking fast. Many of them were looking at their cell phones with their head cocked, looking perplexed. No one seemed to have service.

That was alarming, but I was more concerned by the sudden appearance of men with automatic weapons on virtually every corner and in front of every government building, including the Smithsonian museums. Many wore uniforms with insignia I had never seen before.

We were halfway across the Mall when we heard what seemed like an explosion in the distance.

"I think that came from the White House!" someone in the newly formed mob of thousands exclaimed. "Wrong direction," John said.

A very strange sight greeted us as we approached a highway overpass near our hotel. Cars sat idling with their doors open and their radios turned up. People were looking to the west, where a large black cloud of smoke billowed in the distance.

As we joined the onlookers, we saw that the smoke was coming from the Pentagon, surprisingly close, and another target of the terrorists that day. Sirens blared on the highway beneath the overpass as emergency vehicles headed in that direction.

At the hotel, employees were blocking the lobby elevators. We approached three different staff members before we learned that the FBI had instructed the hotel management not to allow anyone onto the upper floors. (See figure 11.15.)

Frustrated, we joined the large group of people heading into the hotel bar with its televisions and complimentary coffee. As we watched the screens in horror, one of the twin towers at the World Trade Center collapsed.

Without a word, the bartenders opened up the bar and began serving complimentary drinks. No one hesitated to accept one. It was the first time I had drunk hard liquor in the morning.

Word came that the highway bridges into Washington, the Metro transit system and the rail lines were all closed to traffic. But we were allowed to return to our room, where we found a note that had been slipped under the door, apologizing for the inconvenience to the guests. John opined that we might not be able to get out of town for days. I believed him.

Our office manager in Albany at the time, Scott Lorey, worked the phones for us, trying to find a rental car. No luck. So John asked me for

LOEWS
L'ENFANT PLAZA HOTEL
WASHINGTON D.C.

September 11, 2001

Dear Guests:

As a precautionary measure, and for your safety, we have been
advised to evacuate the upper floors of this building.

Your cooperation will be greatly appreciated.

If you have any questions, please call the Operator.

Sincerely,

Skip Hartman

H. A. (Skip) Hartman, Jr., CHA
Regional Vice President/Managing Director

480 L'ENFANT PLAZA, S.W. · WASHINGTON · DC 20024-2197
PHONE 202·484·1000 · FAX 202·646·4468
loewslenfantplaza@loewshotels.com

Figure 11.15. A hotel note. *Source*: author's own material.

50 bucks, which he matched, tipping the hotel concierge 100 dollars to
find us a car. That did the trick.

Racing across town in a cab, we reached the rental agency just ahead
of a crowd of would-be customers. Our reservation got us the last car
available, even as the folks behind us waved fistfuls of dollars at the agents
behind the counter.

Our agent asked, "You are returning the car tomorrow, same time?"

"Of course," we lied.

By this time, another Albany lobbyist had joined us. The three of us jumped into the car and headed out of town. Driving up a strangely empty Massachusetts Avenue past the vice president's official residence in Observatory Circle, we saw another unsettling sight. Three cars parked end to end blocked the driveway entrance. Men with automatic weapons stood behind the cars. Police cars dotted the streets of the neighborhood.

We had heard that the New Jersey Turnpike was closed, so we chose the western route to New York, listening to reports about the day's attacks the whole time on National Public Radio. Some of them described the mysterious crash of another airliner in Pennsylvania, not far from our present location. It was the last plane that the terrorists had targeted that day.

Finally we stopped, exhausted and hungry, at a Holiday Inn just off the highway. There, another eerie experience awaited us.

The hotel staff greeted us as if it were just another day, asking us if we wished to dine in the restaurant or the bar, which served light fare. We chose the bar.

As we entered, a row of guys in cowboy hats eyed us from the bar. Music was playing, and on a large dance floor, dozens of men and women were line dancing. Stunned by the incongruous scene, we staggered out and headed down the corridor to the restaurant.

"Don't they know? Should we tell them?" we asked each other.

At the restaurant, we eavesdropped on the conversations around us but heard not a single conversation about the disasters on the East Coast or the plane crash a short distance away.

When we got our check, I started to hum the theme from *The Twilight Zone*. The others laughed nervously as we headed back to the car and the long ride home.

The next morning, I drove the car to the office and handed the keys to our intern. I instructed him, "Call the rental company and tell them that their car is in Albany, New York. We'll deliver it to an Enterprise outlet nearby if they would like, but we are not returning it to DC."

After a morning of phone calls and repeated threats to our poor intern, the company sent someone over to pick it up.

OUR NEW FRIEND, CHUCK

I knew of Chuck Schumer since his days in the New York State Assembly. He was an ambitious guy who clearly saw a greater future for himself. It was in Albany that the joke started that the most dangerous place at the Capitol was between Chuck Schumer and a TV camera. But the junior senator from New York quickly became an ardent advocate for reducing acid rain and saving the Adirondack Park. It was probably one of the few issues on which he and Upstate New York Republicans agreed. Chuck declared his intention to visit every county in the state at least every year, and has kept that promise. The Council helped arrange events for him in the Adirondacks around our issues when the opportunity arose and kept his Upstate staff informed on new developments.

One incident amply illustrated both the new senator's personality and our good working relationship.

I had just finished a meeting with Polly Trottenberg, Schumer's legislative director, to discuss our plans for continuing the acid rain campaign. As I headed down the hall, around the corner came the senator himself.

I said hello and, to my great relief, he greeted me by name. We both walked on. But I did not want to waste an opportunity, so I turned around and said, "I just want to thank you for putting a hold on the Bush appointment at the EPA."

It remains true to this day that Senate protocol allows a member to put a "hold" on a nomination, usually to gain leverage with the White House for a desired policy. Schumer had temporarily blocked the nomination of Donald R. Schregardus, an Ohio environmental administrator, as the lead enforcement official at the EPA. The reason was that the new Bush administration had been suggesting that the EPA might withdraw from lawsuits against power plants in the Midwest accused of violating federal air-quality standards and contributing to acid rain problems in the Adirondack and Catskill Mountains of New York. Schumer wanted assurances from the administration that the EPA-initiated lawsuits would continue.

I continued, "I know you are getting a lot of heat for holding up the appointment, but you are doing the right thing."

Chuck took several steps back toward me. He leaned in, and in a quiet voice said, "You know what? Fuck 'em."

Our first meeting with Chuck's legislative director had been a good one. Polly had previously worked in Senator Moynihan's office and we talked about our common acquaintances. She seemed interested in what I had to say and offered the prospect of future meetings. She made it clear that Schumer supported the acid rain bill previously sponsored by Moynihan because he wanted to help solve the problem.

As the meeting was wrapping up, Polly commented, "You don't act like a lobbyist."

I replied, "I will take that as a compliment." She did not respond. The exchange unnerved me a little. I truly did not know what she meant.

But we soon developed a solid professional relationship. The Council always tried to meet with her when we visited Washington, and considering the demands on her time, she made herself available quite often. While our talks always focused on the acid rain campaign, the discussion often drifted to other topics.

Polly once demonstrated their new internal instant-messaging system by typing a request for a staff member to come to her office. We laughed about Schumer's fondness for the singing Big Mouth Billy Bass mounted on a plaque that he played endlessly for visitors. She even shared her wedding plans with me.

So it was a surprise when Polly called our Albany office from Washington to talk to me. She had not done that before, and she quickly made clear why she called.

Representatives of several national environmental groups, including the Natural Resources Defense Council, and the Sierra Club, had just met with Senator Schumer. They wanted to discuss an issue that had been building in the environmental community over the past few years. It had become known as 4P versus 2P.

Polly said the groups had told the senator that his sponsorship of the acid rain bill first introduced by Senator Moynihan to control sulfur and nitrogen oxides was out of step with the national consensus. Any legislation that changed the Clean Air Act, they said, had to address not two but four pollutants, including mercury and carbon dioxide. By continuing to sponsor a 2P bill, Schumer was tacitly supporting the policies of the Bush administration and undermining the national groups' effort to address climate change. They asked him to sponsor 4P legislation and dump "the Adirondack Council bill."

Polly was calling to get our assurance that if Schumer dropped his sponsorship of the two-pollutant acid rain bill, the Council would not attack him. I would not give it.

We each made our best arguments, both substantive and political. Polly made it clear that Schumer intended to sponsor the bill supported by the national groups. I then offered a compromise: the senator could sponsor both bills. The Adirondack Council would say publicly that both bills would solve the acid rain problem and that we had no problem with his sponsorship of the 4P bill. I assured Polly that we would love to see action on four pollutants, but we just did not see climate change gaining enough political momentum to get action in the short term. That should be pretty obvious to those working on Capitol Hill, I said.

That's not good enough for the other groups, she said. They want Schumer to drop the 2P bill.

That sent me over the edge, and I raised my voice. "Of course it's not," I said. "They just want you to hurt us." Senator Clinton no doubt was being pressed to do the same, I thought, and we might be left without a rallying point for our acid rain campaign.

She yelled. I yelled back. It ended badly.

When she got off the phone, I turned to our staffer, Scott Lorey, who had been listening in on the call, and, out of my mind, I quipped, "That went well, don't you think?"

Scott came to my office a little later and said that Polly's birthday was in two days. I asked Scott how he knew that, and he replied, "My talents are not fully appreciated." He suggested that we send her flowers along with an apology from me. I quickly agreed and asked him to make it a big bouquet.

On her birthday Polly called me again. It was short and to the point.

"Thank you for the flowers. They are lovely. *Now* you are acting like a lobbyist." And she hung up.

Schumer sponsored both bills.

STATE REGULATIONS STALL

It was taking way too long to get Governor Pataki's new acid rain regulations into final publication. While the surprise announcement in 1999, two years before, had a beneficial effect, we were anxious to sew up the victory and find a way to use that tool in Congress to pry open the Clean Air Act.

Plant operators in the state were quick to object, as we had expected. Several New York utilities had recently sold their generating plants to other companies. The new owners were suddenly facing the prospect of stricter regulations that would require them to retire certain units or install pollution equipment. They launched an effort to water down the proposed rules and stretch out the timeline for their adoption and implementation.

But later actions by some environmental groups caused the greatest concern for the governor's office. In private meetings with the Pataki's staff, some groups carried the Clean Air Task Force message and argued that the governor had not gone far enough—the cuts in sulfur and nitrogen pollutants had to be deeper. In a more fundamental disagreement, they pushed the administration to adopt controls on mercury and carbon dioxide as well as the two pollutants that were the main precursors of acid rain.

Since the 2000 election of George W. Bush as president, the national groups' campaign for a four-pollutant solution to the air-quality problem went into high gear, extending their network into regional and statewide groups in New York. They saw not just the need to satisfy their funders but also the opportunity to piggyback on our initiative with the governor. It was annoying but I can't say I blame them for trying. I would have done the same thing.

The irony was that both the polluting industry and national environmental groups and their New York surrogates were all urging Governor Pataki to delay the regulations. I was surprised when the dispute broke into the open in December 2001. In a letter to Governor Pataki signed by Peter M. Iwanowicz of the American Lung Association, groups that had organized under the banner of the Clean Air Task Force publicly called on the governor to amend the regulations so as to cover all four pollutants. In effect, they were giving the green light for even further delay.

Frustratingly, the word in the Division of Air Resources in the Department of Environmental Conservation was that the problems the power plant operators had raised had been worked out. The department staff made it clear to us that the governor's office was now holding the regulations up solely at the request of other environmental groups.

It had become an intolerable situation for us. We had gone from the sublime—the simultaneous announcement of the new state acid rain regulations at the Capitol buildings in Washington and Albany—to the ridiculous—fellow environmental groups publicly opposing new acid rain controls.

About a month later, I made one more effort to get the draft regulations released. I sent a note to Charlie Fox, Governor Pataki's deputy secretary for energy and environment. I told him that the Council's twice-yearly newsletter was about to be published and that we had a choice of paragraphs to print on acid rain. The text of one praised the governor for the release of the acid rain regulations, and the other condemned the administration for failing to follow through on a promise to New Yorkers made two years earlier.

Within hours, Fox faxed back an alternative paragraph. His version stated that the air-quality regulations had been delayed at the request of virtually every environmental group in New York except the Adirondack Council, in order to avoid giving federal regulators a precedent for a lower level of protection. He then dared us to print it if we wanted our members to know the truth.

And he had copied our correspondence to NRDC and to the Adirondack Mountain Club.

I telephoned him immediately. He had expected the call, but not what I was going to say. I chewed him out for sending other parties our private correspondence. Communication with the Executive Branch was not legally a public document, I said, and his act of disclosure was at least a gross breach of courtesy and protocol. I demanded an apology.

Fox was momentarily stunned by my attack. He never did get around to the question that he really wanted answered: Where the hell did the Council get off threatening the governor?

Before he could recover, I assured him that we loved the governor and that we had already decided that criticizing him would be unfair, because the other groups were causing the delay. I didn't tell him that we had never planned to print the negative paragraph; we had just hoped that it would induce the release of the acid rain rules. In our newsletter, the Council would attribute the delay to opposition by the power companies.

In the end, it would be another year before New York's new acid rain regulations were published, more than three and a half years after they were announced. Several of the same environmental groups that had contributed to the delay issued a news release condemning the governor for breaking his promise to produce the regulations quickly.

THANK YOU, MR. ANDERSON

By the middle of 2001, the new Bush administration had settled in. In what we considered a stroke of luck, one of the president's first nominations was the sitting governor of New Jersey, Christine Todd Whitman, as administrator of the Environmental Protection Agency. As governor, Whitman had generally been supportive of new acid rain controls. New Jersey, however, was not as vocal as some of the other states receiving pollution from upwind sources, because they did their share of polluting their neighbors downwind as well.

It was, we decided, a good time for another visit to the staff that ran the EPA's Acid Rain Market Program. This small staff managed the trading of pollution credits, helped fund stations that monitored air quality, and contributed to research. Overall, it ran one of the most cost-effective regulatory programs ever created by the federal government.

As we prepared for our visit, the Adirondack Council's history of conflict with the EPA was in the back of our minds. Earlier, in the Clinton administration, we had wanted the agency to speed up the release of its analysis of the extent of the problem, as required by the 1990 amendments to the federal Clean Air Act.

That had led to the rude and confrontational encounter at EPA headquarters in which a senior staffer, Brian McLean had challenged us to sue the agency. We did, and the suit was eventually settled. Our most recent visit with Brian, in 1997 during the Clinton presidency, had revealed a congenial McLean, who made it clear that the previous disagreement had been forgotten, or at least forgiven. McLean had warmly greeted us, and after a few minutes of conversation excused himself, reminding his staff to talk to us about "that thing." His staff then informed us in a conspiratorial fashion that senior EPA directors, looking for budget cuts, intended to eliminate funding for the air-quality monitoring stations in the Northeast. At least one in Ithaca had already been closed. This raised the risk that there would be no record of whether the acid rain control program was actually working to reduce pollution.

Now it seemed clear to me why McLean had left the meeting. We were being given information about EPA policy and budget plans that the rank and file obviously did not support, in hopes that we could help block them. If we succeeded, McLean had plausible deniability. The Council had gone from the EPA's legal opponents to brothers in arms.

The agency picked the right folks to ask. We went directly to Senator Moynihan's office. Moynihan had been a major force behind the adoption of the Clean Air Act amendments of 1990, and was particularly instrumental in having Congress require periodic reports on whether the laws were working. The air pollution levels being recorded by the stations in the Northeast were a key part of those reports.

Not long after our visit to his office, Moynihan went to the floor of the Senate and delivered what some characterized as a "tirade" and others a "command performance."

"Upstate New York," he intoned, "has been shocked—I think that is a fair term—and finds itself in near disbelief to learn that the Environmental Protection Agency has closed the Ithaca station, which is part of a broad network of monitoring stations that collect data critical to understanding the impact of acid rain on the Adirondack Preserve."

"If the EPA has the arrogance and the insolence and the stupidity to close the research facility at the site where this whole subject was first understood," Moynihan continued, "I am not surprised that persons are calling for the abolition of the Environmental Protection Agency."

Less than twenty-four hours later, the White House sent Moynihan a letter assuring him that the money would be restored.

With that episode as background, our next visit to the EPA in the Bush era in 2001 was very collegial. That was good, because we had an important question to ask. Who was actually making environmental policy in the new administration?

We learned that agencies were now having their policy decisions and even draft news releases vetted by the White House's Council on Environmental Quality. In the Clinton administration, Vice President Al Gore had run the Council on Environmental Quality (CEQ) as an environmental and energy policy think tank. Now, under Bush, it had become a political colander through which most environmental policy was being strained.

Getting an appointment to visit CEQ was easier than we had thought. Its spokesperson was Sam Thernstrom, who had previously worked in Governor Pataki's communications office and had become acquainted with our John Sheehan. John called Sam, and Sam made the arrangements.

A few weeks later, I was sitting in the office of David Anderson, Council on Environmental Quality's associate director for legislative affairs. CEQ was located in a row of townhouses on Lafayette Park, which sits directly in front of the White House. It was chock-full of young staffers, and my host was no exception.

I was delighted to learn that Anderson had come to CEQ directly from the Chesapeake Bay Foundation, a nonprofit group dedicated to clearing up pollution in the largest estuary in North America. Anderson was both familiar with and sympathetic to the acid rain cause.

We had a good chat. It was a relief not to have to get him up to speed on the topic. I promised some materials on the legislation we were promoting and we agreed to meet the next time I was in Washington.

As we were wrapping up our meeting, something made me remember that Adirondack Council staff meeting when we debated how to get the president involved in our cause.

I circled back to Anderson's desk and said, "Oh, there's one more thing." I reminded Anderson that President George H. W. Bush had signed into law a major revision of the Clean Air Act in 1990—a law that was proving inadequate to the goal of controlling acid rain.

"What a wonderful opportunity that almost a decade later, his son is in the position to complete that legacy and fulfill his father's intent!" I said.

"That's interesting," Anderson said.

I pressed the point.

"I think it would be terrific, you know, given his father's history with the issue, if he finished the job."

"Yes, that's interesting," Anderson said.

My next visit to Washington came sooner than expected, and I easily corralled another meeting with Anderson. He asked me to repeat what I had said about the Bush legacy, and this time he took notes. He pressed me for more details. What kind of additional cuts in pollution would be needed to solve the acid rain problem? What did the federal reports say about the effectiveness of current laws?

And finally, "What is the minimum that would need to be done?"

"At least a fifty percent additional cut in both sulfur and nitrogen emissions from power plants beyond what the law already requires," I told him.

"And you would support that?"

"We already do. That was in the original bill by Senator Moynihan."

"I might want to talk to you some more on this. Can I call you?"

"Absolutely."

2002: A YEAR TO REMEMBER

I got a call a few weeks later, in February 2002. It was Anderson at CEQ, my new best friend.

"The president, and this is confidential, is going to take some action on acid rain. I think you are going to like it. Can you get down to Washington on short notice?"

The president was making a speech at the headquarters of the National Oceanic and Atmospheric Administration in Silver Spring, Maryland. I drove down from New York, and Anderson literally talked me on my cell phone into the parking garage and into the auditorium, where I settled into my reserved seat shortly before Bush stepped to the podium.

I heard what I had eagerly anticipated: the president said he would set "tough new standards to dramatically reduce the three most significant forms of pollution" causing acid rain. It was billed as the Clear Skies Initiative, although, as the official White House transcript shows, Bush referred to his plan as "Clean Skies" throughout the speech.

The president announced, "We will cut sulfur dioxide emissions by seventy-three percent from current levels. We will cut nitrogen oxide emissions by sixty-seven percent. And, for the first time ever, we will cap emissions of mercury, cutting them by sixty-nine percent."

This was wonderful news. The planned reductions were significantly greater than the minimum necessary to turn the problem around, which meant that the recovery of lakes and streams in the Adirondacks would come sooner.

I quickly conferred with our staff to make sure that the Adirondack Council was prominent in praising the initiative. But to our disappointment, most of the media coverage focused on a pledge Bush made earlier in the speech renewing the US commitment to United Nations efforts on climate change and providing additional funding for monitoring. As John Sheehan pointed out, the president's announcement had, from our perspective, "buried the lead"—a newspaper term that means placing the most important point deep in the article.

We got the impression that folks in the administration were not happy with the coverage either. So we were thrilled when they told us a month later that EPA administrator Whitman would visit Albany in early April in a second attempt to promote the Clear Skies Initiative. We were invited to help plan the event and to attend.

John Sheehan did a great job helping the EPA find a venue, the Atmospheric Sciences Research Center of the State University of New York at Albany, and he also turned out the media for the event. The local branch of the Sierra Club, which was protesting the lack of progress on global warming by the Bush administration, posted a few picketers outside, which got them some television coverage.

The March 2002 news conference went well, but was not memorable. Its main value, I thought, was to show that the president was serious about addressing acid rain. I was more impressed with Whitman's tour of the research center after the event. She engaged the staff and interns, discreetly pausing while photographers moved to a better position for their shot. Turning this way and that, she engaged people to provide just the right picture. A talented professional, she was working the media to the max. Impressive.

VILLAINS

Less than a week later, John Sheehan and I were returning to Albany from New York City on the Taconic State Parkway. His phone rang, and after listening for a while he said, "I'm on the Taconic right now. I'll have to call you back."

He turned to me and said, "We got trouble."

A reporter had called for comment. The Clean Air Trust had just announced that the Adirondack Council had been named the "Clean Air Villain of the Month."

The Clean Air Trust was Washington-based nonprofit group seemingly run by one person, Frank O'Donnell. Each month, it identified a legislator, bureaucrat, or organization as a "villain" based on actions or inactions that O'Donnell thought were detrimental to progress on clean-air regulation. The Adirondack Council's crime was supporting the president's Clear Skies Initiative.

"Just last Friday," O'Donnell huffed, "the council's acting executive director [that's me] appeared with EPA administrator Christie Whitman at an event in Upstate New York—while other environmental and health groups showed up to protest!"

The release also stated, falsely, that the Council was bad-mouthing other environmental groups and one of our strongest allies, Attorney General Eliot L. Spitzer, in editorial board interviews. To my knowledge, we were one of the few groups honoring the well-established code in the environmental community of *not* criticizing our colleagues publicly. And we made a point of letting the press and the public know that we were enthusiastic supporters of all the work that our state attorney general and his staff were doing in court to punish power plant operators that were in violation of the current rules.

Finally, O'Donnell claimed that we had undermined Senator James M. Jeffords (I-VT) the year before in the second air-quality "stakeholders meeting" that Jeffords, as the chairman of the Committee on Environment and Public Works, had invited us to attend. The Council had said at the meeting, O'Donnell wrote, that it would accept more pollution than Jeffords was seeking to allow. That was a cheap shot, given that our call for cuts of "at least" 50 percent had been adopted in legislation sponsored by Senators Moynihan, Schumer, and Clinton. We had always called for "at least" that level of cuts.

Prior to Jeffords first stakeholder session on September 11, 2001, each of the twenty-five participants from environmental organizations, power companies, and trade associations was asked to prepare a position paper to share with the other participants. They were distributed just before the Senate office building was evacuated.

Our position paper discussed the minimum cuts necessary to turn around the acid rain problem. We were pleased to see that all participants agreed that cuts of that level or greater were needed in emissions of acid rain's main two precursors, sulfur dioxide and nitrogen oxides. The sticking points were the timing and the extent of the cuts.

Our press release in advance of the second Jeffords meeting praised the fact that the position papers handed out by all the participants before the first meeting had shown that everyone at the meeting, including the power companies, wanted to see cuts in emissions sufficient to stop acid rain.

The Clean Air Trust alleged that our 2001 position paper had "undercut" Jeffords and had "broken ranks" with the environmental community by accepting more pollution than the chairman's bill would have allowed. There was no mention of the fact that we had publicly supported the four-pollutant bill that Senator Jeffords sponsored.

No sooner had John Sheehan learned the news from the reporter than we pulled off the Taconic Parkway and began discussing how to respond to our new moniker. It was the first time the "villain" label had been applied to an environmental group. Certainly some of our board members and staff were going to be upset, and we feared that the attack reflected a new negative relationship between the major national environmental groups and us.

For our formal response, we decided on the "no apologies" approach.

"We don't apologize for working with the president of the United States to solve the greatest environmental threat to the largest state park in the union. New Yorkers love the Adirondacks and will work with anyone willing to help save our park from destruction," we wrote. We also pointed out that no one from the Clean Air Trust had even talked to us before issuing its insulting "award."

Quickly, environmental groups in New York and elsewhere weighed in with their own comments. A recurrent theme was that our being labeled a villain was "too bad, but the Council asked for it." The speed and strong similarities among these responses we thought bore signs of coordination, and we concluded that the attack by Frank O'Donnell had not been his idea alone. The villain award may have spotlighted a split in our movement, but oddly, it became an asset in Washington.

The Democratic majority in the US Senate was short-lived, Senator Jeffords lost his chairmanship, and Senators Inhofe and Voinovich, both conservative Republicans, now led the Senate Environment and Public Works Committee and its clean-air subcommittee. Both had also been previously labeled Clean Air Villains of the Month. Now that the Council was a fellow villain, we became more interesting to them. The next time they saw me, both men made a point of calling me over and joshing about "what we had in common." They clearly trusted us more than before. Our access to both senators improved substantially from that point, and in future meetings the staff was more willing to listen to what we had to say.

That was certainly true of the chief Republican staffer at the Senate Committee on the Environment and Public Works, Andrew R. Wheeler. Andy was always professional in our meetings, but it got easier to schedule a meeting with him after we became "villains." Our meetings were much more casual and forthright. Some Senate staffers called Wheeler "Big Head Andy" behind his back, but inside that cranium there appeared to be a very bright mind. We sparred more than we agreed, but our discussions were respectful and remained focused on public policy. It was clear, however, that he was not going to get out in front of his boss.

I always prided myself on my ability to make personal connections with politicians and their staff members, dealing with them as peers on environmental topics. No matter what their party affiliation or ideology, building a cordial, trusting relationship was the path to achieving the Council's goals. And in our fight against acid rain, I particularly desired good relations with Senator George Voinovich, the Ohio Republican who chaired the Senate Environment and Public Works Committee's clean-air subcommittee. For the first time, after we were declared "Villains" the senator agreed to a one-on-one meeting with me.

But I cannot take credit for how the Council really broke the ice with the Senator. Radmila Miletich, a former legislative analyst at the state assembly's energy committee, had joined our staff. She was a second-generation Serbian-American, and I often overheard her speaking on the phone to her mother in their native tongue.

She soon was accompanying me on lobbying jaunts to Washington. An early stop on our first trip together was Senator Voinovich's office. He came out to the lobby to greet us, and nearly as soon as I had introduced Radmila, the senator switched from English to Serbian. Much to my amazement, he knew immediately she was "family."

It was pretty much Radmila's meeting after that. I remember that Voinovich switched to English at one point to ask if I minded waiting in the anteroom while he walked his newfound family member around his office suite to show her his memorabilia from decades in public office. Of course not, Senator.

The next time I saw Senator Voinovich, he floated the idea of visiting the Adirondack Park. For a variety of reasons, we never got a trip organized.

GOT ANY PLANS FOR APRIL 22?

I had my last meeting with David Anderson at the Council on Environmental Quality just before the Christie Whitman event in Albany.

"Has the president decided where he is going for Earth Day?" I asked.

"Some ideas are being kicked around, but no decisions have been made," Anderson said.

"I think it would be terrific for him to come up to the Adirondacks on Earth Day and declare that he is going to put an end to acid rain," I suggested.

"He already did that" with the Clear Skies announcement, Anderson replied.

I pressed him. "Yes, but you could not have a more receptive audience than Adirondackers, and he can see what he is going to save."

"That's interesting," he said.

Anderson called me a week later. "The Adirondacks are under consideration for an Earth Day event," he said. "It is not a lock, but can you get back to me with some information about airports, places to hold an event, what he could do, etcetera? And the Earth Day location is pretty sensitive at the moment, so can you get me a handle on this quickly without raising too much attention?"

I quickly agreed. That evening I stayed at my desk after the other Council staffers departed (which was not unusual), and phoned the chairman of the Adirondack Park Agency, Richard Lefebvre, at his home.

The agency served as a kind of regional planning board for public and private lands within parks. I wanted to talk to Lefebvre because the APA also operated two visitor centers suitable for a presidential event.

Lefebvre and I got along well. When Governor Pataki appointed him in 1998, he was viewed with suspicion by much of the environmental community because he seemed to be a member of every anti-environmental organization that was interested in the park. But we soon learned he was a fair-minded and intellectually curious person who did not necessarily subscribe to the philosophy of every group he joined, but wanted to know what folks in the Park were thinking.

"Dick, you will not believe why I am calling," I said when I reached him at home.

"Okay, Try me."

"How would you like to host the president of the United States?"

"You are correct," he said. "I do not believe that is why you are calling. Are you serious?"

"Yes"

"Good God!"

I explained the situation and the need for quick and confidential action. A day before I was supposed to get back to Anderson at CEQ, Lefebvre phoned back and said that the best location would be the Visitor Interpretive Center near the hamlet of Paul Smiths, north of Saranac Lake. The Adirondack Regional Airport was nearby, and the center had a sizable auditorium and a brand new boardwalk over a wetland that would provide a good background for photos.

I thanked him and asked him to keep it under his hat for now, because the Adirondack Park was a contender for the Earth Day event, but it was not a sure thing. I told him I would get back to him.

A week or so later, Anderson confirmed that the Adirondack Park event was on and gave me given the cell phone number for J. D. Estes, an official in the White House Office of Public Liaison. I would later learn that J.D. was also known as the "Turkey Guy," a moniker bestowed by the president, because his outreach duties included staging the annual presidential pardon of the Thanksgiving turkey at the White House.

Almost immediately, chaos broke out. Reporters learned of the trip from a member of the New York congressional delegation and called John Sheehan. In rapid succession, I walked down the hall and explained to John that I already knew about the event and had not told him, which thrilled him to no end; broke the news to our Elizabethtown staff, who were stunned, and phoned Dick Lefebvre. His line was busy.

I finally got through to Dick. He said that when the news broke of Bush's plan to visit, he had been forced to admit to the governor's office that he had kept the information to himself for more than a week.

"Were they happy to hear the news?" I asked.

"Happy?" he answered. "No. I got my ass chewed out for almost an hour for not telling them earlier."

I told him I was sorry for the trouble I had caused him.

"Don't be," he said. "It was exciting."

I was happy to hear from Lefebvre that the governor was going to let him attend the event. So was he, I suspect.

As it turned out, the landing of Air Force One at Adirondack Regional Airport was the only part of Lefebvre's plan that survived. The governor's office took over planning for the trip and moved the site to the nearby Town of Wilmington.

THE BIG DAY ARRIVES

It was still early morning on Earth Day, 2002, as I exited the Northway and approached Lake Placid, just a few miles from where the president would speak. I cruised up past the scenic Cascade Lakes, and then past the Olympic Park, and was now coming up on the Olympic ski jumps looming in the foreground.

A lawyer friend of mind called the hilltop towers—295 feet and 393 feet tall—"the symbol of Lake Placid." He had been on the legal team defending the plan to build the towers against a threatened court challenge by the Sierra Club.

The obvious question in both federal and state environmental reviews was whether the huge towers would have an adverse visual impact on their surroundings. To any neutral observer the answer was obviously yes, but the Adirondack Park Agency unanimously approved construction. There was simply too much political pressure to secure the jumps in time for the 1980 Winter Olympics.

Lake Placid was a regular stop when I took the Council's student interns on our orientation tour of the Adirondack Park. I first drove them to the nearby plateau that had once been the farm of John Brown, the militant abolitionist who seized the federal armory at Harper's Ferry, Virginia, in 1859.

Upon exiting the van, I would direct them to focus on John Brown's grave, marked with a large boulder near his cabin and barn. From the farmstead, there is a magnificent 280-degree vista of the Adirondack High Peaks in the distance. I asked the students to humor me and look at first only to the southwest, and then slowly turn to the northeast to take in the inspiring panoramic view. Invariably, they would exclaim how beautiful it was, and then suddenly stop. Looming over the edge of the plateau like an alien spaceship, dominating and ruining the view, were the twin towers of the Olympic ski jumps.

I remember one fellow shouting, "What the hell is that?" Every year, I got a similar reaction. Then I used the experience to explain what an environmental review process was intended to achieve, and what the limitations of those laws were. John Brown's farm was the perfect teaching tool.

But on this day, I buzzed right by the ski jumps and turned right for Wilmington. Tourists come to the town for the trout fishing in the Au Sable River or skiing on Whiteface Mountain, where the downhill events were held in 1980. Some would say that Santa's Workshop nearby also deserves mention as a tourist attraction.

But today Wilmington would be famous for hosting the president of the United States to make a major speech on the environment, on Earth Day. Still, I saw nothing out of the ordinary until I rounded a bend along the Au Sable. Lining the road ahead were dozens of vehicles from the New York State Police and Department of Environmental Conservation. The DEC Rangers, an elite group, would be demonstrating rappelling and other wilderness skills for Bush as he made his way by motorcade from the airport.

As I entered Wilmington—a Republican town—clusters of people appeared holding signs of welcome: Welcome, President Bush! Wilmington welcomes the President. "Thank you for coming, Mr. President."

Some in the crowd held signs with less friendly but important messages: "Stop the War." "Stop Global Warming."

I parked and grabbed my fleece vest and wool ball cap, because the occasional flakes had now become a light, steady snow shower. At the town park, where Bush was to speak, I ran into many people I knew among the invitees: local officials, members of Governor Pataki's staff, and members of my board of directors.

As I stepped into the registration line, the snow intensified significantly. Almost immediately, the word came down: Bush would not deliver his speech at the park. Buses would take all the invitees to Whiteface ski center south of town, which had a large hall.

Credentials in hand, I joined the crowd awaiting shuttle buses to the resort. The snow came down harder and was starting to accumulate rapidly. The temperature was falling as well.

The crowd diminished with every new busload, but I saw that many members of my board of directors had not yet boarded one, including our chairman, David Skovron. Feeling protective and the need to be responsible, I waited for the last bus and made sure that no Council board member, donor, or staffer had been left behind.

The bus was warm, which was a welcome relief. What we overheard as the bus driver communicated with his colleagues was not. The Secret Service had stopped several buses from entering the Whiteface resort because the presidential motorcade was arriving. Worse, it sounded as if the agents were having trouble determining whether all the arriving buses were legitimate.

Indeed, when our bus arrived, the Secret Service members at the entrance seemed startled to see us. Someone had assumed that the previous bus carried the last group of invitees. Our driver, however, talked us in and we gleefully poured out of the bus at the ski center.

Just inside, more members of the Secret Service detail were breaking down the portable metal detectors that all attendees had to walk through. They were even more surprised to see us.

"Who are you?" one asked.

"We are the last bus!" we chirped, almost in unison.

"We can't let you in," the agent said. "The president has arrived and we cannot let anyone else in."

Every cold, wet one of us briefly stood in silent disappointment. Then, some declared their outrage and stormed out of the building, apparently forgetting that they were now miles away from their cars. Others began trying to convince the Secret Service to ignore orders and let them pass. I sought out the head of the detail and asked if he could get me in touch with J. D. Estes, my White House liaison. I had his phone number, but my cell phone had no signal at the ski resort.

My sprits lifted when I was joined by Alexander F. "Sandy" Treadwell, a scion of a wealthy Upstate family who had served as New York secretary of state and was the current chairman of the state Republican Party. Here was a man with clout. Bolstered by his appearance, I told the Secret Service agent just to tell J. D. Estes that Sandy Treadwell was out here.

Within moments, a young fellow raced down the stairs. He asked for Treadwell, apologized, and explained he was authorized to immediately bring him upstairs.

Sandy turned to his bus mates and said triumphantly, "Let's go, everybody!"

"No. Not them. Just you," said young aide.

Sandy looked at the crestfallen faces around him. He turned back and declared, "Either they go, or I don't go." The small crowd burst into cheers and applause for someone who had privilege and refused to use it, a patrician turned, well, republican.

They kept us all out.

Thus did the chairman of the state Republican Party miss the president's speech, as did many other prominent guests, including the chairman of my board of directors, David Skovron.

Most of us waited on the building's ground floor until Bush had departed. I then raced up the stairs two at a time and breathlessly encountered John Sheehan.

"What happened up here?" I asked him.

"Bush thanked the Adirondack Council and promised big pollution cuts to end acid rain. He also reminded everyone that he was a rancher and said that if you own your own land, every day is Earth Day. By the way, what happened to David Skovron? The president was asking for him from the podium."

"You don't want to know," I assured him.

The next day, the *Washington Post* ran an entertaining article by Dana Milbank headlined "Mother Earth 1, Bush 0."

The bulk of the column recounted the wanderings of the buses carrying the White House press corps. The convoy was delayed by the icy weather, was stopped several times by local police as it sped through the countryside trying to make up time, and got lost so frequently that it had to make four U-turns. It arrived at the ski resort two hours and forty minutes late. By that time, the national networks had canceled their planned live coverage of the event due to the weather. When the reporters finally arrived, it was snowing so hard that they could not see Whiteface Mountain in front of them, much less the other beautiful vistas of the Adirondack Park.

In many newspapers, the coverage consisted of a single photo of the president holding an ax aloft as he helped repair a bridge on a hiking trail with young volunteers from AmeriCorps, the successor to the VISTA program. Few of the captions mentioned Bush's acid rain pledge or the Adirondack Park. (See figure 11.16.)

Figure 11.16. President Bush on Earth Day. *Source*: Nancie Battaglia.

In fact, Al Gore had taken much of the bloom off our Earth Day rose. While President Bush was in the Adirondacks, the former vice president was giving a fiery speech in New York City attacking the president's failure to address global warming. Bush had in fact already withdrawn the United States from the Kyoto Protocol, the international agreement to set limits on greenhouse gas emissions by developed countries that the Clinton administration had earlier signed and was no doubt a personal priority for Gore. The diatribe, coming from the man who came within a hair's breadth of defeating Bush for the presidency, got lots of press attention. Gore would make global warming his mission over the following years, rocketing to prominence in 2006 with the documentary *An Inconvenient Truth*.

Gore's Earth Day speech was, in effect, the kickoff for a new, heavily funded four-pollutant clean-air campaign by national environmental groups, including the Natural Resources Defense Council, the Sierra Club, and the American Lung Association.

THE VISITOR

Our hard work to bring the president to the Adirondacks and promote action on acid rain had not paid off as well as we had hoped. Instead, the Council was now between a rock and a hard place within the environmental community.

The doorbell rang at our Albany office later that spring. When I opened the door, she stepped in and kissed me before I could say hello. Then she immediately swept past me into our office, trailed by two staffers. I brought up the rear.

Frances Beinecke had arrived.

I first met Frances in 1980, when I was the executive director of the only full-time environmental lobbying organization in New York, the Environmental Planning Lobby (EPL). The EPL had been created as the lobbying arm for many organizations several years earlier because federal law at the time severely restricted nonprofit organizations from lobbying directly if they offered donors a tax deduction. Each participating organization had a seat on the board of directors.

Frances was then in the early stages of her long career at the Natural Resources Defense Council, where she had eventually would serve ten years as president. Our first collaboration led to the adoption of New York's first coastal management program, and we had continued to work together on a number of environmental policy initiatives over the years.

In our work on coastal management, Frances would come to Albany periodically with Sarah Chasis, a fellow staffer who now directs the NRDC's oceans program. I would set up appointments with legislators and the governor's office and accompany my two experts to the meetings.

EPL also hosted an annual "lobby day" that I helped organize, which assembled a wide range of environmentalists from around the state for a rally and a day of meetings with legislators and their aides. Frances was always part of the elite group that would meet with the governor and leaders of the Assembly and Senate.

Those meetings were almost always frustrating. The leaders always wanted a photo opportunity with environmentalists, but never committed to doing anything. It became an annual ritual for Frances and me to be walking down a Capitol hallway and for her to turn to me and say, "I do not know how you can stand to do this. These people are impossible." I always took it as a compliment.

Frances had also served for years on the Adirondack Council's board of directors and had served as a past chair from 1980 to 1985. I realized I could resume my work with her if, as I was contemplating, and moved from the Assembly staff to join the Adirondack Council staff. Having thoroughly enjoyed my work with her, I looked forward to resuming it at the Council. But to my great disappointment, Frances resigned her post at my first board meeting in 1990. I saw her from time to time after that, but never really worked with her again.

Now, after the dueling Earth Day speeches by Bush and Gore, Frances was in my conference room. As executive director of the NRDC, she was making an effort to reconcile the strategic split between the green groups, as both sides tried to get Congress to revisit the Clean Air Act.

To her credit, she was here in an effort to stop the intergroup bloodshed.

Originally the Adirondack Council had been an organization of organizations, including the NRDC. Over time, the other members had drifted away due to policy differences and tax law changes. When Tim Burke arrived as executive director, he had some success in "getting the band back together" and had even added the Citizens Campaign for the Environment as a first-time member.

Representatives of these member organizations now sat in our packed conference room. Many were eager to meet Frances for the first time. All had heard the story about Frances and Sigourney Weaver that the actor later confirmed years later in a short profile of Frances she wrote for *Vanity Fair* magazine. "I've been fortunate to play some strong women in my career—

protectors, guardians, leaders," Sigourney Weaver was reported to have said. "The no-nonsense Ellen Ripley in *Aliens*. The chain-smoking xenobotanist Grace Augustine in *Avatar*. The real-life zoologist Dian Fossey in *Gorillas in the Mist*. When casting about for the right mix of intellectual rigor and emotional toughness to portray these women, I have often taken inspiration from my former roommate and high-school classmate, Frances Beinecke."[1]

This was the tough, determined woman who now sat ready to persuade the Adirondack Council and our member organizations that we should give up promoting new federal legislation that would address only two or three air pollutants. She wanted us to join the broader coalition led by NRDC and the Pew Charitable Trusts in demanding that any new air-quality law must add controls on carbon dioxide to address global warming—the 4P approach.

I was happy to give her that opportunity. I was taught that groups should resolve their differences through dialogue, and I was optimistic that all of us would reach an understanding that would let us move forward with less strife.

Frances made her pitch, and David Miller, the executive director of the New York chapter of the National Audubon Society, took the floor. Within seconds, Miller threw in the towel, announcing he had come to agree with Frances and we should too. That did not surprise me, given that acid rain was not Audubon's top issue by any means.

But that came as a shock to Tim Burke and to Sarah Meyland, executive director of Citizens Campaign for the Environment. Neither of them was budging. Both argued that the move to solve acid rain was making progress in DC with Bush administration and in the Senate, that acid rain was the one issue our members cared most deeply about, and that—rightly or wrongly—the public did not care about global warming.

This set off a testy debate between Frances and Sarah, who was just as tough, articulate, and determined. Neither persuaded the other, and, finally, Frances shrugged, said her goodbyes, and left with her entourage in tow.

I thought Frances's visit would mark the end of her effort to sway our position. I was wrong.

Frances summered at Long Lake in the Adirondack Park, where her neighbors included not only her longtime friend Sigourney Weaver but also David Skovron, the Council's new board chairman. A few months after the failed reconciliation attempt at our office, David was on a cocktail cruise of the lake with Frances and the conversation turned to the simmering conflict. David soon offered to accompany me to the New York City office of NRDC to meet with Frances and her staff, "to hear what they had to say."

The morning of the meeting, David cautioned me to be nice, but also assured me that whatever happened, the Council would make no decisions on the spot.

John Ernst, the immediate past board chair of the Council, joined us and I found that encouraging. I liked and respected Ernst and his ability to appreciate different points of view. I found John and his wife, Margot, to just be good people, and they were among my favorites at the Council. They hosted a highly successful cocktail party every year for potential high-end donors in their apartment overlooking the United Nations Plaza in New York City, with a guest of honor that over the years included a governor, several state attorneys general, and many prominent legislators. John Ernst also allowed me to lead state legislators and staffers on tours of Elk Lake, their 12,000-acre private forest preserve in the Adirondack Park.

I was unaware that Frances had invited Christopher J. "Kim" Elliman, another past Council board chairman. A Rockefeller cousin, he owned Ampersand Park, a 3,800-acre Adirondack Park in-holding in the High Peaks Wilderness Area. Kim was now president of a land acquisition and conservation organization, the Open Space Institute, which commanded great respect and influence in the environmental community, due in part to its massive endowment from the founders of *Reader's Digest* and aggressive efforts to protect special landscapes. While I knew Kim as a well-respected adviser to my board, a good listener, and an articulate advocate, I also knew he was a good friend of Frances.

Frances had also asked David J. Hawkins, a longtime NRDC attorney who had taken charge of its climate change campaign, up from their Washington office. David was a well-respected figure in the environmental community and in the capital. David had taken the lead in 1993, when the Adirondack Council and NRDC had sued the EPA over its regulations and its failure to implement the 1990 Clean Air Act amendments in a timely fashion. I learned a lot working with him.

I had been warned the day before by our chairman that David might attend the meeting. Out of respect for Hawkins's reputation, I had boned up on my facts and arguments. It was a good thing, too.

Surreally, the meeting evolved into a polite debate between David and me. The other attendees listened and evaluated the discussion, lobbing an occasional question at one of us.

David's arguments were straightforward. It would be better for the environment to simply fully implement the Clean Air Act than to enact Bush's Clear Skies plan, he said, because climate change dwarfed any other environmental issue in importance and must be addressed immediately with 4P legislation. He had to stop at that point and explain to some around the table that the term *climate change*, just coming into wider use, was equivalent to global warming. NRDC had made a political and tactical decision to use the new term, he said, because opponents were jumping on the words *global warming* to confuse the public every time there was a severe cold snap or major snowstorm. He added that the administration would try to insert in any change to the Clean Air Act, retroactive protection for utilities that were known to have already violated the terms of the Act.

I responded that while the Council was actively opposing the administration's attempt to protect lawbreaking utilities, Bush's initiative offered the best chance to make quick and significant progress on the serious problem of acid rain. Full implementation of the Clean Air Act would be great, but that argument was a red herring. There had been ten years of litigation on the Clean Air Act, with no end in sight. The cap-and-trade program adopted in 1990 to address acid rain worked and worked well. Given what we have recently learned of the severity of the acid rain problem in the Adirondacks, we need to lower the cap on power plant emissions. Now.

There was no doubt in my mind, I added, that climate change was real and that human-made emissions were accelerating the problem. But the public was not yet convinced, and without a public consensus the White House and Congress would not act. I pointed out that the unanimous nonbinding vote in the US Senate, 95 to 0, in opposition to the anticipated signing of the Kyoto Protocol on greenhouse emissions by the Clinton administration was some good evidence of that. That was the political reality on the ground, I said.

I offered that while modest, there will be ancillary benefits on climate change from the reduction in the emissions of acid rain precursors from power plants. Installation of new equipment or the shutting down of coal-fired plants will not only reduce heat-trapping nitrogen emissions, but also reduce carbon dioxide emissions of 2–10 percent from those sources. Protecting our forests from further harm preserves their function in sequestering carbon as well.

I also pointed out that the very need to introduce a new name to describe the problem was further evidence that the issue was not politically ripe. If environmentalists take an all-or-nothing stance on a four-pollutant approach, I suggested, we risk ending up with nothing.

We argued to a standstill, and the meeting ended politely. After a quick postgame analysis with my board members on the sidewalk, I left for home confident that our board of directors would continue to support our approach to fighting acid rain.

Frances Beinecke ultimately ended NRDC's membership in the Adirondack Council. I interpreted this as a face-saving gesture and thought that the two of us would soon kiss and make up. I was wrong.

LOONY TUNES

It was August 2002 and I was on vacation with my family near Raquette Lake in the Adirondack Park, but I could not relax. We were in the middle of planning for the first ever conference on the future impacts of climate change on the natural resources of the Adirondack Park. That event was cosponsored with the Wildlife Conservation Society and to be held at nearby Great Camp Sagamore. That was going well. We had good speakers lined up including a keynote by climate change activist and author of *The End of Nature*, Bill McKibben.

On the acid rain front, we had the support of the president of the United States, and still it seemed we were making little progress in Congress. It bothered me. With no cell phone coverage, I drove twelve miles a day to get the *New York Times* (yesterday's news) and the *New York Post* (today's news), so I would not be cut off from events.

I tried to distract myself by visiting the gift shop at Great Camp Sagamore, a national historic landmark. In the early twentieth century, the complex of elaborate wooden buildings in the Adirondacks was the summer home of the Alfred Vanderbilt family. Now it was managed by a nonprofit organization as a retreat and conference center.

The gift shop had a new plush toy. It was a replica of the loon, which for many, including my own organization, was the very symbol of the Adirondack Mountains. Hearing the lonesome call of the loon at night was a singular and spine-tingling experience. (See figure 11.17.)

Squeeze the body, and the Chinese-made loon toy emitted an amazingly realistic loon call—twice. The Cornell Lab of Ornithology had even certified the call. I bought two, one as a gift for my wife Mollie, and the other just to have in my office.

Sitting on the beach that afternoon, I thought back to the session in Maine with David Greenwood and how the Council had continued brainstorming for years about how the loon could be used in our campaign against acid rain. We continued to warn that the acid was leaching mercury

Figure 11.17. Toy loon. *Source*: author's own material.

from the soil into Adirondack lake waters, and that the mercury in its more toxic form of methylmercury was accumulating in fish and endangering the loons that ate them.

The Council had helped secure funding for the state Department of Health to study the mercury in fish populations. Every year, the agency warned that more lakes in the Adirondacks had dangerously contaminated fish populations, and warned the public not to eat some species and to eat much less of others. But the charismatic loon was still gaining more attention than the threat of acid rain to people.

I brought the toy loon into the office on my first day back. "How can we use this?" I asked my colleagues.

The answer came moments later, from an unexpected source. The phone rang. Someone on the staff of the US Senate Committee on Environment and Public Works was calling. Would we like to testify on possible amendments to the Clean Air Act?

Of course we would. And we realized that our new loon was the perfect way to attract wide attention to our issue on a national stage. How do we piggyback a message on the back of the loon? Why on the back of the loon, of course!

The staff in our main office came up with a way to tie a short message around the toy loon. It called for more emission controls to end acid rain and protect the loons. A statistically invalid survey of friends and strangers showed that people not only read the message on the loon, they read it *aloud.*

Now we needed to get 300 toy loons to distribute on Capitol Hill. The then-director of Great Camp Sagamore, Beverly Bridger, said the order was a "hoot" (which is actually one of the loon's four distinct calls). She placed the order and we bought them from the camp.

In a foray to Washington before our scheduled hearing, we met with Senator Chuck Schumer's staff and explained our plan. Chuck's staffers agreed to call down to security if we needed help getting into the Hart Senate Office Building, where their offices were located. From there, we could access the other Senate buildings through underground passages. In appreciation, we left the first of our loon toys for the senator.

Schumer's people came to regret their cooperation. They later told me that Chuck played his loon's call for almost every visitor to his private office. They heard it several times a day for weeks. It was worse, they said, than his plaque with the singing Big Mouth Billy Bass.

On the House side, we met with Robert G. Taub, chief of staff to Representative John McHugh, whose New York district was among the worst affected by acid rain.

Taub said that whatever we were hearing from Schumer's aides about the Senate side, getting our loons into the House office buildings was going to be a problem. It was the post-9/11 era, and he said security guards would never let someone enter with a bag of toys. "They are too skittish now about security. The guards will think it is some kind of diversion," Taub warned.

"So we can't get them into the building?" I asked.

"*You* can't," he replied. "I'll just put them in my trunk, drive them into the garage, and have them waiting here for you. From there, you know, you can just stay underground, avoiding the security checkpoints and you can get to all three office buildings."

The night before our scheduled testimony, our staff gathered in my hotel room to prepare the nearly 300 loons for distribution. We never really thought about the noise. Every loon needed a battery. When the battery was inserted, each loon issued its call—twice.

It took hours. Despite our fears, there were no complaints from the hotel's front desk. But it drove us all nuts.

We met Taub and transferred two large bags of loons to his car. As we packed the loons into his trunk, they squeezed together and began calling. We had visions of gun-toting guards cautiously approaching the car emitting strange sounds. But he encountered no problems, and neither did we after the handoff, as we made the rounds of House offices.

The Senate was another story. Our staffers carried the loons in large, clear plastic bags so the security guards at the Hart building could see them. Occasionally, one would sound off.

As Taub had predicted, the guards believed we were either creating a diversion to smuggle other people into the building or were planning a loud public demonstration. Not on their watch. They detained the loons and our staffers until one of Schumer's aides arrived with Senate ID to take responsibility for us.

I had planned to end my testimony at the Senate hearing, which repeatedly mentioned the plight of the loon, by squeezing one of the birds and having the whole room swoon to their plaintive calls. At the last minute, Andy Wheeler, aide to Senator Inhofe, the panel's chairman, asked me not to; so the loon stayed in my briefcase. I was annoyed to learn later that Andy, no doubt thinking only of his own career, had made the decision himself. The chairman, learning about it after the fact, told me that he was disappointed the loon had been silenced and said it would have been good theater. He was right.

Later, we entered the office of every single senator, holding a toy loon aloft and asking that it be given directly to the senator. It helped to squeeze the loon at that moment. ("No, it is not a duck. It is a loon.") Every staff member in the room stopped what he or she was doing to read the lobbying message attached to the loon's neck—almost always aloud. And, to our distinct pleasure, the staffers pulled many a legislative director or senior aide out of his or her office to meet us, telling them, "You've got to come out and see this!" Most of those senior people would never have given us a meeting. Now we were together chatting about our issue.

As a bonus, I won the hearts of seemingly every Senate staffer who hailed from loon-loving Minnesota, and who had seen the internal broadcast of my testimony. I heard "Minn-a-SOH-tah" accents at office after Senate office we visited that afternoon. They were familiar because my wife's family came from the iron-mining region near Chisholm, Minnesota, and I had gotten used to Mollie and her relatives responding to a question with "Yeah, no" or "You betcha."

Our Adirondack loon handout was undeniably a big success. Many members of Congress kept the loons on their desks, while others gave them away to staffers, who reportedly squabbled over who should get them. Most important, we picked up new cosponsors for our acid rain bill in both the Senate and the House.

2003: BUSH'S PROMISE

My cell phone rang. It was Dana Perino, associate director of communications for the Council on Environmental Quality, one of the persons I made a point of meeting with whenever I was in Washington.

When I had first started meeting with the CEQ in the Bush White House, Dana had clearly been the new person in the room and rarely spoke. But she quickly mastered the CEQ's subject matter and in a very short period of time became the administration's main spokesperson on environmental issues. In fact, as an eager young Republican in Washington, she was always in tune with the administration's message on any topic. By virtue of both her talent and the untimely departure of White House press secretary Tony Snow for colon cancer treatment, Dana became press secretary in Bush's final year in office.

Now she was on my cell phone saying, "Hi, Bernard. Want to run something past you. What if POTUS says the Adirondack Council supports this initiative?"

"Who's POTUS?"

"POTUS, you know. President of the United States."

I asked her to hold on. Here I was, sitting in the back of a packed Lincoln Town Car heading down from the Baltimore airport to a White House event, and an aide is asking me to help tailor the public remarks of the president of the United States. Not bad for a blue-collar boy from Upstate New York.

I savored the moment for a second or two and then got back on the phone.

"Dana, as you know, we support the pollution cuts and cap-and-trade approach to sulfur and nitrogen controls in the Clear Skies legislation, but we don't support the bill as drafted."

"Can he say the Adirondack Council 'supports our approach' to solving the acid rain problem?"

"Okay, that would work," I replied. "See you in a little while."

I didn't blame the White House for trying, but the Clear Skies Initiative, which the president had announced in February 2002 and again on Earth Day in the Adirondacks, had morphed into legislation that was less than perfect.

After the congressional staff and industry lobbyists had gotten a crack at it, the Clear Skies Initiative that had been introduced in Congress by the Republican leadership had the same name but some very different goals from those that Bush had described.

The bill in Congress would reduce sulfur and nitrogen emissions to solve the acid rain problem as we had hoped, but it pushed back the dates for implementation, and its provision addressing mercury emissions could only be described as lame. Regrettably, the sponsors had also added provisions that threatened to undermine federal lawsuits against polluting Midwestern utilities filed by several downwind states suffering damage, including New York.

In the parlance of lobbyists on the Hill, the president's bill was 3P (three pollutants: sulfur dioxide, nitrogen oxides, and mercury) and not 4P (including carbon dioxide).

While it was our growing political sense that only a 2P bill (no mercury) had any chance in Congress in the near future, most of the environmental community would oppose the administration's bill right out of the gate since it did nothing to address climate change.

That would put the Adirondack Council in the middle. That is normally a good place to be politically, if you want to get something done. But there was pressure building steadily on the Council from both the left and the right.

We had been prepared to catch heat from other groups for supporting anything that George W. Bush proposed on the environment. But the add-ons to Bush's original Clear Skies proposal in the Senate posed a very serious problem for the Council. Walking the fine line between endorsing the good ideas and rejecting the bad ones without alienating congressional sponsors was a constant challenge. Our board of directors wanted to continue the momentum of the president's Earth Day announcement, but not at the cost of endorsing rollbacks in other clean-air regulations.

Meanwhile, our staff tried to keep the momentum going. We urged the White House to include a request to stop acid rain in the Bush's second State of the Union message in 2003. Much to our pleasure, the president did mention the need to cut sulfur and nitrogen pollution in his address to Congress.

We also tried to address the "red herring" being advanced by some national groups that the President's Clear Skies proposal would rollback limits on the pollutants that contribute to acid rain, when compared to the full implementation of the existing Clean Air Act.

In fact, with some variations in timing, *all* of the clean-air proposals introduced in Congress, addressing either two or four pollutants, allowed for more of the nitrogen and sulfur dioxide emissions that contribute to acid rain than the Clean Air Act would, if it ever became fully implemented. Even the bills introduced by clean-air advocates Senator Jeffords of Vermont and Senator Carper of Delaware would not match the theoretical cuts in acid rain emissions by full implementation of the Clean Air Act.

We ended up producing our own chart comparing the provisions on acid rain in each proposal and distributing it to hundreds of organizations up and down the East Coast. It helped "clear the air" and helped brace us against the tide of misinformation.

Now in September 2003, we were heading to the White House, intending to jump-start the Council's efforts to win over the administration on the need to return to Bush's original Clear Skies plan, or something very similar. Now that we had the president's ear, we needed to use every opportunity to send that message.

Various stakeholders had been invited to meet inside the White House with the president, including our executive director, after which Bush would deliver a speech in the East Garden to express his desire for action by Congress that year.

I joined several of my board members at the White House gate on that typically warm and humid summer day. It was my first time inside the building, and we were ushered through a series of hallways, guided at each turn by members of the military in dress uniforms. We were eventually led out into the East Garden.

Chairs had been set out for the guests. We greeted each other and then sat down. The men in our suit coats. In the full sun. Meanwhile, the Adirondack Council's executive director, Brian L. Houseal, was waiting for Bush inside the air-conditioned Blue Room.

I sat alone in the sun with my thoughts. My shirt was soaked with sweat, but I did not care. I had gotten our executive director a face-to-face meeting with the president of the United States. I fondly recalled brashly plotting with my colleagues to involve the president in our cause. We had done well.

To the relief of those assembled, water and soft drinks were eventually served under a canopy nearby. I crowded together in the shade with the others, now with our coats off, as we awaited the arrival of the president.

Brian would tell me later that he found George Bush to be a likable guy. At one point, he said, he had confided to the president that the Adirondack Council was taking a lot of abuse from our fellow environmentalists. Brian said Bush replied, "*You're* getting abuse? Tell me about it."

Brian told me he asked Bush as they left the meeting whether the administration intended to also address climate change. "Next term," he answered.

In time, the guests in the garden were informed that the president was on his way, and Brian and others proceeded to take prime seats in the front. The coats went back on.

The podium was set up so that the president could look directly into the assembled television cameras. The audience was actually behind him. He looked relaxed, although he stumbled a few times reading his prepared speech. Most importantly, Bush delivered the language I had discussed with Dana Perino just as promised. "The Adirondack Council is here," he said. "They support the approach." I relaxed. Despite Bush's nudge, it was growing increasingly apparent that the additional baggage the Senate had added to the Clear Skies legislation had weighed down the bill in committee.

One big problem was a provision aimed at bailing out utilities. Power companies across the country had upgraded their equipment and increased electricity production without adding new pollution controls, as required by federal law. Attorneys general in New York and other states were vigorously pursuing cases against those companies, with great success. So the Republican leadership in Congress had inserted an amnesty provision, perhaps hoping it would not be noticed or that it could later be used as a bargaining chip in negotiating pollution levels. Whatever their strategy, the provision was doomed.

The environmental community did not take long to flag this provision as unacceptable, and newspapers across the country were amply covering the state lawsuits. Members of Congress were increasingly on the defensive about the notion of bailing out lawbreaking polluters.

The anemic mercury provisions of the Clear Skies bill were also being picked apart. The EPA had proposed trading mercury emissions between locations, a plan similar to the cap-and-trade program for sulfur and nitrogen. But mercury is toxic. Anything other than cuts in emissions at every site was not going to be accepted by public health professionals and biologists or by the voters.

Meanwhile, the national environmental groups were continuing to pound Democratic and Republican lawmakers alike for their failure to add carbon dioxide limits to the bill to address climate change.

Those groups had briefly glimpsed a glimmer of hope on carbon dioxide. For sixteen months starting in June 2001, Democrats had held a Senate majority, and in that period the Senate Environment and Public Works Committee narrowly approved the Clean Power Act, introduced by Senator Jeffords, which placed new limits on the emissions of carbon dioxide as well as mercury and oxides of sulfur and nitrogen.

Senator Hillary Rodham Clinton, at our request, had amended the bill during the committee mark-up session, where members agree on a bill's language before a final vote. The Clinton amendment gave the EPA the authority to monitor and even overturn trades of pollution credits if it was found that sensitive receptor areas, like the Adirondacks were being adversely affected. It was what the Council had previously requested of the EPA but had failed to get the EPA to include in the regulations implementing the Clean Air Act amendments of 1990.

The Adirondack Council strongly supported that bill. But soon afterward, Republicans regained a Senate majority and the Clean Power Act withered on the vine.

A year later, Senate Republicans on the environment panel were refusing to budge from their increasingly unpopular version of Clear Skies. We had hopes that the poor publicity and rapidly expanding scope of the lawsuits would convince the Senate leadership to strip the offending get-out-of-jail-free provision for polluters out of their proposal. But to our chagrin, the staff and leadership in the committee would not budge from the bill as drafted.

But it was also clear that the moderate Republicans in the Senate and on the Committee on the Environment and Public Works were now uncomfortable. Chairman Inhofe and subcommittee chairman Voinovich were having problems getting the necessary votes to move the bill out of committee. The bill looked like it was headed for oblivion, taking the acid rain limits for which we had fought for a decade down with it.

Then the new acid rain regulations in New York went into effect. And the EPA released a report, demanded by members of Congress from both sides of the aisle, showing that all the major air-quality bills introduced in Congress would address the chronic acidification of lakes in New York state. Then Christie Whitman resigned.

Christine Todd Whitman, administrator of the federal Environmental Protection Agency, was strongly in favor of the Bush administration's efforts to address global warming, a goal President Bush noted when he announced his Clear Skies Initiative to control acid rain early in his first term. But apparently, Whitman was among the last in the administration to know that Bush, without her input, had backed away from any action on the issue. She resigned in June 2003 as gracefully as she could, only revealing in a 2007 interview that she had left because Vice President Dick Cheney had insisted on easing air-pollution controls at power plants.

Whitman's resignation left the president with the need to nominate a new EPA administrator.

That summer, John Sheehan got a call from a reporter for an environmental news service. It seemed that a list of possible EPA nominees was circulating in Washington—and my name was on it. Did the Adirondack Council have any comment? John rushed into my office and told me what was up.

"Really?" I asked. "That's a hoot. Tell him not to waste his time."

"No, let's play along," John said. "Just tell him you can't talk about it. It will be fun."

I picked up the phone and proceeded to evade the reporter's questions.

As John perhaps knew, but I did not even suspect, that was only the first inquiry. The hounds of the media had been unleashed. Over the next few days, the calls poured in.

I got pretty good at being evasive.

"Have you had any private conversations with the president?" a reporter would ask.

"If I did, would I be telling you?'

"If you were asked to serve by the president, would you serve?"

"I think anyone who is asked to serve his country by the president of the United States has an obligation to seriously consider the request." (I really meant that.)

And so on. John would often sit in my office as I took the calls, chuckling as I came up with more and more witty responses. But the situation turned more serious when Tim Burke, our executive director, asked me weeks later if I was really pursuing the position. It was then that I realized I had never mentioned it to him.

Alarmed, I reassured him. "It is not real, Tim. No one in the administration has talked to me at all. Either the Bush administration floated my name so that there would be one true environmentalist on the list, or one of the national environmental groups had someone suggest me as a clever way of harming our reputation with Democrats."

It was not until I heard myself offering these explanations to Tim that the truth of what I was saying registered in my own mind. Under either theory, playing my teasing game with the reporters was just helping someone's damned plot along.

My doubts were confirmed when on a trip to Washington I met with Dana Perino and her colleagues at the White House's Council on Environmental Quality. I intentionally made a reference to the circulating list of EPA candidates to see how they would respond. The White House officials looked at each other with a comical expression, their cheeks sucked in as if they had swallowed a passing bird. I wasn't sure how to interpret that, but it didn't make me feel good.

While I enjoyed the attention that the rumor brought me the sense that this crazy adventure was getting out of hand became ever more evident. At a conference, local Republican officials of Adirondack Park towns lifted their glasses to me in a humorous toast. George Canon, supervisor of the Town of Newcomb, delighted his companions by asking me if I would hire him as my Washington chauffeur.

Soon, I stopped volunteering any remarks on the situation, and if anyone asked me about it, I told them the truth. But the rumor had taken on a life of its own. Not only was it no longer fun, the albatross that this story had become was getting heavier and heavier. Way too many people were convinced that I really was campaigning for the EPA job. So *that* was why Melewski was so cozy with President Bush on the acid rain issue, some said. The journalist and environmental activist Bill McKibben wrote an article for the popular magazine *Adirondack Life* in which he held up my obvious quest for the position (he didn't name me) as an example of the perils of compromise with those in power. Apparently, no one told McKibben it was a joke.

Soon thereafter, another lobbyist, an active Democrat who I considered politically savvy, confronted me. "You're kidding yourself! You don't have a chance!" he declared. I told John that our playacting was finished, but I knew that I had pulled the plug far too late.

I was reminded of a saying I learned while growing up in then-rural Halfmoon, New York: "Never piss into the wind."

And then, a total surprise.

We were invited by the Council on Environmental Quality to a meeting in DC. We were not told of the purpose of the meeting. There for the first time, Chairman James L. Connaughton was in attendance. He told us that the president was serious about keeping his Earth Day promise to New Yorkers to end acid rain. The EPA would begin developing regulations that would achieve the very cuts in emissions that we had first proposed to David Anderson at CEQ. If Congress failed to act on acid rain, Connaughton said, the EPA would go forward with the regulations.

The EPA's proposed Clean Air Interstate Rule contained nearly identical emission cuts to those in a bill then sponsored by New York Republicans in the House whose districts included parts of the Adirondack Park. The legislators, John McHugh and John Sweeney, together with Sherry Boehlert, had dubbed themselves New York's "Acid Rain Team." The rule would also impose pollution reductions sooner than had been proposed in the Clear Skies legislation.

The EPA made its public announcement of the Clean Air Interstate Rule (CAIR) in December 2003, and the draft rule was published in the Federal Register the next month.

The Adirondack Council traveled to public hearings on the proposed rule in March 2004 in Illinois, Pennsylvania, North Carolina, and Virginia. We closely coordinated with two other highly motivated nonprofit groups, the National Trust for Historic Preservation and Trout Unlimited, on testimony for the hearings and turning out local attendees.

In August, EPA administrator Michael O. Leavitt accepted the invitation of the Adirondack Council to speak at a conference at Paul Smith's College in the Adirondack Park. There, Leavitt declared his intention to finalize CAIR by the end of the year.

In fact, the final rule was soon to be delayed by three months. Senate Republicans had asked the White House for one more chance to take action on the Clear Skies bill.

In February 2005, the Council was once again at the witness table before the Senate Environment and Public Works Committee. In his testimony, Brian Houseal, our then executive director, told the committee: "Today, we are here to make three requests as you consider new legislation in order to help solve the acid rain problem. First, action to stop acid rain must be taken this year. Second, it must be as good as or better than the Environmental Protection Agency's Clean Air Interstate Rule. Finally, no individual state's current enforcement mechanisms should be eroded."

On the eve of possible action by the committee, the Council wanted to make clear that the timelines for pollution cuts were too long and that the language in the bill that would interfere with enforcement of past violations of the Clean Air Act by utilities was unacceptable. Houseal also reminded the senators that the issue of acid rain controls was more than ripe for action, and that a decade ago, Senator Moynihan had introduced a bill virtually identical to CAIR. He insisted that a lack of consensus in the committee on how to address climate change should not be used as an excuse for failing to act on acid rain.

One month later, the committee met in a final attempt to mark up the bill's final language. In the decisive vote, it deadlocked. The bill would not move forward.

The next day, the EPA finalized the Clean Air Interstate Rule. George W. Bush had kept his promise.

SO THEN WHAT HAPPENED?

The mere proposal of the Clean Air Interstate Rule by the administration of President George W. Bush had an instantaneous impact. The volume of pollutants from out-of-state sources falling on the Adirondack Park started to decline as utilities started to install antipollution equipment or close older plants in order to drop their emissions below their allocation and collect pollution credits to sell in the emerging emission credits trading market. The price of the allowances had soared, making the installation of pollution control devices even more attractive. The EPA reported that power plant sulfur dioxide emissions would fall below the total allowed under the federal cap for the first time and years ahead of schedule.

In New York, the attorney general and the governor took additional steps to force several in-state power plants to curb their contributions to the acid rain problem.

But the continued existence of the acid rain rule remained in legal limbo for almost another decade. Lawsuits brought by power companies and some states worked its way through the federal court system for years. In 2008, the US Court of Appeals for the District of Columbia Circuit allowed CAIR to stay in place, but ordered the US Environmental Protection Agency to revise the rule's underlying analysis. The EPA ultimately developed a similar rule, the Cross-State Air Pollution Rule. In August 2012, the same court vacated that rule as well. But on appeal, on April 29, 2014, the US Supreme Court reinstated the EPA effort. The NRDC, Sierra Club and the American Lung Association, among other national groups, supported the rule throughout the court battles, and CAIR ultimately survived.

While the reduction in acid deposition will benefit the waters, forest, and wildlife of the Adirondacks, it will take a long time to recover. For a definitive scientific and environmental history of acid deposition in the Adirondacks, the reader should consider the publication *Acid Rain in the Adirondacks: An Environmental History*.[2]

Meanwhile, Congress, despite near unanimous worldwide scientific consensus on the need for action, has failed to take any action on climate change, and the Executive Branch has adopted conflicting positions under successive administrations. In 2015, President Barack Obama committed the United States to the United Nations–sponsored Paris Agreement, which has been accepted by most nations in the world. The Paris Agreement required signatories to determine the steps they must take to mitigate global warming. The same year, the Obama administration released the Clean Power Plan, a set of regulations to reduce carbon dioxide emissions from power plants. Various states, coal-mining companies, and utilities have twice challenged those regulations. The first challenge was turned back by the US Supreme Court, which confirmed that the EPA had legal authority under the Clean Air Act to issue the regulations. The second challenge contended that even if the EPA possessed the authority to control carbon dioxide emissions, the EPA's regulations were improperly formulated. That lawsuit remained at the federal appeals court until then-newly elected President Donald Trump announced the United States' intention to withdraw from the Paris Agreement, and his EPA administrator, Scott Pruitt, initiated the formal process to withdraw the Clean Power Plan regulations in their entirety. After the one-year notice period, the Trump administration completed the withdrawal from the Paris Agreement in November of 2020. Newly elected President Joe Biden rejoined the Paris Agreement on behalf of the United States in 2021.

CHAPTER 12

THE ART OF LOBBYING

My lobbying career was unique. I worked solely on environmental issues for environmental and conservation groups—in other words, I was a classic "tree hugger.

I came to lobbying gradually. After earning a BA in political science from Siena College and spending a semester as an intern in the state Senate, I graduated from Syracuse University College of Law in 1976. In my senior year there, I was persuaded by a fellow law student to join him and another classmate in a new clinical program on the environment. Our faculty adviser, Professor Richard Goldsmith, an environmental attorney in the early days of that developing field, was a wonderful mentor and advocate. The three of us in the Environmental Law clinic represented the Sierra Club, on draft rules the state had prepared to govern the environmental review of major projects being proposed for the state. I also testified before a state legislative committee on a separate issue as part of my legislative seminar.

After graduating and working for the Legal Aid Society of Albuquerque in New Mexico, I joined the New York Public Interest Research Group (NYPIRG) in 1978, as its Syracuse-based regional director. While there, I learned lobbying techniques that would prove very useful.

NYPIRG had received a federal grant to investigate allegations that private insurance companies were systematically withdrawing property coverage in some of the state's urban communities. I was chosen to manage NYPIRG's statewide research project on property insurance redlining.

This introduced me to one of the most cherished techniques in the advocacy world: thoroughly researching an issue that needs reform, publishing the results, and releasing the report (using a catchy title) to the media. With the media coverage in hand, we would visit the politicians or bureaucrats who could produce the change we were seeking and explain why reform was needed.

Although our research produced no smoking guns, it did lead to private discussions with the chief executive officers of every major insurance company in the country, presentations before the National Association of Insurance Commissioners, coverage by the nationally syndicated columnist Jack Anderson, and meetings with legislators, including members of what was then the New York State Black and Puerto Rican Legislative Caucus. Legislation that prohibited property insurance redlining in New York was adopted that year, and the National Association of Insurance Commissioners proposed similar model legislation for the benefit of its members.

This early success in producing even a modest change in the law through good research and informed policy recommendations intoxicated me and I never looked back.

A move to Albany to join my future wife would land me, with the help of my college mentor, a position on the legislative staff of a state senator. In only a few months, a notice in the *Legislative Gazette* led to in my hiring as the next executive director of the Environmental Planning Lobby, a statewide environmental advocacy organization. It did not hurt that the chairman of the search committee, Robert Kafin, had been a law partner of another of my former professors at Syracuse Law, Neil Needleman. When I was hired in 1978, I was a staff of one and the only full-time environmental lobbyist at the New York state legislature.

During the decades that followed, I lobbied on most of the major environmental issues facing the state, including the two campaigns to protect the Adirondack Park.

In waging these battles, I learned that a bundle of cash isn't the only tool that can change minds. Even a low-budget group can push big policy changes forward by providing the right information to the right person at the right time. Political savvy is also vital, because any official will be keenly interested in how your idea can provide them with a boost in the next election. The way I looked at it, I needed to find a way to make my goal, their goal.

I also learned a lot about how different advocacy groups can work together on a common cause to amplify their influence—and what happens when allies work at cross purposes.

With environmental lobbying, when everything goes right, the rewards are substantial: not just personal satisfaction, but better health and recreation for everyone.

There is a public stereotype of lobbyists: They wield lavish expense accounts to wine and dine legislators at expensive restaurants; they provide travel on corporate jets; and they arrange for large campaign contributions. In return, they get new laws or contracts that repay their investment handsomely. That notion is, by and large, true.

But not when you lobby for a nonprofit environmental group.

The organizations for which I worked had small budgets, and even the larger ones ran as lean machines. Donations and grants went to pay staff and overhead. Their board members were typically unpaid, serving as directors because they care about the cause—and because their backgrounds in the law, science, or other professions give them access to individuals or foundations that might support the organization financially.

The Adirondack Council, for example, did not, and does not, make campaign contributions or endorse candidates, nor does it obtain grants from government. But it did recognize the importance of having an in-house lobbyist working at the state Capitol (me) who was granted considerable leeway to speak for the organization and make commitments. That was a big factor in successfully influencing policy.

As a Capitol lobbyist, I had no real entertainment or expense budget, though my fellow Council staffers and I might take an elected member or staffer out for a beer. I shared an office with three or four other staff and, acting as a team, we gave out calendars every year featuring beautiful photos of Adirondack Park landscapes. Those were very popular. If we were really flush, we'd sponsor a small reception for legislators and staff providing food, beer, and maybe even music by a featured North Country musician.

Without open wallets to get the attention of legislators, we turned to other tools. One was to organize public opinion. We praised and condemned lawmakers' actions in statements released to the press. We circulated petitions, delivered them to the Capitol, and released them to the press. We rallied our members with "action alerts" to call or write their representatives at critical times. We joined with allied groups to stage "lobby days," where hundreds of supporters would descend on the Capitol to hear speeches and then go door-to-legislator's-door to plead our case.

Another tool was good old-fashioned customer service. At the Adirondack Council, we trained everyone to acquire and share accurate information on a wide range of issues with others in the Capitol community, in order to establish ourselves as a source that could be relied on. Some lobbyists had no compunctions about making stuff up to support their cause. We also made it a high priority to provide requested information as soon as possible. Many lobbyists tended to do nothing in hope that they would not be asked again.

But mostly we dealt heavily in one of the legislature's most valuable currencies: inside dope. A key bit of news—say, an imminent announcement by the governor involving a legislator's district—had real value and might earn you a "chit," meaning that the other party felt obligated to provide a similar favor in the future.

One corporate lobbyist in Albany drove this barter system to new heights.

He would sidle up to me and say, "Bernie, I thought Senator X supported you guys."

"He does!" I would reply.

"Then why is he introducing a bill that you won't like?"

It took me most of a legislative session to learn this lobbyist's secret. He was wining and dining not the members or their senior staffers, but the clerk of the Assembly—the person responsible for entering draft bills into the computer system for printing. The clerk was one of the first to know when bills would be introduced and which committees would consider them. This lobbyist's largesse won him a wealth of information to use himself, and to amass chits from others throughout the Capitol.

An odd thing about representing a nonprofit group is that valuable information would sometimes fall into our lap. Business lobbyists would describe their plans, assuming we wouldn't really care because there was no financial advantage to be gained. Ah, but someone always cares! Unless we had promised confidentiality, we spent that information to earn our own chits.

Happily, green groups have one informational tool that business lobbyists cannot match—ready access to news reporters, who often had a sympathetic view of environmental issues and were receptive to many of the story ideas we peddled virtually every day.

The power of press clippings has long been a fact of life at the Capitol. Although the news business has largely shifted online, in the 1990s policy makers still had their staff collect news stories and editorials from newspapers around the state. Everyone from the governor's staff to the lowliest legislative interns read "the clips" every day.

To have a positive article or editorial about our current issue appear in the right newspaper at the right time helped grease the wheels. Sponsors of bills we backed were encouraged and found it easier to attract support. Of course, the occasional negative story would do just the opposite.

A close relative to a negative story, and much more appealing to me as a lobbying tool, was the political cartoon. A single well-done political cartoon can carry a message that resonates with a broad audience. It is especially effective as satire.

The very definition of *satire* in the *Oxford English Dictionary* says it all: "The use of humor, irony, exaggeration, or ridicule to expose and criticize people's stupidity or vices, particularly in the context of contemporary politics and other topical issues."

We made sure to circulate political cartoons that we came upon that favored our point of view. Why we even commissioned a few. A picture is worth a thousand words.

Since the media needed news as much as we needed publicity, we had to learn how to tailor our approach to generate the right kind of attention. The keys for our success were the coordination of our lobbying activity and our communication outreach.

From our office near the New York State Capitol in Albany, we reviewed and commented on any legislation that might affect the Adirondacks. It was important work. Every year, some group or legislator would make an effort to roll back protections for the Park. Even well-intentioned ideas often had the potential to create unforeseen damage. Fortunately, it is easier to kill a bill in the state legislature by bottling it up in a committee than it is to pass anything. We killed a lot of bad bills.

State agencies generated some of the best and some of the worst ideas every year. We were a regular and visible presence at the agencies. I worked with our professional staff both in Albany and in our main office in Elizabethtown to monitor state permits and comment on any new regulations. We also paid close attention to activities at the Adirondack Park Agency, which controlled most development of public and private lands inside the Park. We commented on many of the projects submitted to the agency for approval, and occasionally would participate in formal adjudicatory hearings about those that may have had significant environmental impacts.

Developing friendly contacts with staff was essential, and we carefully maintained our own stable of insider leakers and blabbers in state agencies. It was our early warning system.

The other key activity was our communications capability.

It was especially critical to educate and inform the media. When I was named acting executive director in my first year at the Council, I used my newfound temporary authority to increase our efficiency, reorganizing our staff to give each professional naturalist and fundraiser in Elizabethtown a dedicated administrative assistant. But I thought it was even more important to have a full-time communications director. If something went wrong, you wanted to have plausible deniability and an opportunity to correct a gaffe. Separation between the executive director and the media liaison at those moments was important. The board of directors agreed with me, and we started interviewing potential candidates for the position.

It was the fall of 1990, and I had one last interview to conduct. It was with John Sheehan, managing editor of the *Malone Telegram* in Malone, New York. I had spoken to him over the phone and felt that he deserved a personal interview.

We arranged to have dinner at the Deer's Head Inn in Elizabethtown, just down the street from our main office. A heavy snowstorm made us both an hour late, but it was worth the trip.

I soon realized that John was an excellent candidate. He was a quick study, had a voice that was perfect for radio, could obviously write well, and possessed a detailed knowledge of the Adirondack Park. When he said he was originally from Troy, New York, I mentioned that I spent several years in Troy as a college student.

He asked me where I had lived. I told him that a bunch of guys from the neighboring university, Rensselaer Polytechnic Institute, and I had gotten a great deal on a former bordello on Fourteenth Street. John said he had grown up around the corner.

I quickly realized that he was none other than "Little Johnny," one of the neighborhood kids.

John asked, "Were you in the house with the strange doorbell?"

Bruce, an electrical engineering student who lived with us, had wired speakers to play a recorded message whenever someone rang our doorbell. Our messages would range from silly holiday greetings to martial music to faux threats. "Hey! Get off our porch!" was a typical one.

John said, "My friends and I would ring the doorbell just to hear the messages and then run away."

I laughed. That happened more than he knew.

"We got used to that," I said. "I caught our mailman doing the same thing. He just couldn't move as fast with that heavy bag of mail on his shoulder."

I knew then that John and I would work well together.

The Adirondack Council became one of the few environmental organizations in New York with both a full-time lobbying operation and a full-time communications person. John's talent gave us an important edge in getting our message out to the public and to politicians alike. He was always available to reporters to comment on a breaking story on deadline, and as a former editor, he knew what they needed. We got plenty of free media coverage in addition to our own publications and news releases. Our media presence not only helped influence events, but made our organization attractive to donors as well.

It was, as they say, a good hire.

GET THEM TO THE 'DACKS

In the policy trenches, information can be an activist's most important weapon. The Council operated on the principle that "if you don't know, you don't care." We always sought to educate journalists and policy makers.

As a nonprofit and politically nonpartisan organization, the Council worked with all political parties, but made no political endorsements and offered no campaign contributions. That meant that some of the most powerful tools used by other lobbyists were not available to us. But there was one unique arrow in our lobbying quiver: the Park. While our daily presence and our publications were important, letting folks see for themselves what we were trying to protect was a key part of our job.

Most people across the country—and most New Yorkers, for that matter—have never visited the Adirondack Park. But the idea of the Park often occupied a special place in their minds. One of my favorite stories involves the experience of a couple of our North Country staffers when they took a cab in New York City. Upon learning they worked to protect the Adirondack Park, the cab driver observed, in a heavy accent, that he hoped to visit the Adirondacks one day. He said he loved the idea that a "forever wild" forest, free to all people, was less than a day's drive away.

The Park also enhanced our access to politicians and the media. While it was always difficult to get the attention of the overstimulated Capitol reporters, who are pitched a new story every hour, newspapers outside the capital were usually receptive to us. Twice a year, we invested time in a press tour from Long Island to Buffalo and throughout the North Country. We always were cordially received, and occasionally a roomful of editors and reporters gathered to hear us. We would share our perspective on the issues of the day and make the contacts we'd need to peddle a future story. A local editorial might someday influence a key legislator or even the governor's thinking.

At the legislature, we used old-fashioned shoe leather to make things go. We tried hosting receptions in Albany and Washington, but they were always lightly attended, typically attracting brief stop-bys from a few legislators on their way to another event hosted by campaign contributors. Likewise, distributing swag—in the form of a slick color calendar produced by *Adirondack Life* magazine or frame-worthy color photographs of natural resources that needed protection—just was not bringing us enough attention.

So I pushed hard to add a line in our annual budget to stage tours of the Adirondack Park for legislators and their staff. Some of our directors generously offered to host our tour travelers at sites such as John Ernst's Elk Lake Lodge in the eastern part of the Park and Barbara L. Glaser's Great Camp Uncas in the west. These were some of the finest places on Earth, much less the Adirondacks. (See figure 12.1.)

The Albany staff organized what we called "black fly tours," after the swarms of biting insects that plague the region each spring. Often using my own family minivan, we put the Black Fly Tours sign in the windshield as we pulled up to the Capitol and our waiting guests. We then drove in a large arc through the Park. A tour would usually start in the east at Lake George with stops at Elk Lake. Elk Lake Lodge donated the first conservation easement to the State of New York in 1963, which protected the lake

Figure 12.1. Black Fly Tour sign. *Source*: author's own material.

shoreline. The remainder of the 12,000 acres would be similarly protected in 2012.[1] Then it was onto the Keene Valley in the High Peaks region, Lake Placid with its prominent ski jumps and the John Brown farm, and then into the lake country—Saranac Lake, Tupper Lake, Long Lake, and Blue Mountain Lake. It was always a long day.

If our guests could stay overnight, our final destination for the day was one of the Great Camps near Raquette Lake. William West Durant built Great Camp Uncas and Great Camp Sagamore in the late 1800s, on peninsulas jutting into private lakes amid forested lands now owned by the state. Uncas became the summer home of J. P. Morgan, while the Sagamore was a Vanderbilt family retreat for over fifty years. Both are now National Historic Landmarks, and while Uncas remains in private hands, Sagamore is open to the public and run by a not-for-profit. Waking to the call of loons during an overnight stay there is always special. (See figure 12.2.)

One year, a state constitutional amendment had been proposed involving a swap of private and public land in the Keene Valley. The swap had the support of local governments and the environmental community, but the measure was bottled up in the Assembly. Then key staff people came on a Black Fly Tour.

Figure 12.2. Main Lodge at Great Camp Sagamore. *Source*: Nancie Battaglia.

The sticking point in Albany was a lingering dispute over responsibility for the repair of a dam on the affected lands. The state would take ownership of that dam if the amendment were to pass. An alarming report on dam safety released the previous year showed that the state was already facing a significant financial burden to maintain and repair the many dams it already owned across the state, so the idea of taking on another one was not attractive.

We stopped at the site with our guests and showed them that the structure was just a "crib dam" made mostly from logs and standing no more than three feet high. Surprisingly, nobody had pointed that out to the staff in the legislature. After seeing it, the staffers advised their bosses to drop their objection.

The amendment went to the voters and passed easily, and the land swap went forward. The Town of Keene was able to expand its cemetery adjacent to state land, and in return the town gave the public a nice roadside rest area and swimming hole above the dam.

On another trip in late autumn, we took a group to Elk Lake, the day after the Lodge closed to the public. The view in autumn with the trees aglow in color is so awesome that the Lodge sells place mats featuring a color photograph of it. (I own four.)

Our group walked down to the lakefront. As if on cue, a solitary loon swam around a bend, into view close to shore, turned its head toward us and sang its gorgeous song.

"Release the loon!" chortled one of the cynical senior staffers. We all had a good laugh, imagining a Council diver lurking underwater, releasing his captive loon upon our arrival.

Several of our tour mates later confessed that they had never before seen or heard a loon, the ideal wilderness ambassador. Perfect. (See figure 12.3.)

On another occasion, early in the fight for new federal controls on acid rain, Adirondack environmental groups jointly hosted congressional staffers on a retreat at Blue Mountain Center on Eagle Lake. The artists' retreat and conference center was formerly Eagle Nest, a Great Camp built by the Hochschild family on a shoreline tract previously owned by Durant. We were pleased to get quite a few attendees from the House and Senate. We fed them a steady diet of beer, sandwiches, and fresh chocolate chip cookies, a famous and delicious tradition at the center. We subjected them to a few lectures, but left them plenty of time to hike, canoe, and soak up the natural beauty we were asking them to help preserve. At night, we all stood on the porch far from urban lights and watched a satellite travel across the sky. Very special.

Figure 12.3. Elk Lake. *Source*: Gary Randorf.

So were the floatplane trips that Helms Aero Services in Long Lake provided virtually from our door. A low-level flight is the best way to appreciate the vast water resources of the western half of the Adirondack Park. Peter Bauer, the executive director of another group, was to take the staffers out three at a time and show them dead lakes destroyed by acid rain, which ironically from the air were a beautiful blue color.

Peter fell ill at the last minute and asked me to lead the flights. I agreed, not letting on that I had never been up in a floatplane before and that I did not like flying—or even heights in general. I did know that the safety record for floatplane charters by the Helm family was impeccable, because I had looked it up when I thought I might be a passenger. A few reluctant guests were reassured to hear me say that I was overcoming some of the same fears they had.

On each flight, I talked pretty much the whole time to keep my fear under control, prattling on about acid rain or the attributes of this or that lake.

When we were disembarking from the last flight, the pilot asked me if I was a lawyer. When I confirmed I was, he said, "I thought so. You talk too much."

Our opponents in the legislative arena often accused us of "Chicken Little" tactics—overstating our case in "the sky is falling" terms to attract media attention. To that, all I can say is that we knew how to market our issues.

There was one topic, we learned, that was a fail-safe media magnet—threats to charismatic megafauna. Save the wolf! Save the moose! And in the case of the Adirondack Park, home to a bird that stirs the emotions of anyone who hears its haunting call on a secluded lake at dusk: Save the loon!

Appeals on the behalf of wildlife never failed to rev up public support. It didn't hurt that they usually raised a ton of money from private donors as well.

Another key to maximizing influence is understanding the political rhythms of the legislature. In New York state, all seats in the Assembly and Senate are up for election every two years. This offered us a regular window of opportunity.

Every election year, members in both houses, Democrats and Republicans alike, sought to establish their environmental standing as they geared up their campaigns. We tree huggers held a trump card, because most New Yorkers expect their elected officials to protect the environment. And we didn't hesitate to play it, widely distributing a "voters' guide" just before the election that rated legislators' performance on environmental issues over the previous two years.

So in even-numbered years, incumbents had to have an environmental bill or two to sponsor and promote. That was the time for us to play offense and persuade lawmakers to write our priorities into legislation.

The odd-numbered years were a different story. The big-money benefactors who mostly funded legislators' campaigns had to be rewarded after the election, and that meant environmental consciousness often took a backseat. The green lobby turned its focus to playing defense and fighting harmful bills.

Each legislative session in Albany also has its own political rhythm—a slowly gathering wave that can overwhelm an unprepared lobbyist.

New York's legislative session officially convened in January, when the governor delivered his State of the State address. Some bills were introduced on Day One, but the legislature's workweek grew only gradually from two days to five as spring arrived. Until April, the members focused their attention primarily on the state budget, which was usually adopted after its April due date and just before a lengthy spring recess.

For a lobbyist interested in environmental legislation, these were not idle months, but time to execute a carefully conceived plan.

Preparing for a successful legislative campaign begins the previous summer. Well before the session opens, you meet with your clients to develop goals. You identify strategic objectives to help you reach each goal, the tasks needed to achieve those objectives, and benchmarks to evaluate progress.

In the winter and early spring, all that planning was put into action. There were continual strategy meetings with colleagues. Coalitions were painstakingly built with other lobbyists who supported your effort. And there were endless visits and discussions with the people who could actually help your goals become laws—members of the legislature, their staffs, the folks in the governor's office, and sometimes even the governor himself.

In June, everything built to an unpredictable crescendo.

In the final month of the legislative session, members are increasingly anxious to finish their business and get home in time to appear at the Fourth of July parades in their district and turn to their other lives. (Although New York lawmakers put in enough hours to be considered full-time workers, according to state law they are working only part time for their salary. This makes them legally able to earn outside income, and most of them do.)

By June, committees had begun sending bills to the floor of each chamber. The daily agenda expanded, the floor debates got livelier, and workdays expanded into the evenings. For almost twenty years, I did not see my family much during the month of June. The days and nights were spent walking the marble hallways of the Capitol complex.

Soon, signs began to appear that the legislative climax was near. Leaders in both houses began to restrict the introduction of new bills, a hint that members needed to start wrapping up legislative business. The Assembly speaker, the Senate majority leader, and the governor began meeting in earnest to seek agreement on the host of remaining issues. These gatherings are traditionally known as "three men in a room," a description that remained historically accurate until Andrea Stewart-Cousins was named Senate majority leader in 2019.

The key clue that the process was nearing an end was the Great Blowup. One of the three men in the room would stomp out and declare that the other two were impossible to work with. Sometimes one of the two majority legislative leaders would threaten to shut down his chamber and have his members leave the Capitol.

The Great Blowup would always be followed by a "reconciliation" and a "productive meeting." Once the three men had agreed in concept on most major issues and no further deals seemed possible, it was time for the senior staff to hammer out the exact text of new legislation and make the deals necessary to ensure a majority vote. There would be a hectic final week of round-the-clock negotiations, conferences, and debates until the closing gavel was struck.

Things happened quickly in this period, so most professional lobbyists spent their time moving between members' offices and the Senate and Assembly chambers. You made yourself available to the staff and members and snagged anyone passing by that might give you an update on the progress of your issues. You gave your card to the ushers in the hope that a member would come out of the chamber to talk. Word spread like wildfire in the lobby (yes, the lobbyists hung out in the lobby) when a new list of bills to be debated on the floor of the chambers was released. But mostly you waited. And worried, until the Final Day, the day all loose ends would wrap up in votes.

When Warren M. Anderson of (a Republican from Binghamton) was Senate majority leader, he would signal the Final Day of the session by wearing an outlandishly ugly jacket. Unfortunately, that unique tradition left when he left the office.

For a lobbyist, the Final Day brought only three possible outcomes:

- *Victory was yours!* You got a new law passed or obtained funding for your cause.

- *You compromised.* The law that passed was not as good as it could have been, or the budget appropriation was a fraction of what was needed.

- *You went belly-up and got nothing for your client.* Rookies take note: This is another way of saying that you failed to compromise, the heart of the legislative game. Get what you can, because there is always next year to build a bigger coalition; shoot for more funding; find a way around this year's roadblocks.

In some ways, now is the best time to be a citizen lobbyist. The tools for the citizen activists have only improved over the years. You have:

- Instant communication via cell phones.

- Action alerts through email and social media to organize your supporters. A petition with thousands of signatures from constituents still gets the attention of state politicians.

- The capability, via the internet, to conduct in-depth research of your issues, to find similar legislation in other states, to explore the demographics in any district, and to track campaign contributions.

- The knowledge, offered here by example, that the path to federal reform is often begun through state legislatures.

- Open meetings laws that require notice and public discussion of important government decisions.

- Freedom of information laws (FOIL) that permit the average citizen to research and obtain documents critical to the action (or inaction) by state and local governments.

Three keys to success remain constant:

- Know your issue. Not just why you support it, but why others may not.

- Know the players. Where did the legislator grow up? Did the family have a farm or a business? Education? Hobbies? What does the spouse do for a living? (Don't underestimate the power of pillow talk.) This knowledge can only help your political relationships.

- Use your knowledge of the player to inform them, educate them, and to maintain a cordial exchange of views. It will be worth the effort.

But it is still true that the more things change, the more they remain the same. Some politicians are motivated to act in the public interest, though many will only act if their constituents or their donors demand it, while others only want publicity to advance their careers. Goal one remains: to convince legislators that your goal should also be their goal. Getting there, that is, lobbying, remains an art form.

NOTES

NOTES TO THE INTRODUCTION

1. Adirondack Council, "Our Mission," 2020–2021, State of the Park, 3.
2. Adirondack Park Agency, "About the Park," http://www.apa.ny.gov.
3. Adirondack Council, 2020–2021, State of the Park, 4.
4. Adirondack Council, 2020–2021, State of the Park, 4.
5. New York State Constitution, Article XIV, Section 1.
6. Adirondack Council, 2020–2021, State of the Park, 4.
7. "The Future of the Adirondack Park," the Temporary Commission on the Future of the Adirondacks, 1970.

NOTES TO CHAPTER 1

1. *The Adirondack Park in the Twenty-first Century*, Commission on the Adirondacks in the Twenty-first Century, State of New York, April, 1990.
2. Robert F. Flacke, "Minority Report," the Commission on the Adirondacks in the Twenty-first Century, April 12, 1990.
3. Adirondack Council, 2020–2021, State of the Park, 4.
4. John B. Oakes, "Last Stand for the Adirondacks," op-ed, *New York Times*, June 19, 1992.
5. Elizabeth Kolbert, "Cuomo Plans to Acquire Adirondack Tract," *New York Times*, December 29, 1988.
6. Bill Deval, *Clearcut: The Tragedy of Industrial Forestry* (New York: Random House, 1994).

NOTE TO CHAPTER 10

1. New York Department of Environmental Conservation, press release, February 8, 2019.

NOTES TO CHAPTER 11

1. *Vanity Fair*, interview with Sigourney Weaver, October 2014.
2. Jerry Jenkins, Karen Roy, and Charles Driscoll, *Acid Rain in the Adirondacks: An Environmental History* (Ithaca, NY: Cornell University Press, 2007).

NOTE TO CHAPTER 12

1. *Adirondack Daily Enterprise*, January 4, 2013.

INDEX

Note: Page numbers in *italics* indicate illustrations.

Abrams, Robert, 150
Acadian swordgrass moth, 137, 139
Acid Deposition Control Act (1997), 156
Acid Deposition Standard Feasibility Study Report to Congress (1994), 151–152
acid rain, 148–152, 247; ad campaigns on, 175–179, *176, 177*; brochures on, *169, 178*; effects of, 6, 150–154, 169–170, 173, 192, 222–223; emission credits and, 150–152, 164–168, *166, 185,* 185–186, 230; mechanics of, *149.* *See also* water pollution
Acid Rain Market Program, 203
Adirondack Campaign, 20, 42–43, 141–145
Adirondack Lakes Survey Corporation, 191
Adirondack Landowners Association, 98, 134–135
Adirondack League Club, 111–112
Adirondack Mountain Club, 51, 76, 129, 203
Adirondack Museum (Blue Mountain Lake), 166

Adirondack North Country Association, 30
Adirondack Park Agency (APA), 4, 32; authority of, 13; on Champion International Paper sale, 83; Cuomo and, 14; Flacke on, 11; Glennon at, 31; management classifications of, 84–85; subdivision plans and, 76; on timber blowdown, 64; Whitney estate sale and, 76–78; zoning laws and, 32
Adirondack Park Agency Act, 32
Adirondack Planning Commission, 31, 33
Adirondack Solidarity Alliance, 21, 23–24
air pollution, 6, 183–184; bond act for, 71; emission credits for, 150–152, 164–168, 185–186, 230; four-pollutant approach to, 183–184, 188, 191–192, 200–202, 217, 220–221; monitoring of, 137, 166–167, 230; Pace University symposium on, 154. *See also* acid rain; climate change
Albany Pine Barrens, 137

255

Allinger, Steve, 99
Amax Coal Company, 165–166
American Lung Association, 188, 202, 217, 234
American Whitewater (organization), 125–126
Ampersand Park, 220
Anderson, David, 205–206, 211, 233
Anderson, Fred, 132
Anderson, Warren M., 250
Appalachian Voices (organization), 190–191
Association for the Protection of the Adirondacks, 4, 27, 28, 129
Audubon Society. *See* National Audubon Society
Ausable Chasm, 128–129
Ausable Club, 98–100, 102
Au Sable Forks, 147
Au Sable River, 213

Baker, Maynard, 22
Barcelona Neck, 78
Bauer, Peter, 79, 247
Beamish, Dick, 18–19, 37, 42
bears, 138, 141
Beaver River, 127, 129
Beebe, Mary-Arthur, 121–124
Beinecke, Frances, 217–222
Berle, Peter A. A., 8, 9, 13, 20, 52
Biden, Joe, 235
Big Moose Lake, 170, 181–182
black flies, 5, 36–37; cluster flies and, 20
"black fly tours," *244*, 244–246, *245*
Black River, 109
Blue Line Council, 16, 21, 31, 32
Blue Mountain Center (Eagle Lake), 246
Blue Mountain Lake, 166
Boehlert, Sherwood "Sherry," *177*, 179, 193, 233

Boreas Ponds, 93, *94*
Borrelli, Peter, 56
bottle/can deposits, 50
Bowes, C. V. "Major," 170
Bridger, Beverly, 222, 224
Brodsky, Richard L., 41–43, 64–67; on emission credits, 168, 184; Pataki and, 65; Stafford and, 168, 184
brownfields, 73–75
Bruno, Joseph L., 55, *166*
Bruno, Peter J., 134
Burke, Timothy J., 39–40, 49; on acid rain, 219; on air pollution, 183; Citizens Campaign for the Environment and, 218; Hubbard Brook report and, 193, 194; resignation of, 147–148; wilderness classifications, 85, 87
Bush, George H. W., 149, 150, 187–188, 205–207
Bush, George W., 183, 187–188, 205–206; Clear Skies Initiative of, 206–208, 220–221, 227–231; Earth Day (2002) and, 148, 211–217, *216*

Cahill, John P., 82, 84–87, 180
campaign contributions, 133, 239, 243–244, 251
Campbell, Gregory, 64, 76, 78
Camp Eagle Nest, 165–166
Camp Sagamore, 55, 222, 224, *245*
Camp Topridge, 52–53, *53*
Camp Uncas, 55, 244, 245
Canachagala Lake, 111, 112
Canal Corporation, 107, 111, 112
Canon, George H., 88–89, *89*, 232
cap-and-trade program. *See* emission credits
Carpenter, Bruce, 125–130
Carper, Thomas, 228
Carr, Calvin, 21, 23

cell-phone interceptions, 86
Champion International Corporation, 81–84, 92
Chasis, Sarah, 218
Cheney, Dick, 231
Chesapeake Bay Foundation, 205
"chits," 86–87, 240
Christmas tree exemption, 133
Chub Lake, 112
Citizens Campaign for the Environment (CCE), 73, 113, 162, 172; Burke and, 218, 219
Clark, Frank, 98–100
Clean Air Act (1990), 149–150, 159, 193, 204, 221
Clean Air Interstate Rule (CAIR), 233–234
Clean Air Task Force, 160, 188, 201–202
Clean Air Trust, 208–209
Clean Power Act (2001), 230
Clean Power Plan, 235
Clean Water/Clean Air Bond Act (1996), 71–75, 72
Clear Skies Initiative, 206–208, 220–221, 227–231
climate change, 200–201, 219–222, 234; Bush on, 200, 207; Gore on, 217; Kyoto Protocol on, 184, 217, 221; Paris Agreement on, 235. See also air pollution
Clinton, Bill, 150, 204
Clinton, Hillary Rodham, 181–183, 230
Clinton Correctional Facility, 33, 115
Clintonville Pine Barrens, 137
cluster flies, 20. See also black flies
Commission on the Adirondacks in the Twenty-First Century, 5, 7–10, 12–13
Connaughton, James L., 233
conservation easements, 14, 97–102, 101

Conservation Fund, 90–92
Cooke, William, 73, 114–115; Citizens Campaign for the Environment and, 162, 172; D'Amato and, 159, 162–164; Pew Charitable Trusts and, 189
Council on Environmental Quality (CEQ), 205, 206, 211, 226
Covewood Lodge, 170
Covid-19 pandemic, 106
Cross-State Air Pollution Rule, 234
Cuomo, Andrew, 92, 94–95, 105
Cuomo, Mario M., 7, 8; Adirondack proposals of, 14, 30–31, 37–38, 38; at Blue Mountain Lake Museum, 35–37, 36; on canal reservoir violations, 111; Environmental Protection Fund and, 51–52, 56, 56–58; on Marino, 54
Cutler, Leonard M., 44–45, 48–49, 55

D'Amato, Alfonse, 154, 156–159, 161–164, 163; Acid Deposition Control Act of, 172, 173
Dannemora prison, 33, 115
Darrin Freshwater Institute, 123
Davis, George D., 9, 21, 22
Diamond International Corp., 14, 29
DiNunzio, Michael, 67
Donohue, Gavin J., 85–87
Driscoll, Charles T., 191–193
Duck Hole, 91

Earth Day, 147, 161–162, 211–217, 216
Earth First! (organization), 22
earthquake (2002), 147
electric vehicles, 70
Elk Lake, 220, 244–246, 247
Elliman, Christopher J. "Kim," 80, 220

Emerson, Ralph Waldo, 90
eminent domain, 15–16, 78
emission credits, 150–152, 164–168,
    166; Clinton amendment to, 230;
    GAO report on, *185*, 185–186
Empire State Forest Products
    Association, 134, 136
Environmental Advocates of New York,
    161
environmental bond act (1996),
    68–75, *72*
Environmental Defense Fund, 175
Environmental Planning Lobby (EPL),
    217–218
Environmental Protection Fund, 54–
    56, *56*, 69, 81
Erie Canal reservoirs, 107–112
Eristoff, Andrew P., 81
Ernst, John, 220, 244
Estes, J. D., 212

Farb, Nathan, 59
Federal Energy Regulatory
    Commission, 126
Finch, Pruyn paper company, 92–93,
    105, 134–135
Fink, Stanley, 29
Finnegan, Michael C., 69, *150*; on acid
    rain, 154, 180; on brownfield issue,
    74–75; Whitney estate sale and, 80
Five Rivers Environmental Education
    Center, 142
Flacke, Robert F., 11–13, 16, 31
Follensby Pond, 90, *91*
Forest Legacy program, 137
Forest Products Association, 135
"forever wild" clause, 3–4, 61–62, 108,
    133, 138, 243
four-pollutant (4P) approach to air
    quality, 183–184, 188, 191–192,
    200–202; Gore on, 217; Hawkins
    on, 220–221

Fox, Charlie, 202–203
Freedom of Information Law (FOIL),
    116

Genier, Lisa M., 49–50, 55, 127;
    on canal reservoir violations,
    108, 110–111; on Christmas
    tree exemption, 133; tourism
    promotion and, 103–104;
    Whitney subdivisions and, 79
Gerdts, Donald H., 22, 24
Gerhardt, Doug, 108
Gibson, David, 28
Glaser, Barbara L., 5, 244
Glennon, Robert C., 14, 31–33, 42
global warming. *See* climate change
Goldsmith, Richard, 237
Gore, Al, 150, 183, 184, 187;
    Council on Environmental
    Quality and, 205; on global
    warming, 217
Grannis, Pete, 35, 42–43, 104
Grant, Tom, 38–40, 104, 133
Grasse River, *82*
Gray, Alyse, 28–30
Great Blowdown disaster (1950),
    61–62
Great Blowup (legislative tactic),
    249–250
Greenwood, David, 148, 166, 175,
    223–224

Hawkins, David J., 152, 220–221
hazardous wastes, 69, 73, 88
Heartwood Forestland Fund, 92
Henderson Lake, 87–89, *89*
Hendrickson, John, 76–80, 93–95
Heurich family, 29, 48, 56, 57, 90
Hicks, Alan, 142–144
Hinchey, Maurice, 28, 29, 35, *36*
Hochschild family, 165–166
Holtzman, Elizabeth, 156

Houseal, Brian L., 88, *89*, 228–229, 233–234
Hubbard Brook Ecosystem Study, 191–192

incinerators, garbage, 46
Inhofe, James M., 172, 180, 209–210
International Paper, 90–92, 135
Iwanowicz, Peter M., 202

Jacangelo, Dominic, 138–139
Jakubowski, Roger, 52
Javits, Jacob K., 156
Jeffords, James M., 194, 208–209, 228
Jerry, Harold A., Jr., 9–11; Randorf and, 18; resignation of, 41; Stafford and, 40–41, 47
Johnson, Owen H., 138–139
Jorling, Thomas C., 15, 25–26, 142, 150, 165

Kafin, Robert, 238
Karner blue butterfly, 137
King, Kevin, 134
Kligerman, Tom, 117
Kyoto Protocol, 184, 217, 221

LaBastille, Anne, 21
LaGrasse, Carol, *17*
Lake George, 104, 105, 244; milfoil control in, 121–124
Lake George Commission, 40–41
Lake Placid, 104, 105, 147, 213, 245
Lake Tear of the Clouds, 87
Lambert, Kathy Fallon, 191–192, 193–194
Lassiter Properties Inc., 14
Lazio, Rick, 181
lead poisoning, 6, 170
Leahy, Patrick, 185
Leavitt, Michael O., 233
LeBrun, Fred, 25, 26

Lefebvre, Richard, 211–212
legislative calendar, 133, 240, 248–250
Lehrman, Lewis E., 100–101, *101*
Likens, Gene E., 191
"Lilliputian effect," 10
Lithophane lepida lepida, 137–139
Little Tupper Lake, 75–81, *77. See also* Tupper Lake
lobbying, 237–251; campaign contributions and, 133, 239, 243–244, 251; "chits" and, 86–87, 240; ethical conflicts with, 2; Freedom of Information Law and, 116; keys to success of, 251; media savvy and, 239–243
Long Island Lighting Company (LILCO), 164–165, 167–168, 186
Long Island Pine Barrens, 138
loons, 141, *223*, 246, 248; acid rain effects on, 153–154, 169–170, 222–224
Lorey, Scott, 88, 192, 201

Mangia, Angelo J., 44–47, 55
Marcellino, Carl L., 132, 168
Marino, Ralph J., 44–50, 54–56
Marsh, Langdon, 52
Martens, Joe, 31, 50
McCormick family, 90
McGinty, Katie, 183–184
McHugh, John, 224, 233
McKibben, Bill, 222, 232
McKinley, William, 88
McLean, Brian J., 150–151, 172, 204
Merchant, Natalie, 179
mercury: acid rain and, 6, 153, 169–170, 200, 222–223; legislation on, 183–184, 207, 227, 229–230
Meyland, Sarah, 219
Milbank, Dana, 216
Miletich, Radmila, 210

milfoil control, 121–124
Miller, David, 219
Miller, Melvin H., 27–30
moose, 6, 141–145, *145*, 248
Morgan estate, 90, 245
Morse, Richard D., 2, 71
Moshier Reservoir, 127–128
moths, endangered, 137–139
motorized vehicles, 84, 93
Moynihan, Daniel Patrick, 150, 153–
    156, 162, 172, 204, 234
Mucha, Zenia, 74
Murray, Frank, 31–33, 38
muskies, 127–128

National Acid Precipitation Assessment
    Program (NAPAP), 170–173, *173*,
    219
National Audubon Society, 9, 20, 129,
    175
National Energy Deregulation
    Conference, 156–157
National Trust for Historic
    Preservation, 175, 233
Natural Resources Defense Council
    (NRDC), 188, 203, 234; on acid
    rain, 150–153, 175; Beinecke on,
    217–218; Gore and, 217
Nature Conservancy, 26, 47, 51, 80;
    Clintonville Pine Barrens and,
    137; Finch, Pruyn acquisition
    by, 92; pine pinion moth and,
    138–139
Needleman, Neil, 238
New York Public Interest Research
    Group (NYPIRG), 237
New York Rivers United, 125, 129
New York State Barge Canal, 107
Niagara Mohawk Power Corporation,
    36, 76, 126–127, 165
9/11 attacks, 195–198
NL Industries, 87–89

Northern Forest Alliance, 154
North Lake, 109

Oakes, John, 14
Obama, Barack, 235
O'Donnell, Frank, 208–209
OK Slip Falls, 92–93, *93*
Olympic Games (1980), 213
Open Space Institute (OSI), 56, 80,
    87–88, 90, *91*, 220

Pace University School of Law, 154
Paris Climate Agreement (2015), 235
Parment, William, 135
Pataki, George, 58–59; on acid
    rain, *148*, 154, 165, 167–168,
    180–181, *186*; Brodsky and, 65;
    on clear-cutting, 68; on electric
    vehicles, 70; environmental
    policies of, 59–75; Marino and,
    55–56; on proposed prison, 113–
    114, 118; Saratoga fundraiser of,
    162–163; on timber theft, *136*;
    tourism promotion by, 103–105
Patterson, David A., 92
Pedersen, Ronald, 118
People v. Fisher (1908), 108–109
Perino, Dana, 226, 229, 232
Petty, Clarence, 5, *63*, 63–64, 68
Pew Charitable Trusts, 188–192, 219
pine pinion moth, 137–139
Plumley, Dan, 7–8, 149, 159
Post, Marjorie Merriweather, 52
Preston Ponds, 90, *91*
prisons, 6, 33, 113–119
Property Rights Council of America,
    17
Protect the Adirondacks, 95
Pruitt, Scott, 235
Public Utility Holding Company Act
    (PUHCA), 157, 161, 164
Purdue, Richard, 33

Race, Bradford, Jr., 60–61, 67
Rainbow Falls, 128–129
Rait, Bonnie, 179
Randorf, Gary, 5, 20, 98, 159; Jerry
    and, 18; on proposed prison, 114,
    117–118
Raquette River, 90, 129
Repas, Peter G., 34, 38–39, 116
Residents' Committee to Protect the
    Adirondacks, 79
Rockefeller, Nelson A., 4, 13, 20–21,
    166
Roosevelt, Theodore, 88

Sacandaga Lake, 109, 129
Sacandaga River, 129
Sauer, Klara, 51
Scenic Hudson (organization), 51
Schaefer, Paul, 57
Schregardus, Donald R., 199
Schumer, Charles E. "Chuck," 164,
    179, 198–201, 224
September 11th attacks, 195–198
Sheehan, John, 23, 60, 110–111;
    Clean Air Trust and, 207–209;
    on Earth Day (2002), 215–216;
    on EPA acid rain report, 151;
    hiring of, 242–243; on Hubbard
    Brook report, 192; LeBrun and,
    25
Sierra Club, 54, 188, 234; on clear-
    cutting, 67; Environmental Law
    clinic and, 237; Gore and, 217;
    on proposed prison, 117–118; on
    Whitney estate sale, 80–81
Silver, Sheldon "Shelly," 71
Siy, Eric, 20, 37, 42–43
Skinner, Peter, 125–126
Skovron, David, 148, 215–216,
    219–220
Snow, Tony, 226
snowmobiles, 84, 93

Solomon, Gerald "Jerry," 153, 154,
    158, 161, 172
Sonar (herbicide), 121, 122
Spitzer, Eliot, 134, 208
Stafford, Ronald B., 23–24, 33–35,
    39–41, 43–44; Ausable Club and,
    98–100; on emission credits, 168,
    184; Environmental Protection
    Fund and, 56; Grannis and, 104;
    Jerry and, 40–41, 47; Marino
    and, 47, 48, 49; Pataki and,
    55–56; on proposed prison, 113,
    115, 117–119; on timber rustlers,
    132–133, 135
Stark, Lynette M., 104, 118
Stewart-Cousins, Andrea, 249
Stillman, William James, 90
Sweeney, John E., 179, 185, 233

Tahawus Tract, 87–89, 89
Taub, Robert G., 224–225
tax abatement program, 78–79
temporary revocable permits, 108–110
Thernstrom, Sam, 205
timber industry, 6, 109; clear-
    cutting by, 14, 64, 65, 67–68;
    conservation easements and,
    97–98; People v. Fisher case and,
    109; removal of downed trees by,
    61–62, 64
timber rustlers, 6, 132–136, 136
tourism promotion, 103–106, 119–
    120, 127; loons and, 141, 223,
    246, 248; moose and, 141–145,
    145, 248
Treadwell, Alexander F. "Sandy," 215
Trottenberg, Polly, 199–201
trout, 127, 129, 213; acid rain effects
    on, 152, 173; brook, 76–77, 94
Trout Unlimited (organization), 129,
    175, 233
Trump, Donald, 235

Tupper Lake, 76–77, 94; prison proposed at, 6, 113–119; Wild Center at, *119*, 119–120, 137. *See also* Little Tupper Lake
2020 Vision policy guide, 9, 84–85
Twenty-First Century Environmental Quality Bond Act, 15–16, 26–27

Ulasewicz, Thomas A., 124

Vaccaro, Vincent J., 15
Vacco, Dennis C., 132, 134, *171*
Vanderbilt family, 55, 222, 245
Voinovich, George V., 180–181, 209–210

water pollution, 6, 32, 69; from black fly spraying, 5; bond act for, 71; from milfoil herbicide, 121–124. *See also* acid rain
Waxman, Henry, 193

Weaver, Sigourney, 218–219
Weprin, Saul, 35
What Environmentalists Want, 11
Wheeler, Andrew R., 210, 225
Whiteface Mountain, *66*
Whitman, Christine Todd, 203, 207, 208, 210, 230–231
Whitney, Marylou, 75–81, 93
Whitney estate, *93*, 93–95
Wild, Scenic and Recreational Rivers program, 5
Wild Center (Tupper Lake), *119*, 119–120, 137
wilderness classification, 9, 21–22, 84–85, 93, 129, 243
Wilderness Society, 175
"wild forest," 3, 4, 84
wolves, 248
Woodworth, Neil, 51, 53, 55

Zagata, Michael D., 61, 68
zoning regulations, 4, 13, 32, 135